MAMMALS OF BRITAIN
Their Tracks, Trails and Signs

MAMMALS OF BRITAIN
Their Tracks, Trails and Signs

M. J. Lawrence
R. W. Brown

BLANDFORD PRESS
London

Acknowledgments

A special feature of this book is the section of colour photographs of mammals in their natural habitat. For this we are most grateful to Mr. G. K. Kinns for allowing us to select from his outstanding collection of British mammals. We are also indebted further for the numerous black and white photographs Mr. Kinns has made available.

Other photographic acknowledgements are due to Jane Burton 1:7, 1:14, 3:5, 3:6, 3:7; Eva Crawley 5:4, 5:32 and photographs from which figures were taken; Janet Hornby 3:17, Plate 16; Joyce Pope 3:11, 4:40; C. Atherton IV A–D, 5:87, 5:88, 5:89; R. Balharry 2:20; J. Collins 2:37(c), 2:34, 3:19, 4:38; R. Hewson 2:13, 2:14, 3:8; K. Hunt i, ii, vi; H. G. Hurrell 2:15; I. Linn 2:28; P. Livesley 4:18, 4:20, 4:21, 4:28, 4:30, 4:39; R. Mahoney 3:28A, 3:28B, 5:25, 5:90; J. Mason 4:7, 4:8; E. G. Neal 2:10, 2:11, 2:12, 2:16, 2:17; G. Quedens 2:36; R. Stebbings 1:13; N. Tinbergen 2:2, 2:3; N. Utsi 4:19, 4:31, 4:37; J. van Wormer and B. Coleman 2:27; by kind permission of Her Majesty's Stationery Office 3.20, 3:21, 3:35 (A), (B), (C); J. Zool, 1:8, 1:9, 1:10, 1:11, 1:12. We are also indebted to Mrs. Joyce Pope for her constructive criticism in reading through the manuscript.

We would like to express our thanks to the many people who have helped us in the preparation of this book, and in particular to acknowledge the kind advice and assistance given by the following people: Professor M. Abercrombie, Mrs. Patricia Ferguson, Mr. R. B. Freeman, Dr. K. A. Kermack, Mr. R. Mahoney, Mr. Edwin Perry (All of University College, London); Mr. John Ferguson, Dr. P. A. Morris, Mrs. Valerie Kielty, Miss Clare Lloyd, Dr. G. B. Corbett (British Museum: Natural History); Mrs. Patricia Brown (formerly Miss Patricia Hughes); Mr. I. Linn; Dr. D. Pye; Mr. C. Tett; Mr. H. G. Hurrell and Miss Elaine Hurrell; Mr. Utsi; The Reindeer Co. Ltd., Inverness; Mr. Hallam, Riber Castle Zoo, Matlock; Mr. H. A. Snazle and the Staff of Chessington Zoo; Head Keeper Styles, London Zoo; Mr. R. Balharry, Anacun Field Station, Loch Maree, County Ross; Mr. Talbot, Deer Keeper to His Grace The Duke of Bedford, Woburn Abbey; Dr. E. W. Bentley and the Staff of the Ministry of Agriculture, Fisheries and Food, Tolworth; Miss Eva Crawley.

M.J.L. and R.W.B.

First published 1967
© Blandford Press 1967
Revised edition 1973
Second revised edition 1974

ISBN 0 7137 0659 7

A

Printed in Great Britain by Fletcher & Son Ltd, Norwich

Contents

NOTE

The illustrations bear two reference figures, one refers to the chapter number and one to the figure number, e.g. Fig. 3:10 refers to chapter three and is the tenth illustration in that chapter.

Preface to the First Edition

The arrangement of this book is such that one chapter is devoted to one pair of Orders of mammals, namely Insectivora–Chiroptera: Carnivora–Pinnipedia: Lagomorpha–Rodentia: Artiodactyla–Perissodactyla. At the end of the book a long chapter is devoted to 'indirect' signs, such as skulls and other bones which may make field identification of mammals possible.

In the chapters which deal with the various Orders the following series of sections are considered for each species (there are departures from this general scheme in some Orders, but where this is so the introduction at the beginning of each chapter explains why).

First there is the terminology for each species: the family, common and scientific names and names for the sexes and young.

The next section deals with occurrence. This states if the animal is very common, common, uncommon, rare or very rare. This also accounts for the various limiting factors on the species' distribution and give as accurately as possible the localities in which the animal occurs.

The information following deals with habits. Here are considered such factors as whether the animal is gregarious or solitary, the time of day at which it is active and whether regular paths and feeding habits are maintained.

The habitat deals with the type of terrain in which the species lives – in woodland, grassland, bleak mountain top moors and so on. This section also considers the animal's relationship to man's habitat where appropriate.

The section dealing with tracks consists of illustrations with a brief description. The proportions of the track, relative and actual, are stated where possible since these provide an important means of identification in some cases.

Under the heading 'Trail' are given details of such factors as the length of stride at the various gaits with which the animal moves.

The final information generally included for each species is that entitled 'Signs', which deals with the other indications denoting the presence of a species in an area. These vary widely from things such as latrines, runs, playgrounds, feeding remains, shed hair on fencing and in the case of some carnivores the strong musky odour which is often associated with their presence. Droppings are also very important. From the shape, size, number, colour, texture and odour it is possible to identify a dropping as belonging to one of a very limited number of species.

The dwelling place is considered. This section describes the types of shelter the animal utilises or makes, and gives it the correct technical name. The location is also taken into consideration.

The final sections of the book are of a more general nature. Chapter 5 deals with the various signs indicating a species' presence which have not already been considered under more specific headings (these consist largely of those animal traces found in the feeding remains and droppings of other creatures). Then comes a glossary which defines some of the technical terms used throughout the book and finally there is a bibliography of the mammal books which may be of value for reference and further reading.

Where possible the drawings of trails are life-size; otherwise they are made to a set scale 1 : 5.

Finally, it must be stressed that the material shown here is based entirely on the authors' own field work (*with a few exceptions which are indicated in the appropriate places*), and therefore relate to specific examples. Throughout the book certain generalisations have been made, for example, the drawing of a Brown rat trail may be said to be life-size. An observer using the book may then encounter something which has all the characteristics of a Brown rat trail, except that it is smaller or larger than the one shown here. This does not mean that this cannot be the trail of an individual of this species, but merely proves that this individual has different proportions. Therefore the statistics given here cannot be taken as rules, merely as *guides*. This applies to all sections of the work, except that dealing with anatomical matters (although even here there will be variations in proportion). Used as a guide to the subject, it is hoped that this book will prove reliable though not totally infallible.

PREFACE TO THE SECOND EDITION

A second edition of this book has made it possible to make major additions and corrections. Indeed, recent research and new information have made revision essential, and the publishers have kindly agreed to this.

Modifications have been made to the existing text and complete new sections have been added where required. The final chapter has been expanded so that it now forms a complete key to all species of British Mammals. In this edition we have added information on recent introductions and on the less common seal and whale visitors to our coast.

We have removed the diagrams showing ideal tracks from the text on the individual species concerned and have organised these into more meaningful keys. Our original maps have also been removed, and we recommend readers to refer to the Interim Maps published by the Mammal Society of Great Britain, which can be obtained from most Public Libraries.

The bibliography and glossary have been revised and considerably enlarged. We hope that the additions and revisions will increase the usefulness of this second edition considerably.

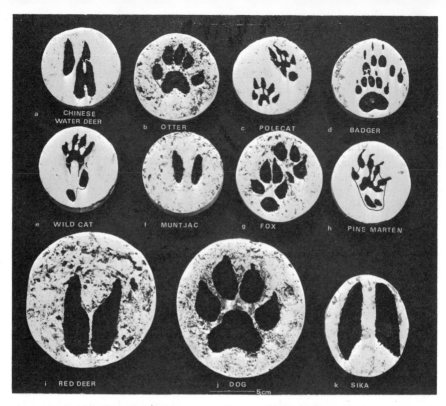

i and ii Examples of plaster casts of 'near perfect' mammal tracks.

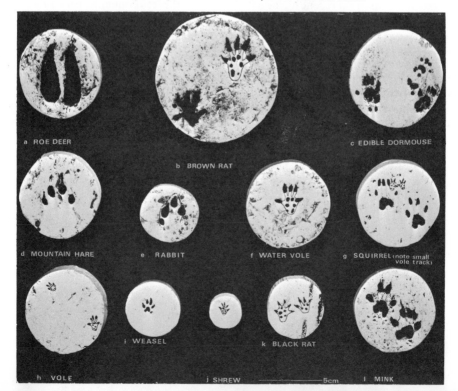

Introduction

The value of field work

In order that the material presented in this work is used to its full advantage it is necessary for the reader to understand the methods involved in collecting it. Perhaps the most interesting aspect of mammal study lies in field work and the authors consider it essential that sufficient material is given to make it possible for the information given in this book to be used in a practical way. To facilitate this the following brief introduction explains the ways in which tracks, trails and other signs may be collected in the field. The systematic layout of the book makes it possible for anyone to identify a mammal species without ever actually seeing it. Since the concern of this study is not with the characteristics of the animals themselves no detailed descriptions of the species have been given. There are many excellent works on this aspect of mammal study already in existence (see Bibliography).

Recording in the field

To deal efficiently with material found in the field the following procedure should be adopted. When a track is found the whole area around it should be examined carefully for other tracks and evidence of the animal. If a series of individual prints are found the trail should be drawn out *before any plaster casts are taken*, and as many measurements between individual tracks as possible taken (all measurements in this book are given on the metric scale since this is the scientific standard and may soon be adopted for common use in this country). These records are important and notes of the soil conditions, the terrain and exact location should also be taken. It is also useful to note the weather, time of day and the gait of the animal (e.g. walking, running, bounding). If droppings, remnants of kills, shed fur or some other signs are found near to the trail these should be measured and drawn *in situ*, their precise relation to the trail and the surroundings being noted and, if necessary, the evidence should be collected for analysis and more detailed study. Only after this has been done may the tracks be cast. Choose the best track (i.e. the one which is the most clearly impressed and seems to be the most complete), but also look for interesting tracks, that is tracks which seem unusual (see Fig. 2 : 21d) and perhaps characterise the trail (e.g. clusters of fore and hind feet parallel to each other across the median line which is typical of the *Mustelidae*). The subject of casting is considered below in some detail since the use of tracks for identification is the most important single aspect of the book.

Making plaster casts

In the preparation of material for this book, all the tracks were cast in plaster of Paris which may be obtained from almost any chemist, and costs between twenty and thirty pence for a seven-pound (3 kg) tin. The pink plaster used for walls and ceilings was avoided, since this does not register the very fine detail required when taking the tracks of small mammals, e.g. shrew.

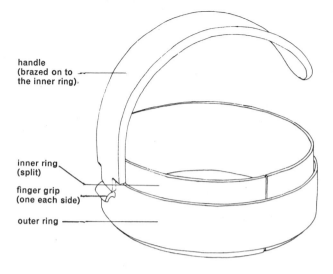

handle
(brazed on to
the inner ring)

inner ring
(split)

finger grip
(one each side)

outer ring

iii Casting ring. The ring illustrated is made of brass and consists of a solid outer ring with a split inner ring. The inner ring contains the plaster over the track and when it is pushed clear of the outer ring it will expand releasing the cast.

Preparing the frame

The main problem in casting with plaster of Paris is in obtaining the correct consistency so that air bubbles are eliminated and detail is well shown. The second problem is in finding a suitable material for containing the plaster over the track. Strips of cardboard can be used, but these have a very short life.

To overcome this last problem a series of metal rings (Fig. iii) and frames were constructed (Fig. ivb), the rings ranging from 2 to 25 cms. in diameter, the rectangular frames from 8.5 by 15 to 25 by 75 cms. (these were made so that trails and elongated tracks could be cast without wasting plaster). When a suitable track, or group of tracks were found, in the case of Fig. iva a group of coypu tracks) the frame was placed over them so that there was a clear margin between the prints and the edge of the tray (Fig. ivb). The frame was then pushed gently into the soil so that a plaster-tight seal was formed (if the ground proved to be too hard for this then an additional seal of softened earth, built up around the outside of the frame, was used).

Adding the plaster

The plaster of Paris was mixed so that it could be poured into the tray to take the *negative* impression of the print. Since the plaster has to be poured into the frame so as to cover the whole of the area to a depth allowing at least half of an inch of plaster above the highest point of the track, care must always be taken to mix enough plaster, and to make it of the consistency of evaporated milk. When the plaster is poured in (Fig. ivc), the edges of the frame are gently tapped to dislodge air bubbles. When mixing plaster it is better to add powder to water. After pouring the plaster it must be left *for a minimum of 15 minutes*. A useful means of discovering whether the plaster is set is to feel it periodically. As it hardens an exothermic reaction takes place; the plaster first of all becomes warm and then cools rapidly (endothermic reaction). Only when it has completely cooled

iv (A, B, C, D). Method
of casting a trail (see text
for explanation).

after the generation of heat may the cast be lifted in safety. When the plaster has
set hard the cast can be removed from the frame (Fig. ivd) and the greater part
of the adhering soil removed. The cast shown has been coloured to emphasize the
detail. The detailed cleaning should be delayed until the cast has been taken to the
laboratory or home. Newspaper is the most useful thing to wrap the casts in since
it is cheap and helps to absorb any excess moisture. When it has been cleaned up
the cast should be clearly labelled, and the actual impression of the print picked
out in some suitable colour so that it may be seen in sufficient detail to facilitate
identification (see photographs, p. 14).

Surface conditions for castings

One other point which may be mentioned is that not all surface conditions are
suitable. Snow and very soft silt often give the best tracks, but in the first case the
heat given out by the plaster, and in the second the weight of the plaster make it
impossible for casting to take place. The granular nature of sand also makes this a
poor medium. The authors have attempted to overcome this problem by using a
colloidal spray before pouring the plaster over an unsuitable surface, but this has
not achieved very much, apart from making it possible to just identify some of the
larger tracks from the casts made of them in such circumstances.

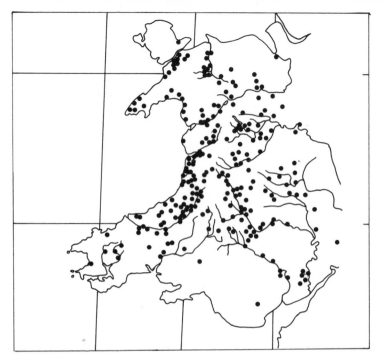

va   Map showing precise sightings of species.

vb   Map showing range of species.

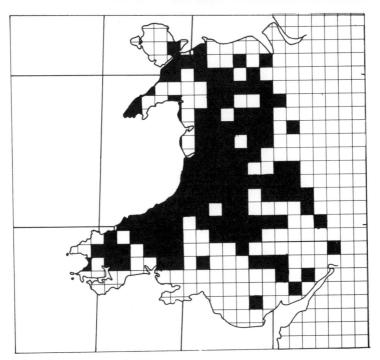

vc   10 x 10 km grid, each black square means 1 or more sightings (as used by the Mammal Society).

vd   A modification of the 10 x 10 km grid. This gives more detailed information on the distribution.

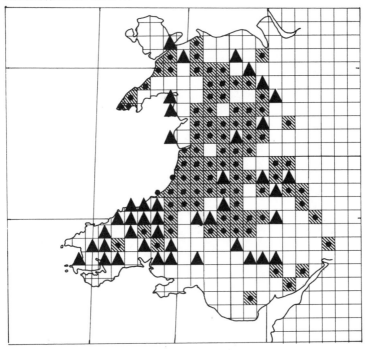

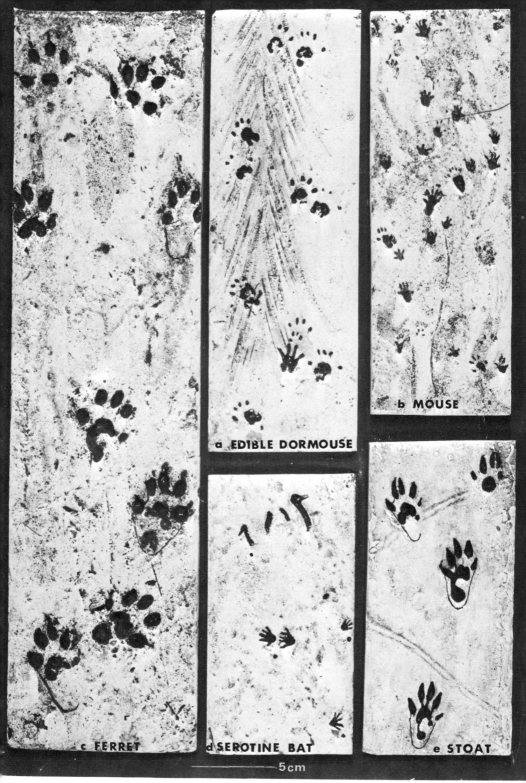

a EDIBLE DORMOUSE

b MOUSE

c FERRET

d SEROTINE BAT

e STOAT

5cm

vi Photograph of casts taken of mammal trails to show how much the quality of tracks may vary within a short distance.

Interpretation of distribution data

In the preface it was suggested that the Mammal Society of Great Britain's maps be used. It is as well, however, to comment on the problems which accompany the different methods of representing distribution on maps. Data taken from Walton's work of the Polecat in Great Britain (1968) serves to illustrate the different methods.

By far the most accurate map is the type which records the location of every siting of the species concerned (Fig. va). This obviously is very time-consuming and requires a force of workers in the field to obtain meaningful data.

Perhaps the least accurate method is the range map (Fig. vb) in which the total area over which the species occurs is drawn in monotone. This is useful in that it gives an indication of the area in which a species *might* occur, but it can give no idea of density or precise location. Sometimes several tones are used to represent different densities.

The grid square method represents a very satisfactory compromise. The Mammal Society has adopted a 10 by 10 km. grid based on the National Grid. Fig. vc shows the simplest form of this in which every square in which a record is made is blocked in. This gives a fairly tightly defined distribution of the species, but again gives no idea of density. The system shown in Fig. vd is a modification in which the use of symbols and shading allows different densities of population to be represented.

Criticisms of the 10 km. sq. system are that the area is too large to be of value, but intelligent use of the ecology of the species concerned normally allows fairly precise positioning to be made.

These are the main types of maps encountered and providing the limitations are borne in mind each is useful.

1 Insectivora and Chiroptera

ORDER INSECTIVORA

The insectivores are an extremely interesting Order in that they range from generalised and primitive types such as the shrew in which there is no reduction in the digits and the dentition is unspecialised, to the mole with its highly specialised digging forelimbs. Many habitats are represented in this country and insectivores are found in almost every one. Although the distribution of some species is limited, representatives of the Order occur as burrowers and ground dwellers as well as inhabiting freshwater. It is not unlikely that all the species of this Order (with the exception of the Scilly shrew) may be found to exist within a comparatively small area when conditions are favourable.

Three families of the Insectivora are present in the British Isles, two of them, Erinaceidae (hedgehog) and Talpidae (mole) represented by single species only. Four species of Soricidae (shrew) occur.

One of these, the Scilly shrew, a white-toothed shrew confined to the Scilly Isles, is included here for the sake of completeness. Its very restricted distribution makes it an object of interest to only a few trackers.

All members of this Order, excluding the hedgehog, are small. The nature of the mole's habitat, and the size and habitat of the ground shrews make the likelihood of finding tracks small. Hedgehog and Water shrew tracks are common in suitable areas but to find the tracks of all species provides an interesting challenge. Very little material, except for the obvious mole runs, hedgehog nests and shrew holes, is likely to be encountered in the field, and it will often be difficult to assess whether certain signs indicate the presence of Pygmy or Common shrew. Reasons other than inaccessibility make this an extremely demanding Order on one's tracking ability.

Talpa europaea   Family: Talpidae

Mole

OCCURRENCE Widely distributed in the British Isles, up to altitudes of 600 metres in favourable conditions. Present on the Isle of Wight, Anglesey, Skye, Mull, Jersey and Alderney. Absent from Ireland, the Isle of Man, the Hebrides, Orkney and Shetlands.

HABITS Solitary in existence, only one individual occupying any given tunnel system. The forelimbs are used to excavate the tunnels, the earth being moved, and thrust up into heaps on the surface with them (see also 'Signs' and 'Dwelling Place'). The home range is small in the females (10–12 metres), a little larger in males (15m.) and may be extended considerably in the spring at the onset of the breeding season. Active by day and night, resting periods spent sleeping in the nest. Tunnel systems are elaborate: deep, permanent tunnels are constructed in the vicinity of the fortress. Further out, shallow runs near the surface are made which in rare cases are so close to the surface that the roof collapses. The animal is an excellent swimmer. The eyesight is poor, and may even be non-existent, and, although the hearing and smell may be good, the sensitive vibrissae, which enable slight vibrations of the ground

Plate 1 Young hedgehogs.

Plate 2 Mole showing clearly the fore and hind feet.

Plate 3 Lesser white-toothed shrew or Scilly shrew.

Plate 4 Water shrew.

to be detected, constitute the most important sense. On occasions the animal may come to the surface, especially for water in summer.

HABITAT Below coniferous forests. Very common on arable and pasture lands as well as some open heath and woodland. The mole does seem capable of living in heavy waterlogged soils (Brown, 1972).

TRACK Very unusual. Although there are five toes on both fore and hind feet the powerful front limbs have been considerably modified, so that the animal tends to walk on the side of the fore feet. The hind impression on hard ground is in the form of an 'L', with three toes in a line and two others below in a line. The dimensions of this shape are about 1.1 cms. wide, 1.5 cms. long.

TRAIL This consists of the hind tracks straddled very wide astride the median line, the fore feet showing inside them. There are extensive scuff marks where the body of the animal has dragged over the ground. Generally very little movement takes place at the surface, but where it does the animals appear to take strides of between 3 and 4 cms. when walking (see D. W. Yalden 'Running in the Mole–*Talpa europaea*').

SIGNS The food consists almost entirely of animals which live in the soil, insects, worms and slugs. Broken hills have revealed large knots of damaged earthworms, presumably stored by the mole. Droppings are extremely unlikely to be located at the surface. The large mounds of earth commonly seen in the countryside are the fortresses. Small piles of earth in a line indicate deep tunnelling while continuous lines of earth at the surface indicate shallow tunnels, usually in hunting for food in the root zone. Open furrows are the result of excited rushes at the surface during the breeding season. Piles of earth which have been extruded will be colonised by grass and will often become ant nests or rabbit latrines.

DWELLING PLACE The nest may be in an expanded tunnel underground, or in areas where the water table is high in a large surface mound up to half a metre high and two metres in diameter. The nest may be actually in the mound, at surface level, or below ground.

Erinaceus europaeus   Family: Erinaceidae

Hedgehog

OCCURRENCE Widespread throughout the British Isles, although sparse in the Scottish Highlands. It is found on many islands off the coast: the Isles of Wight and Man, Anglesey, Shetland, Orkney, Skye, Bute, Mull, Coll and Canna, although probably as an introduced species on several of these.

HABITS Largely nocturnal, although may be active at dawn and dusk. A very noisy animal, frequently heard snuffling in ditches and woodland litter. Relies largely on hearing and smell as the eyesight is poor. It is a good swimmer and climber, as well as being able to dig. Hibernation occurs but is not deep and often does not begin until December, ending in March or April, and during this period individuals will frequently be seen abroad. There seems to be a very restricted home range and territory; it is uncertain if these are defended. The animal coils up into a ball when attacked or alarmed presenting its protective spines (really modified hairs).

HABITAT Common in open country which has sufficient shelter for making nests

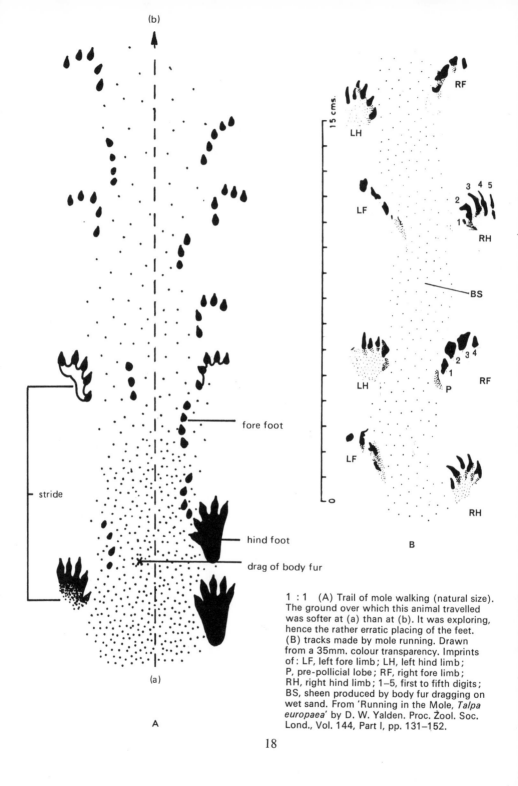

(b)

15 cms.

RF

LH

LF

3 4 5
2
1
RH

BS

LH

2 3 4
1
P
RF

LF

RH

B

stride

fore foot

hind foot

drag of body fur

x

(a)

A

1 : 1 (A) Trail of mole walking (natural size). The ground over which this animal travelled was softer at (a) than at (b). It was exploring, hence the rather erratic placing of the feet. (B) tracks made by mole running. Drawn from a 35mm. colour transparency. Imprints of: LF, left fore limb; LH, left hind limb; P, pre-pollicial lobe; RF, right fore limb; RH, right hind limb; 1–5, first to fifth digits; BS, sheen produced by body fur dragging on wet sand. From 'Running in the Mole, *Talpa europaea*' by D. W. Yalden. Proc. Żool. Soc. Lond., Vol. 144, Part I, pp. 131–152.

18

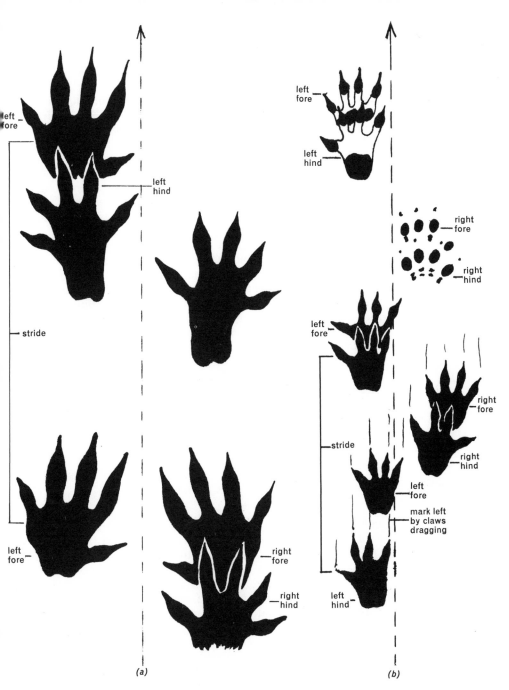

1 : 2 Trail of hedgehog (*a*) adult, (*b*) young, cast in very soft mud. Note drag of the claws and absence of the thumb on the fore foot. In the young hedgehog the thumb does not reach the ground and hence it will not show in the tracks. (Natural size.)

19

(e.g. copses and ditches). Grassy heaths, cultivated land, open wood, scrub and sand dunes are inhabited. Quite common in open spaces in and around built-up areas (e.g. parks and cemeteries) and will even live in large gardens. Dense woodland, marshes and high moorland are not often frequented.

TRACK The fore and hind feet are approximately the same width, but the hind foot is slightly more elongated (e.g. fore foot 4 cms. long; hind foot 4:5 cms. long). The toe marks are short and are separated from the pads by a space. The pads are large, if anything, larger on the fore foot. Two small pads may show on the hind feet, far back on the heel. The claws are long, sharp and usually show.

TRAIL When moving at the running gait the animal's body is held clear of the ground, an average stride of about 10 cms. being taken. When feeding and exploring, the animal tends to rest closer to the ground so that the marks of spines may show to the outside of the tracks. The feet are straddled across the median line and tend to turn out slightly. Registration does not always take place.

SIGNS The animal takes many invertebrates for food. It will also take frogs, reptiles (usually the adder) and small mammals such as young mice and voles. It may also break and eat small birds' eggs, but it is unlikely that hen eggs are taken as they are too large for the animal's jaws to encompass. Horse droppings and cow pats which have been broken up, rubbish and dung heaps which show signs of being disturbed may be the work of a hedgehog searching for food. The droppings are deposited at random, are up to 1 cm. in diameter and up to several cms. in length, are black in colour, rounded at the ends and contain the elytra and other remains of insects. The sound of crashing through ground vegetation in an unconcerned way at night, or the sound of small, clawed feet moving along a road or path at speed may indicate the presence of a hedgehog.

DWELLING PLACE The nest is usually a ball of grass and leaves under cover, in the roots of a tree, under a bush, or in a dry ditch for example. It may be in a burrow. The breeding nest may occur in a pile of vegetation, or even bonfire piles, but will be compact and well hidden.

Neomys fodiens   Family: Soricidae

Water Shrew

OCCURRENCE Found on the mainland of the British Isles, but seems to be absent from Ireland and all islands except Anglesey, Arran, Kerrera, Islay, Skye and the Isle of Wight. There is evidence to suggest that this species may occur to considerable altitudes where there is water, but it is uncertain what the maximum altitude may be.

HABITS Solitary, with overlapping home ranges. Seems to range over distances of about 160 metres. Diurnal activity, but probably maximum movement takes place at night. Regular runs and swims are adopted. Short excursions are made into the water, and a great deal of time is spent on the bank in grooming the fur.

HABITAT Usually in banks next to streams; known to prefer watercress beds. Will spread to other habitats, especially woodland, often far away from water, and records of specimens two miles away from any expanse of water have been made. Confirmed reports have been made of individuals living in mountain streams.

TRACK The fore and hind feet have five toes, the second, third and fourth point-

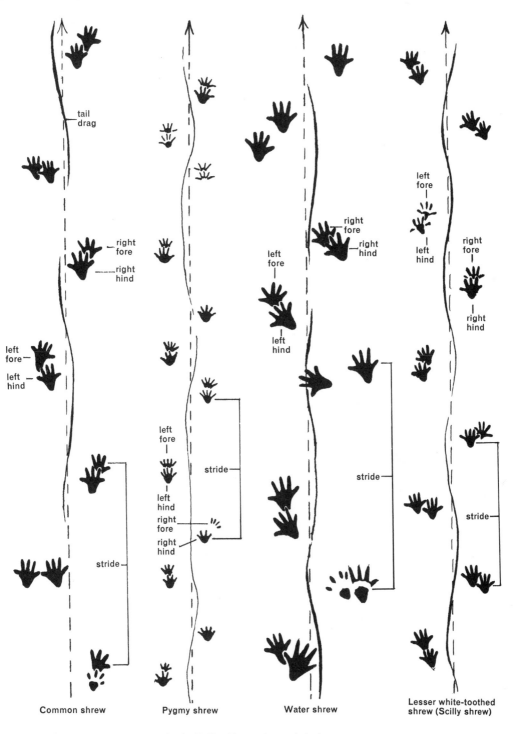

1 : 3 Trails : Shrews (natural size).

ing forward, the first and fifth forming angles with these. The hind foot is slightly longer than the fore (e.g. 1.4 cms. to 1.2 cms.), and is more likely to show the claws. There are six pads on both feet, four near to the toes, two further back on the heel. The tracks of this species (as with all shrews) can be differentiated from those of the smaller rodents in that (apart from the fact that the shrews have five toes on fore and hind feet) there is a much shorter length of foot behind the toes.

TRAIL The normal gait is a run, when a stride of about 4.5 cms. is taken. The hind feet register imperfectly on the fore and are placed fairly wide astride the median line. The tail shows in the trail.

SIGNS Known to eat small mammals, crustaceans and molluscs (the remains of snail shells may be found near the holes). The droppings, which are black and cylindrical and may occasionally contain the remnants of insects, are deposited near the edge of water, or at random in habitats away from water. Regular runs may exist in the vegetation on the stream bank. A line of bubbles may indicate that an animal is swimming under the water, but as there is no way of distinguishing whether it is a Water shrew or vole unless it emerges, this is of little use.

DWELLING PLACE Extensive shallow burrow system in river bank and often some distance 'inland' in the litter zone. The entrance is in the river either above or below the water. The tunnels are flattened in cross-section, as are those of other shrews, but this may be recognised by its large size. The tunnel is made very narrow, and this is probably to help squeeze the animal dry.

Crocidura suaveolens   Family: Soricidae

Lesser white-toothed Shrew (Scilly Shrew)

OCCURRENCE Within the political boundary of the British Isles, excepting Jersey and Sark, this species occurs only in the Scilly Isles, and is the only species of shrew found there. It is unlikely that the reports of this species occurring on the extreme southern tip of Cornwall have any foundation. The islands known to be inhabited are: St. Mary's, Tresco, St. Martin's, St. Agnes, Bryher, Tean, Annet, Samson and some of the smaller islands.

HABITS Very little is known about the activities of this species, but they are probably similar in many respects to those of the other shrews. It is certainly active during the day, and is perhaps more gregareous than *Sorex araneus* and *S. minutus*, the Common shrew and Pygmy shrew respectively.

HABITAT Found in all habitats on the Scilly Isles from pebbly beaches to the floor of bare pine plantations. Concentrations seem to occur in heathland, where there is bracken and bramble and a litter zone.

TRACK The tracks are slightly smaller than those of *S. araneus*. Claws, toe tips and pad marks will show in good tracks and, as conditions are adverse to finding tracks generally, any which are found are likely to be excellent.

TRAIL When running gait is adopted the tracks register, and a stride of about 3.5 cms. is taken. Tail marks are evident. At bounding gait the tracks will be in groups of four.

SIGNS Feeds on insects and other litter zone invertebrates, sand hoppers being taken on sandy beaches. Droppings extremely small, and contain the hard parts of insects.

DWELLING PLACE Little is known about this, but extensive runs are probably constructed in the litter zone, and nests are made from soft vegetation (e.g. grass) in covered places in heath conditions.

Sorex araneus   Family: Soricidae

Common Shrew

OCCURRENCE Common, occurring over much of England, Wales and Scotland. Absent from Ireland, the Isle of Man, Scillies, Lundy, Outer Hebrides and some of the Inner Hebrides. Found on the Isle of Wight, Anglesey, Skomer, Islay, Jura, Arran, Bute, Mull, Skye, Raasay, South Ronaldsay, Scalpay and Ulva. Considerable concentrations may occur locally.

HABITS Swift, almost invisible movement when exploring for food with sensitive vibrissae. Eyesight poor, scent little used in tracking food. Extensive runs are made in litter zone, tunnels are dug and those of other species utilised. Most activity takes place in the litter level. The animal is a good swimmer. It is solitary and aggressive except in the mating season, and individuals will fight on meeting. The home range is large for such a small animal, up to 145 metres in males. In spring the males may move even further afield. Active throughout twenty-four hours, but probably most active at night, and least active in the early afternoon. Almost all time is spent in search for food, which is held on the ground between the front paws to be eaten. Surplus food is stored, usually (if insect or invertebrate food) in a maimed form, the shrew having first taken a bite from it.

HABITAT Found in most types of habitat up to at least 600 metres. Most common in areas of thick grass, woodland, scrub, hedgerows and banks.

TRACK The tracks are very small. The hind foot is longer than the fore (hind foot 1 by 1 cm.; fore foot 0.8 by 0.9 cm.). Although not normally found, except in soft silt, or other very soft medium, good tracks will show the tips of toes and claw marks clearly. The hind foot and fore foot both have six prominent pads.

TRAIL The running gait is the most usual. The hind foot registers and an average stride of 4 cms. is taken. The feet are slightly straddled across the median line, but much less so than in the case of the Scilly shrew. At bounding gait the feet are placed in groups of four, with a distance of 4 to 5 cms. between them.

SIGNS Food consists largely of invertebrates of the soil and litter zone, especially beetles and earthworms. The droppings are small and may be distinguished from those of mice by the insect remains they contain. Tunnels and nests may be found under fallen trees and general surface litter. The tunnels are small and horizontally flattened. Very often, a high-pitched squeaking noise is the first sign that shrews are present.

DWELLING PLACE The nests are loose balls woven from grasses, built either below ground, or under cover at the surface. Ordinary nests are flimsy while the breeding nest is more solid. Nests may be found in matted vegetation, under fallen trees, roots or rubbish.

Sorex minutus   Family: Soricidae

Pygmy Shrew

OCCURRENCE Widely distributed over the British Isles, being absent only from the Scillies, Channel Islands and Shetlands. This species is found in almost all habitats, is common in many areas and may be very common in favourable localities.

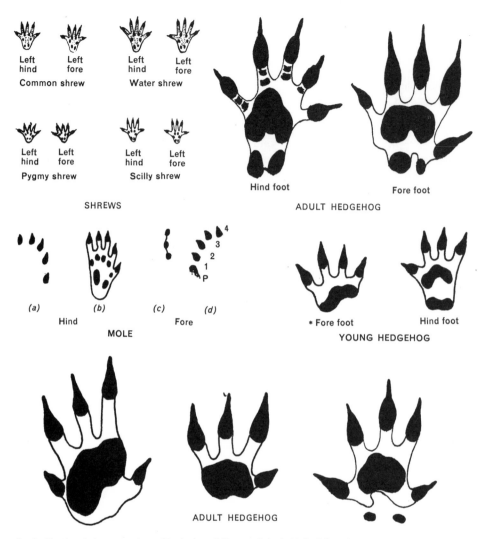

Left
hind

Left
fore

Common shrew

Left
hind

Left
fore

Water shrew

Left
hind

Left
fore

Pygmy shrew

Left
hind

Left
fore

Scilly shrew

SHREWS

Hind foot

Fore foot

ADULT HEDGEHOG

(a)

(b)

Hind

(c)

(d)

Fore

MOLE

4
3
2
1
P

* Fore foot

Hind foot

YOUNG HEDGEHOG

ADULT HEDGEHOG

1 : 4   Tracks of shrews, mole and hedgehog (all natural size). Mole (a) on hard mud, (b) on soft mud, (c) on hard mud, (d) on soft mud. 1, 2, 3, 4, indicate digits. P, pre-pollicial lobe.
See 'Running in the Mole, *Talpa europaea*' by D. W. Yalden for further information.
*Note that the thumb prints do not show in the track of young hedgehog. This is characteristic of the young.

HABITS Similar to those of *S. araneus*, the animal being solitary and aggressive except in the breeding season. Relatively more active during the day with frequent, short, resting periods, but there is evidence of considerable night activity also. An average radius of the area an individual will range over is about 30 metres. This species does not make its own burrows, but utilises those of other species just below or at ground level in the litter zone. The animal is an agile climber and probably swims well.

24

1 : 5   Common shrew (showing the feet clearly).

1 : 6   Pygmy shrew.

HABITAT Every type of terrestial habitat is occupied, from high moors to sandy coasts. In general, this species is more common in open types of habitat and is never found in woodland or scrub as frequently as *S. araneus*. It is commonly found in young growing plantations.

TRACK The tracks are extremely small. The hind foot is 5 mm. long, and the fore foot is 4 mm. long. The tracks are as wide as they are long. There are six pads on each foot, and claw marks will show clearly. These tracks will be found only in the finest silt.

TRAIL The hind foot registers and the tracks straddle across the median line. The tail drag shows and is rather like a fine thread. The average stride is about 2 cms.

SIGNS and DWELLING PLACE: See *Sorex araneus*.

ORDER CHIROPTERA (Bats)

In many ways the bats may seem to be somewhat beyond the scope of this book. They are the only group of mammals which have attained the power of sustained flight and the resulting skeletal modifications have led to a way of life which makes this the least likely Order to move over the surface of the ground. It is, however, extremely important to consider all of the material, however rarely it occurs, which is likely to be encountered in the field, and for this reason the bats are dealt with as fully as possible here. The bats hunt on the wing and eat and rest in roosts (a hollow tree, cave or the roof of a building with direct external access), usually suspended upside down by the hind feet. The likelihood of finding signs anywhere outside of a known roost is not great, although broken bodies of beetles, found under trees, hedges and fences may be the remnants of prey taken on the wing. Tracks are extremely rare as it is difficult for bats to land on flat ground; it has been reported, however, that individuals have been seen to land by the edge of a pool or on cow pats in search of insects. Once on the ground, however, they can move with considerable speed and leave a distinctive track (see Fig. 1 : 17). It would be of no value to deal with the tracks of all the species considered in this chapter since some of them are extremely rare, and there is little variation, except in size, from species to species. There are two families of bats in the British Isles, the Vespertilionidae, or smooth-faced bats, and Rhinolophidae, or Horseshoe bats.

The forelimb is the most greatly modified. The forearm is long and curved, the first digit is short and has a long claw, digits being elongated and supporting a membrane which reaches down to the ankle and on to the tail. The upper part of the sternum has a well-developed keel to which powerful muscles are attached. The clavicle is strongly attached to the humerus and the bones of the neck and back are strong, some of them being fused for extra strength. In some bats the first and second ribs are joined not only to the backbone and sternum, but to each other to form a solid supporting ring of bone. The pelvis, legs and tail are weak, and the thigh bones are twisted round so that the knees bend in the opposite direction to that of most mammals.

General features of movement

Bats move over the ground in the same way as do most terrestrial mammals, i.e. with the fore- and hindlimbs moving as diagonally opposite pairs. The left forelimb is moved just before the diagonally opposite right hindlimb. As the right hindlimb comes forward it forces the right forelimb to rise at an angle to the ground. This series of movements takes place whenever the animal moves (Fig. 1 : 8).

The tracks of the forelimb show as a single thumb mark or dot, the hindlimb tracks are five-toed and claw marks are usually present.

Walking

This type of gait was demonstrated by *E. serotinus* only and by *P. pipistrellus* occasionally.

The forelimbs are held close to the body and the tracks are therefore the width of the body apart. When walking the forward movement of one hindlimb tends to make the animal unstable. To correct this the tail is pressed on to the ground and

1 : 7 Haunt of whiskered bat.

used as a fourth point of contact, which extends the base-area and so stabilises the body. The form of the trail is shown in Fig. 1:17. The tracks appear as pairs (fore and hind) diagonally opposite each other, and are placed astride the median line. Between each set of diagonally opposite tracks is the mark of the tail and this appears as a dot on the side of the median line of the forefoot most extended, i.e. that side on which the instability occurs when the hindlimb approaches the ipsilateral forelimb. Also in the trail are two lines made by the calcars, these lie between the tracks and the median line.

In the trail of the Serotine (Fig. 1 : 17) the animal had rested after walking and this produced an interesting result. The forefoot tracks not only showed the thumb and wrist but also the anterior part of the digits. When bats rest on the ground they very often lay their heads on it and the mark of the lower jaw may show.

Running

The type of gait is performed by *N. noctula* and *P. pipistrellus*. It was observed under two circumstances, '*normal*' and '*restricted*'.

In the normal running gait the forelimbs are not held close to the body but at an angle to it. This means the forelimb tracks appear to the outside of the hindlimb tracks, alternate fore and hind, and are widely spaced (Fig. 1 : 10a). The running animal is much more stable because of its speed and less acute angle of the limbs. As one limb is moved forward the tail is raised and kept clear of the ground and is thus not used for supporting the animal (Fig. 1 : 10–1 : 11).

In the restricted gait the forelimbs, unlike those in normal gait, are kept close to the body. This type of gait results in the tracks appearing precisely one behind the other (fore and hind, fore and hind) . . . and equally distant from the median line (Fig. 1: 12a). In this type of movement, even though the limbs are held close to the body as they are in walking gait, the hindfeet are not brought so far forward, and the forelimbs are consequently held at a less acute angle.

Leap-frogging

This type of gait was observed briefly on one occasion only in the noctule (*N. noctula*). In all previous gaits the limbs have moved in the following manner: right fore, left hind; left fore, right hind; right fore, left hind; left fore, right hind; etc. While in this gait they move thus: left fore and right fore; left hind and right hind; left fore and right fore; etc. (Fig. 1: 12b). The fore- and hindlimbs thus move as opposite pairs. What part, if any, the tail plays in lending support to the body when the hindfeet are moving forward is as yet undetermined, but it does leave a faint central mark. The tracks appear as pairs and as widely spaced across the median line.

Family Rhinolophidae

Rhinolophus ferrumequinum

Greater Horseshoe Bat

OCCURRENCE Found in England and Wales, and may be locally common in south-west England, south and west Wales. Occurs in the southern counties as far east as Kent. Not generally found in East Anglia, and is totally absent from Scotland and Ireland.

28

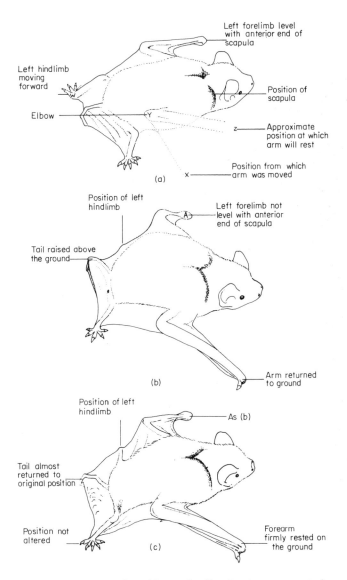

Left forelimb level
with anterior end of
scapula

Left hindlimb
moving
forward

Position of
scapula

Elbow

Y

z

Approximate
position at which
arm will rest

Position from which
x arm was moved

(a)

Position of left
hindlimb

Left forelimb not
level with anterior
end of scapula

A

Tail raised above
the ground

Arm returned
to ground

(b)

Position of left
hindlimb

As (b)

Tail almost
returned to
original position

Position not
altered

Forearm
firmly rested on
the ground

(c)

1 : 8   Drawings taken from 16 mm. cine film showing movement of
limbs.

29

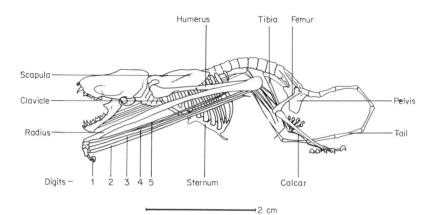

1 : 9   Skeleton of bat seen from left side.

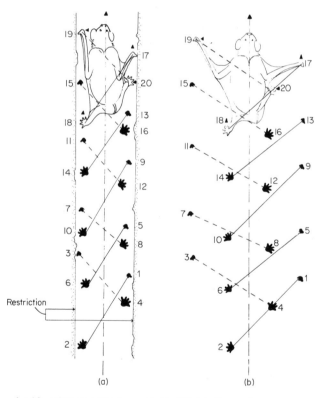

(a)   (b)

1 : 10   Diagram of tracks and trail of Pipistrelle running
(a) restricted; (b) normal.
▲ Foot about to move forward; ◀ foot just making contact with
ground. Numbers indicate order in which feet moved.

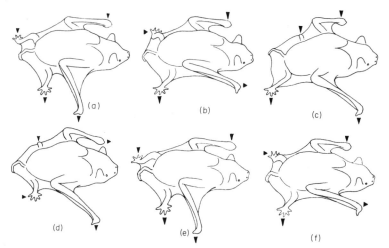

1 : 11 Stages of movements when unrestricted (*N. noctula*)
▶ Foot moving forward; ▼ foot pressed firmly on the ground.

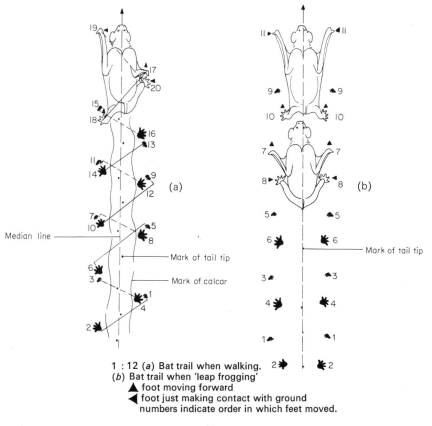

Median line

Mark of tail tip

Mark of calcar

Mark of tail tip

1 : 12 (*a*) Bat trail when walking.
(*b*) Bat trail when 'leap frogging'
▲ foot moving forward
◀ foot just making contact with ground
numbers indicate order in which feet moved.

31

Plate 5 One Greater
and two Lesser
Horseshoe bats
sleeping.

Plate 6 Pipistrelle bat
with young.

Plate 7 Long-eared bat in walking position.

Plate 8 Whiskered bat.

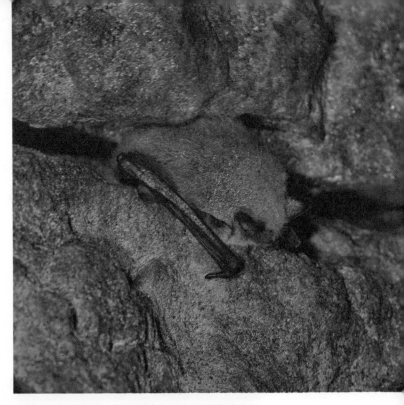

Plate 9 Hibernating Daubenton's bat. Note the condensation which has taken place on the fur.

Plate 10 Leisler's bat in walking position.

Plate 11   Fox.

Plate 12   Scottish Wild cats. (Male and female).

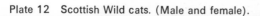

HABITS Lives in colonies, emerging late and flying throughout the night. Usually flies low, taking beetles, moths and other nocturnal insects as well as spiders. Some prey is caught by the bat dropping to the ground with outspread wings, and the animals have been seen settling in grass to take beetles on cow dung. Small prey is eaten on the wing, larger creatures dismembered at the roost.

HABITAT Caves and mine tunnels during hibernation; often found in barns, lofts and attics between May and October. In some cases the same habitat is used throughout the year.

Rhinolophus hipposideros

Lesser Horseshoe Bat

OCCURRENCE Covers much the same area as *R. ferrumequinum* but extends further north into the Midlands and Yorkshire. Occurs in isolated parts of East Anglia and Ireland, where it seems confined to western limestone districts.

HABITS Similar to *R. ferrumequinum* but flying period begins earlier. Lives in smaller colonies than *R. ferrumequinum*. Flight is low to medium; beetles, spiders and moths are taken and eaten in the same way as by *R. ferrumequinum*.

HABITAT Similar to *R. ferrumequinum*.

Family Vespertilionidae

Myotis mystacinus

Whiskered Bat

OCCURRENCE Common over most of the British Isles; said to be rare in Scotland and East Anglia although colonies have been recorded in Norfolk.

HABITS Emerges early and activity seems to take place during the whole night, although it may be intermittent. Sometimes seen abroad by day, especially in the spring. Usually solitary, but may be gregarious. Small insects of various kinds are taken on the wing, or else plucked from foliage. Low to medium flight.

HABITAT May hibernate in caves, crevices in rock faces and cellars, but will spend the summer in buildings and trees.

Myotis nattereri

Natterer's Bat

OCCURRENCE Quite common in England and Wales, and has sometimes been recorded in southern Scotland. Frequently recorded in many parts of Ireland.

HABITS Emerges early and flies periodically throughout the night. Active on mild nights in winter, but only for a short period. Gregarious in summer, solitary in hibernation. Food consists of various small insects and moths which are taken on the wing, or sometimes from foliage.

HABITAT Favours well-wooded areas and will inhabit holes in buildings and trees as well as caves, the latter especially for hibernation.

Myotis bechsteini

Bechstein's Bat

OCCURRENCE Very rare, and until the end of the Second World War only recorded

1 : 13 Nathusis Pipistrelle (a new species to Britain).

in Hampshire, Isle of Wight, Berkshire and Sussex. In recent years specimens have been recorded in Dorset, Somerset, Gloucester, Wiltshire and Shropshire.

After R. E. Stebbings (1968). Now found in Devon (Hurrell, 1966) and will possibly continue to increase its range.

HABITS Probably emerges fairly late. Low flying. Gregarious, living in colonies of up to 20. Feeds on moths, catching them on the wing, and also taking resting insects from the foliage of trees.

HABITAT Probably woodland, favouring holes in trees as a roost. Little known about hibernating habitat.

Myotis myotis
Mouse-eared Bat

OCCURRENCE It is uncertain if this species is migrant or resident in England, but it is certainly very rare, being recorded in Cambridgeshire in 1888 and in Dorset in 1956, where further records have been taken. Phillips and Blackmore (1970) found nine Mouse-eared Bats in Sussex in October 1969. In November they recorded thirteen and then a further five. In January 1970 twenty-eight specimens were recorded.

HABITS Very little is known about it in this country, but since it has been known to travel many kilometres there is no reason to suppose that migration does not take place.

HABITAT Various buildings and caves.

Myotis daubentoni
Daubenton's Bat

OCCURRENCE Fairly common in most counties in England, Wales and Scotland. Just as common in Ireland, but over more restricted areas, probably due to lack of information.

HABITS Emerges late and hunts over water, sometimes in large numbers. Gregarious, colonies of several hundred not being uncommon in summer. Hibernates in small colonies or alone. Low flight, circling over water. Feeds mainly on aquatic insects taken on the wing.

HABITAT Streams, rivers, ponds and caves.

Eptesicus serotinus
Serotine Bat

OCCURRENCE Confined to England and is locally common in Kent, Surrey, Sussex and Hampshire. Extends westwards into Cornwall, and eastwards into Sussex. Recorded as far north as Cambridgeshire.

HABITS Time of emergence varies and activity occurs at periods throughout the night. Medium to high flight. Gregarious, colonies of up to 50 having been recorded. Hibernates from October to March. Food consists mainly of beetles and moths. The animals may actually land on foliage to pick off insects. Food may be eaten in the air when on the wing.

HABITAT Buildings and hollow trees, with a few records of caves being used for hibernation.

Nyctalus leisleri

Leisler's Bat

OCCURRENCE Locally common in parts of Ireland and records indicate a fairly wide distribution in England, ranging from Cheshire and Yorkshire in the north to Devon and Kent in the south.

HABITS Emerges early and flies for about an hour while a second flight may be taken just before dawn. Solitary in flight, but may be gregarious or solitary in roost, colonies of up to 100 individuals being recorded. Roosts are sometimes changed. A medium to high flier. Food consists mainly of beetles, moths and flies, often eaten during flight.

HABITAT Lives in holes in trees, in roofs or holes in buildings. Hibernation from September to April. Does not often frequent caves.

Nyctalus noctula

Noctule Bat

OCCURRENCE Common over most of England and Wales but, although recorded as far north as Morayshire, is nowhere common in Scotland.

HABITS Emerges very early and flies for about an hour to an hour and a half; a second flight sometimes being made before dawn. Colonies often migrate to other places. Flight medium to high. Food is taken on the wing and consists of any insects, but the larger beetles seem to be the most favoured. The roost often has a rancid smell about it.

HABITAT Holes in buildings or trees, hollow trees in summer. Caves not much frequented, and even when selected for hibernation are only used by individuals.

Pipistrellus nathusi

Nathusis Pipistrelle

OCCURRENCE Discovered in October 1969 at Furzebrook Research Station by R. E. Stebbings (*J. Zool.* 1970) as a new species to the British Isles. He gave details of measurements taken and compared these with *P. pipistrellus*.

Pipistrellus pipistrellus

Common Pipistrelle or Pipistrelle Bat

OCCURRENCE Found almost everywhere in the British Isles, and is by far the most common species.

HABITS Emerges at or just before sunset. Probably sporadic activity throughout the night. Flight medium to high. Gregarious, colonies of several hundred animals occurring. Hibernates from October to March. Gnats and many other small insects are taken on the wing, but larger prey is taken back to the resting place to be eaten. May occasionally be seen during the day.

HABITAT Usually found in confined spaces – under roofs or even in disused chimneys, in hollow trees or small caves.

1 : 14   Moths' wings that have accumulated under a bat roost.

Barbastella barbastellus

Barbastelle Bat

OCCURRENCE Found only in England and Wales and, although fairly widespread in areas as far north as Cumberland, it tends to be localised.

HABITS Emerges at or just after sunset and is active until midnight, in August and September at least. There is a further period of activity just before dawn. Usually solitary but small colonies may be formed in the summer. Low to medium in flight, the prey usually being taken on the wing.

HABITAT Buildings, caves and hollow trees. Roosting may occur behind the bark of trees in summer.

1 : 15   Horseshoe bat droppings.

1 : 16   Hedgehog after being taken from its hibernating nest to be photographed.

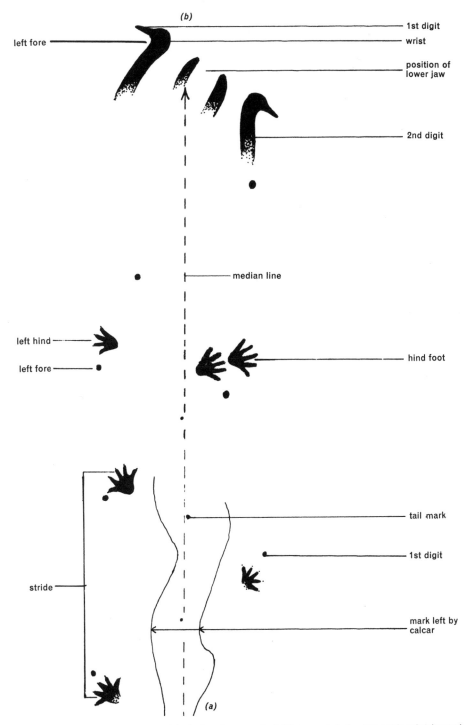

1 : 17 Trail of Serotine bat (natural size). See photograph vi. After a period of walking this animal rested. This explains the excellent impression of the fore arm and the unusual mark left by the lower jaw. The ground was harder at (a) than at (b).

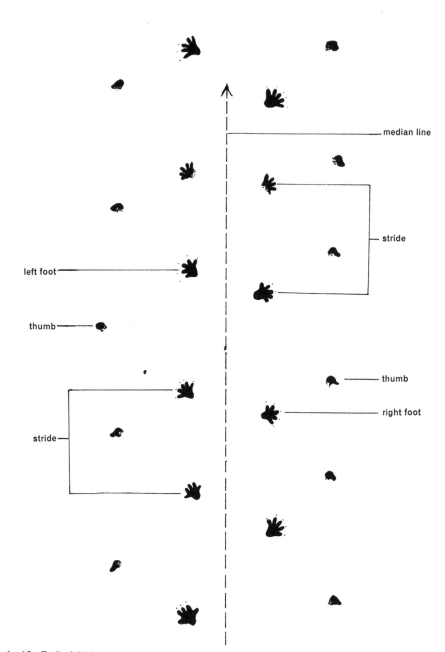

median line

stride

left foot

thumb

thumb

right foot

stride

1 : 18   Trail of Pipistrelle bat (natural size) moving at speed on the ground. Note the absence of tail and calcar marks.

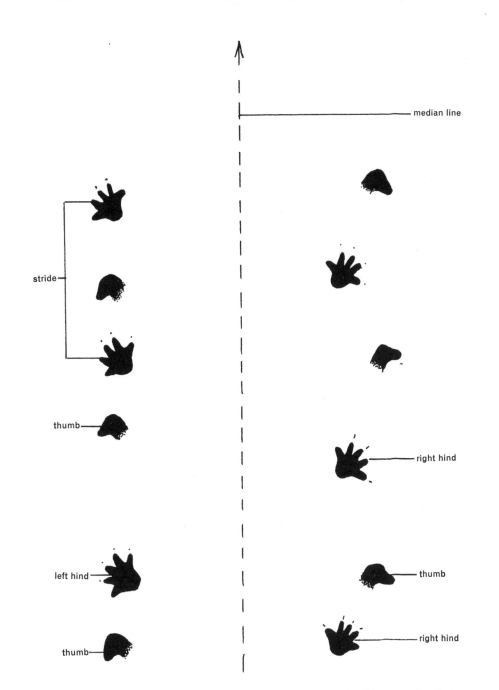

median line

stride

thumb

left hind

thumb

right hind

thumb

right hind

1 : 19 Trail of a running Noctule bat (natural size) its movement restricted between two twigs. Note total absence of tail and calcar marks.

Plecotus auritus

Long-eared Bat

OCCURRENCE Common and very widely spread over the British Isles.

HABITS Emerges after sunset, and is sporadically active throughout the night. Hibernates from October to March, but sometimes flies on mild winter nights. May be migratory. Gregarious in summer and autumn, but usually hibernates alone. Moths, butterflies, beetles, crane flies and other small insects are taken, usually from tree trunks or foliage. Small prey is eaten on the wing; larger prey is taken to the roost.

HABITAT Roosts in house and church roofs are sometimes inhabited all through the year, but caves may be used as hibernating locations.

Plecotus austriacus

*Grey Long-eared Bat

OCCURRENCE Little is known about this at the moment. The species was only recognised as being separate from *Plecotus auritus* (in this country) in the last few months. It is uncertain to what extent the characteristics of this species differ from those of the Long-eared bat.

HABITS ⎫
HABITAT ⎭ See *Plecotus auritus*.

* Was first named by Fischer (1829), but then seems to have been overlooked until quite recently when G. B. Corbet (British Museum, Natural History), rediscovered its presence in this country.

2 Carnivora and Pinnipedia

ORDER CARNIVORA

In many ways the carnivores are, perhaps, the most interesting Order of British mammals to study, not because of their great diversity in form but because they present the greatest challenge to the tracker and general naturalist. This Order includes our rarest species of mammals, and almost all of them keep their activities concealed from man, owing to constant persecution by him. This chapter deals in detail with each species of the Order Carnivora, but before individuals are dealt with, there are several general features worth considering here.

In this country there are three families: the *Canidae* or dogs, the *Mustelidae* or weasels, and the *Felidae* or cats.

The dogs contain only the fox as a wild species, and many breeds of the Domestic dog, *Canis familiaris.*

The *Mustelidae* consist of weasels, stoats, martens, polecats, badgers and otters, and represent the bulk of our carnivores. These have certain features in common with each other.

When a weasel, stoat, polecat or pine marten makes a kill, it nearly always eats brain of its prey first; hence the cranium of many of their kills when found will be bitten through at the base.

All carnivores have musk glands at the base of their tail, and in the *Mustelidae* these are particularly well developed. In some species, notably the polecat, this has a very strong and unpleasant odour, but with the majority there is simply a musty smell. The fresh droppings of this family also bear this musty odour.

There is only one truly wild member of the cat family to be found in the British Isles – the Scottish wild cat. Its smaller domestic relatives sometimes revert to the wild state, but are not true wild cats. The only general feature of the cats which need to be considered here is that the claws are retractile, and are usually kept covered. Hence on feline tracks the claw marks are rarely visible.

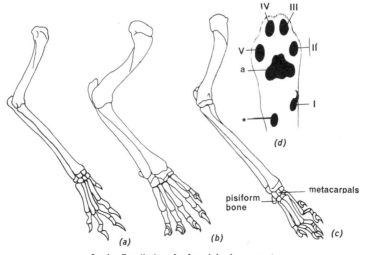

2 : 1   Forelimbs of *a* fox, *b* badger, *c* cat.
In *d* the under-surface of a cat's right fore paw is sketched to show pads.
I, II, III, IV, V indicate the five toes, I being the pollex. Trilobed pad (*a*) lies beneath the distal ends of the metacarpal bones. *Pad beneath the pisiform bone of the wrist (after Mivart).

2 : 2 Place where hedgehog has retrieved buried eggs.

2 : 3 Rabbit hidden by fox near earth.

Key to Carnivore Tracks

This key refers to perfect *adult* track. Careful note should be taken of the position of the pads and of the lobes on the hind pad. Reference to the illustrations is advised.

1. Four-toed   Felidae/Canidae 2
   Five-toed   Mustelidae   4
2. Claw marks absent   ...   . Cat
   Claw marks present (over 3 cms. in width)   3
3. Toes approximately same size as hind pad; hair marks often present between toes and hind pad.   ...   . Fox
   Toes smaller than hind pad, which is tri-lobed.   ...   ... Dog
4. Large (4 cms. and over)   5
   Medium (over 2 cms. but less than 3.5 cms.) 6
   Small (under 2 cms.)   7
5. Toes form shallow curved line; claw marks strong; wider than longer; toes point forward.   ...   . Badger
   Toes strongly curved in arc; webbing between toes ...   ... Otter
   Toes strongly curved in arc; webbing not present   ...   ... Pine Marten
6. Webbing between toes ...   . Mink
   Webbing between toes absent ...   . Polecat
7. Over 1 cm. and less than 2 cms.   ...   . Stoat
   Under 1 cm.   ...   . Weasel

2 : 4 FOUR-TOED TRACKS

WILDCAT (Felidae)
Claw marks absent. Hind pad three lobed, the
middle being larger. Toes pointing in a straight
line, i.e. they do not spread out.
Size : Up to 6 cms. wide, 6 cms. long.

DOG (Canidae)
Claw marks present, toes radiate out slightly.
Hind pad consists of three lobes. Each toe is
equal in area to one lobe on the hind pad, i.e.
area of three toes is equal to that of the hind
pad. Claw marks point outwards.
Size : Varies greatly.

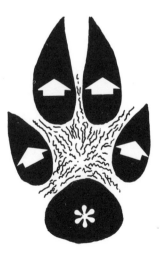

FOX (Canidae)
Claw marks present. Outer toes show a slight
radial tendency. Hind pad single lobed, one
toe equal to the area of the hind pad. Toes
grouped closely together. Hair traces often
present between pads and toes.
Size : 4 cms. wide, 6 cms. long.

43

BADGER (Melinae)
Toes form a very shallow curve, do not radiate; claw marks parallel. Span of toes smaller than or equal to width of hind pad. Hind pad 'Bean shaped'. Five toes equal in area to area of hind pad. Toes do not descend beyond hind pad. Size: About 4.5 cms. wide, 4 cms. long.

OTTER (Lutrinae)
Toes widely spaced and radial about the hind pad; webbing marks show between toes. Claws short and blunt also radiating. Span of toes greater than span of hind pad. Two outer toes extend beyond the area of hind pad and below or on a level with the top of hind pad. Web marks are above the toe line.
Size : 6 cms. wide, 5.5 cms. long.

PINE MARTEN (Mustelidae)
Toes widely spread about pad. Web marks absent. Claw marks short, blunt but clearly defined. Width greater than length. Fore foot tracks show toes evenly distributed around hind pad. When webbing shows it appears below the toe line.
Size: About 6.5 cms. wide, 6 cms. long.

44

TRACKS

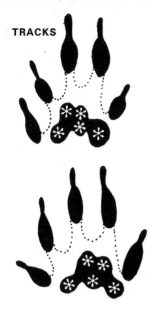

POLECAT/FERRET (Mustelidae)
Toes form a curve around the hind pad which has four lobes and is irregular in shape. Span of toes greater than width of hind pad. Area of toes far greater than area of hind pad. Claw marks very long and often joined to toes. Fore track longer than it is wide. Hind track as long as it is wide. Middle three toes above hind pad, outer two toes on a level with hind pad. If web marks show, they lie below the toe line.
Size : 3.5 cms. wide, 3 cms. long.

MINK (Mustelidae)
Toes form an arc. In the fore track the two middle toes lie close together, the hind track has the middle three toes in an almost straight line. Web marks show clearly between toes and lie above the toe line, also the claw marks which are relatively slender.
Size : About 2.5 cms. wide, 2.5 cms. long.

STOAT/WEASEL (Mustelidae)
Tracks small and five-toed. The Weasel has the smallest tracks, about 0.9 cms. wide, 0 cm. long. Stoat tracks 2 cms. wide, 1.5 cms. long. Toes widely spaced around hind pad. Claw marks long and prominent.

* Toe does not always show in Mink tracks.

Vulpes vulpes   Family: Canidae

Common Fox

The male is termed Dog, the female, Vixen, and the young, Cub.

OCCURRENCE Common over most of the British Isles, often near to human settlement. There are specimens, hill forms which live in isolated areas of Scotland, which are larger than the lowland animals.

HABITS Largely nocturnal, but may be seen during the daytime. Follows regular paths, usually through well covered areas, where its presence may be concealed. Will often raid farms, and is prepared to pass through, or near human settlement. Changes locality frequently, except when the vixen has young. Usually family groups keep together.

HABITAT Prefers wood and copse, highland and lowland, but will inhabit high, rocky country when the former are unobtainable.

TRACK The pad is triangular, with four toes arched tightly around it. The toes show the claws clearly, and there is a tendency for the two central toes to point inwards. The print is neat, and in really soft mud hair traces may show around the track, and between the toes and pad. The fore foot is larger than the hind.

TRAIL When trotting the tracks are evenly spaced along either side of the median line, with an average stride of 46 cms. When stalking its prey the fox creeps, placing the feet very close together. When bounding the feet are put down as a group of four with a distance of 60 cms. between each group. When trotting, the fox trail follows a purposeful course and may hence be distinguished from that of dog, which tends to be erratic with frequent pauses.

SIGNS The feeding remains consist of bones, fur and feathers which are found outside the fox earth together with droppings. There is a very strong smell from these food remains. The musty smell which is characteristic of the fox, can be detected where the animal has recently passed by. The red hair and scratch marks around burrows and fences shows the digging activity of the fox. The droppings or 'castings' are long and twisted with tapered ends, but do not coil. The colour varies with composition, but may be greenish-grey to brownish-blue, and will usually show insect and bone remains, plus hair. There is also a strong musty odour present with these.

Tinbergen (1965) records food burying by *Vulpes*, including eggs (of Blackheaded gulls), rabbits and birds. The eggs were not taken until the breeding population of gulls had left and food (gulls) had become scarce. The food is buried over a very wide area and this reduces robbery. The food is not always literally 'buried'; it is sometimes just placed under a bush or hedge. Hedgehogs were also recorded digging up these eggs, although they never buried them.

DWELLING PLACE The 'earth' is built in ditches, under tree roots, and in rocky places. Sometimes rabbit warrens are taken over and enlarged. Badger sets may also be intruded upon.

Canis familiaris   Family: Canidae

Domestic Dog

The male is termed Dog, the female, Bitch, and the young, Puppy.

OCCURRENCE Dogs are found almost everywhere in the range of human habitation,

46

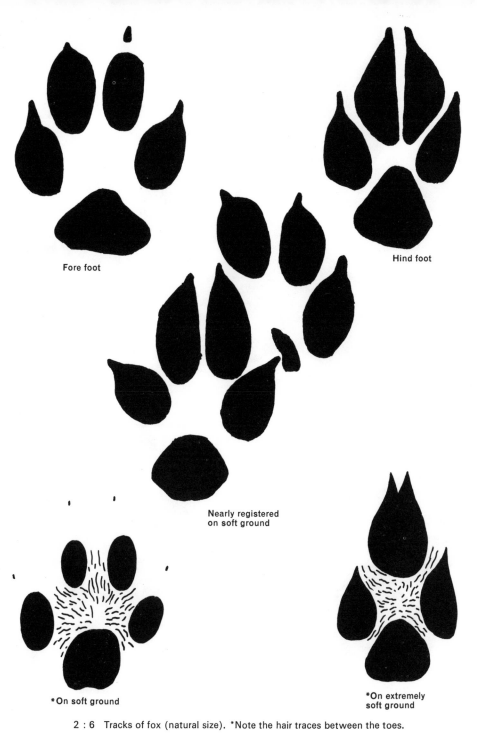

Fore foot

Hind foot

Nearly registered
on soft ground

*On soft ground

*On extremely
soft ground

2 : 6   Tracks of fox (natural size). *Note the hair traces between the toes.

47

Large

Small

Medium

An extremely unusual track since the first toe has shown. Found in soft sand.
Left fore foot

2 : 7   Tracks of domestic dog (natural size).

Plate 13 Sleeping Pine marten. Note the details of the feet.

Plate 14 Polecat.

Plate 15 Stoat.

Plate 16 Crow's nest on a stone wall showing the remains of rabbit skulls. It is unusual to find this, and there is some doubt as to whether or not the crows would have killed the rabbits. In all probability carcases were carried back to the roost. Crows tend to scavenge rather than kill. Forty skulls were counted.

and are common. Their distribution is governed by that of man.

HABITS Very much an animal of the day, as is its master. Wanders at random, in the town or country, making frequent stops and deviations from course to investigate and sniff around. Dogs rely very much on the sense of smell in their activities.

TRACK Great variation in size according to breed, but generally speaking a triangular pad (much larger than toes) with four toes arched around the front, and usually rather spread out. Claw marks frequently show. The distinction between the tracks of domestic dogs and the fox is to be found largely in the wide spread of a dog's toes around a large pad; in the fox, the formation of the toes is tighter in front of a pad which is not much larger than they are.

TRAIL When walking the feet are unregistered, placed at random on either side of the median line, but at a diagonal to this. This feature occurs as a result of the peculiar 'crab walk' of dogs, in which the hind quarters are carried slightly to one side of the fore quarters, although the direction is in a straight forward line. When trotting, registration and wider spacing of tracks, characterise the trail. When bounding, the feet are placed roughly in groups of four, but not symmetrically, about the median line, with a large space between each group. No distances are given since there is great variation.

SIGNS Apart from scratchings in grass and earth the only signs are those of urination against buildings, posts, trees and so on, and the droppings. The droppings are sausage-shaped, neither twisted nor coiled, and vary greatly in colour and size.

DWELLING PLACE In human habitations.

Meles meles   Family: Mustelidae

Badger

The male is called the Boar, the female, the Sow, and the young, the Cub.

OCCURRENCE Common over most of the British Isles with the exception of highland areas, and probably more common than is generally supposed. Records are uncertain north of the Central Lowlands of Scotland, but it seems likely that the animals colonise the lower straths and favourable coastal flats in considerable numbers. Has declined in numbers over the last ten years (Neal, 1965).

HABITS There is a very highly organised social system and set paths and runs are followed. Regular playgrounds, latrines and sunning places are adopted. The animal is almost entirely nocturnal, except in undisturbed areas where a casual wanderer may accidently disturb a badger sunning or on its way to a latrine. It is its night-time activity which misleads, and gives the impression of the badger being absent in an area where in fact it is common. Hibernation does not take place as is often thought, but the animal will lay up in very cold weather for days (even longer sometimes) without food. The badger is very clean in its personal habits, and spends much of its time scratching and washing.

HABITAT One important locating factor in the sites of 'sets' is the workability of soil. The ground must not be too crumbly, but at the same time it must not be so hard and heavy as to make it impossible for extensive excavation. Woodland is preferred, especially when it is derelict, neglected and floored with heavy undergrowth, but open ground must also be readily accessible.

TRACKS The most solid of all Mustelid tracks. The pad is large and has five toes arched some distance above it, and unlike the other Mustelid species no toe is set far back from the others. The size varies greatly with sex and age, but in all cases the print is broader than it is long, usually in the ratio 6 : 5.

The hind foot is smaller than the fore, and claw marks are frequently visible on both feet.

TRAIL When walking the tracks tend to register, hind over fore, and are placed close astride the median line and always pointing inwards. It is impossible to give any average size; pattern identification, not specific identification will have to be used. In galloping, the tracks are close together with a continuous and almost exact process of registration. At the trot, the tracks are usually imperfectly registered and far apart.

SIGNS Feeding remains, such as bones and feathers outside the set are rarely the work of the badgers living there, but signify that a fox is sharing the home. Small mammals, birds, insects, roots and plant material are taken. A wasp or bee's nest that has been torn open usually signifies the work of a badger's powerful digging claws. Near the set the bark on the lower part of sycamore trees is stripped off for the sweet sap. Droppings vary in size, content and colour, but are always firm and resemble those of dogs in shape. They can usually be identified by the undigested remains in them (e.g. beetle elytra). The snaffles (shallow holes scraped to get at roots) found near a set show recent activity, so do the black and silver and white hairs found on twigs and fences. Posts with deep scour marks in them show where claws have been sharpened and cleaned. Regular paths, often made over centuries, are trodden into the grass and undergrowth and are conspicuous. These usually lead to drinking places or regular latrines where the droppings build up into mounds. There is a faint musty odour accompanying the badger, and this will be smelt in the piles of ferns and grass (bedding) thrown out of the set holes. Finally one will often hear a badger in the dark without seeing it, for the grunts, clumsy crashings through the undergrowth and scratching can hardly be mistaken for anything else. Black and silver hair found at the entrance of the set indicate badger diggings and not fox.

DWELLING PLACE The set, as the home is called, is a series of holes and tunnels in the ground under tree roots, in ditches or embankments which will often be centuries old and may cover many hundreds of square feet. It is perhaps the most obvious home of any British mammal, and cannot be confused with that of any other. The holes are large, and outside them huge mounds of excavated material and bedding build up. There are often more than 20 holes which are used and cleaned in sequence. There is, however, one hole in more or less constant use, this being the front door as it were.

Lutra lutra   Family: Mustelidae

Otter

The male is termed Dog, the female, Bitch, and the young, Cub.

OCCURRENCE This species occurs widely throughout the British Isles. It is declining due to habitat destruction and river pollution, and *possibly* the spread of the American Mink.

50

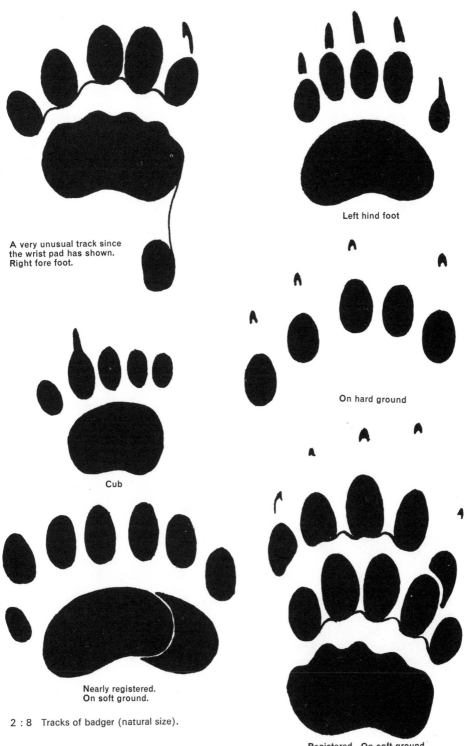

A very unusual track since
the wrist pad has shown.
Right fore foot.

Left hind foot

On hard ground

Cub

Nearly registered.
On soft ground.

2 : 8   Tracks of badger (natural size).

Registered. On soft ground.

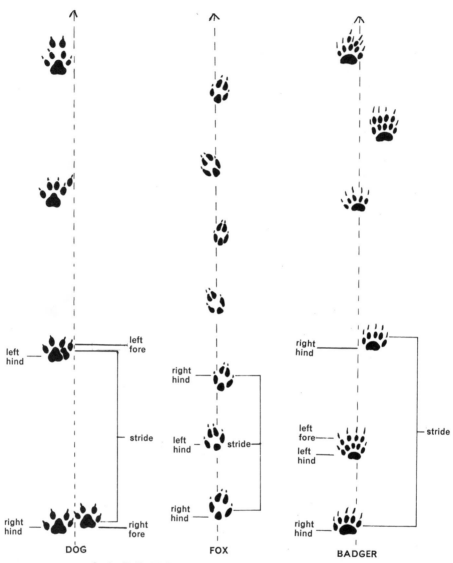

2 : 9 Trails. Walking gait of dog, fox and badger (reduced).

HABITS The otter is most active at night, but is occasionally seen in daylight. Solitary except in the mating season. There is a tendency to follow regular runs, but they do tend to move from one stretch of river to another.

HABITAT Otters prefer slow-moving rivers to rocky mountain streams, although they are found in both. They prefer stretches of rivers alongside which there is plenty of ground cover, so that they can go undisturbed.

TRACK The diagrams below embody the essential features of typical otter tracks. The length and width of the track is in the proportion 1 : 1. The pad is large, with

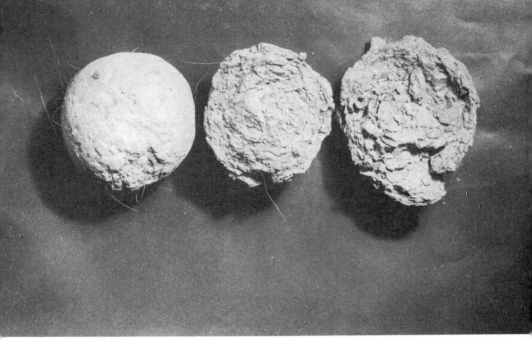

2 : 10   Badger balls (clay). The purpose of these is not clearly understood !

five toes arched around the front of it. If the ground is moderately soft, claw marks will be present: if there is very soft mud the webbing may show.

TRAIL When the animal is walking there is an average stride of about 36 cms. At this gait the fore and hind feet nearly register. When galloping, the stride is about 50 cms. and there is no registration. When bounding all four feet are bunched together, and there is a distance of 80–100 cms. between each group of tracks.

2 : 11   Badger path.

2 : 12   Badger sett.

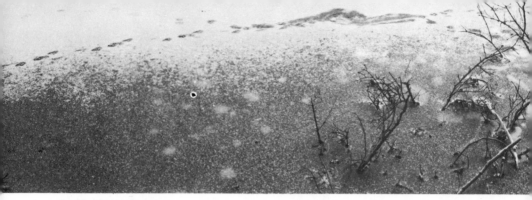

2 : 13   Otter trail on ice.

SIGNS The food remains consist largely of fish bones, crustaceans and molluscs. A regular feeding place is used, a rock in mid-stream, which will be recognised by the assorted food remains. Otters have regular sprainting places where they deposit their droppings or spraints. They will choose a boulder, tree stump or any other convenient place along one of their regular runs. Otters, as do many carnivores, enjoy play. One of the marks of this play is the 'otter slide'. These are long troughs of wet mud on river banks, also found in snow, down which the otter slides into the water. The spraints are cigar-shaped and from 3 to 10 cms. long, and vary in number from 1 to 4. When fresh they are black and very mucilaginous. They contain fur, bones and fish scales. There is usually a characteristic musty odour with fresh spraints. Erlinge (1967).

Rolling Places. At the rolling places the otters dry and groom themselves, roll on their backs, whirl round and deposit scent material. These places are usually in the immediate vicinity of water, generally with a distinct path leading from the water.

Runways and *travelling routes.* Erlinge states that the otter has regular pathways which are easily seen. These connect with invisible swim-ways. The routes follow the shore but sometimes the otters cut off part of the distances by swimming straight across.

Sprainting spots and sign heaps. The otters generally leave their scented excrements on obvious places: stones, tufts of grass, mounds, tree trunks, etc.

Fishing holes in ice, grass twists, signal spots. The depth of fishing holes varies from 3 to 6 in. (75 to 150 mms.) normally, but may be as much as 18 in. (app. 45 cms.) in cold months. The twists consist of vegetation which is loosely gathered

2 : 14   Otter couch.

2 : 15 Otter wisps or twists.

with the stems parallel. Sedges are commonly used, although rhododendrons and ferns are also used. These twists are close to the water, often inaccessible and are added to throughout the year.

Food includes fish: salmon, pike, eel, carp, perch, trout, stickleback; birds: wagtails, thrushes, dippers, geese, ducks, moorhen, grebes, game birds; mammals: moles, shrews, voles, rabbits and hares. Frogs and crayfish are also taken in large numbers.

Otter couches (Hewson, 1969). These are oval or rectangular, ranging from 12 by 18 in. (30 by 45 cms.) to 24 by 36 in. (app. 60 by 90 cms.).

DWELLING PLACE This is called a holt, and is usually a hole in the bank with an entrance under water and overhung by alders and herbage. Where the otter lives near the sea the holt may be in cliffs and rock piles. Otters living near the sea have taken to a marine rather than freshwater existence.

2 : 16 Otter trail on river bank.   2 : 17 Otter slide on bank.

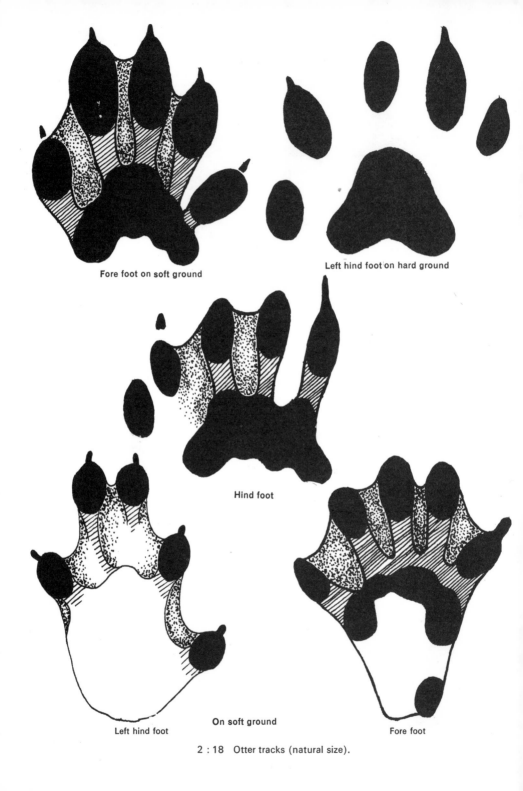

Fore foot on soft ground

Left hind foot on hard ground

Hind foot

Left hind foot   On soft ground   Fore foot

2 : 18   Otter tracks (natural size).

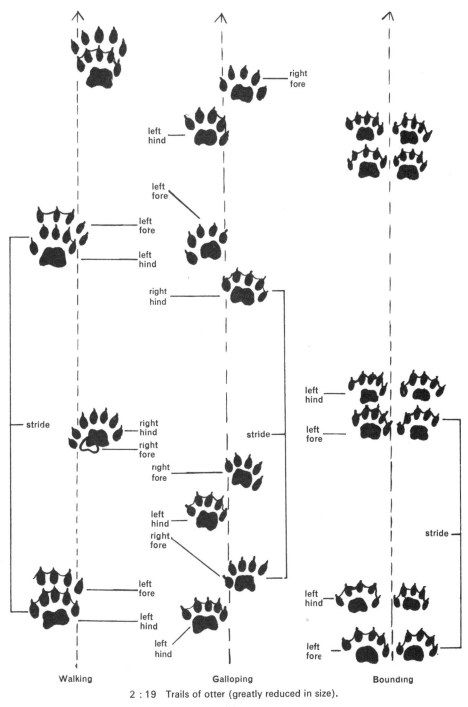

right
fore

left
hind

left
fore

left
fore

left
hind

left
fore

left
hind

right
hind

stride

right
hind

right
fore

right
hind

right
fore

stride

right
fore

left
hind

left
hind

right
fore

left
fore

left
hind

stride

left
fore

left
hind

left
hind

Walking

Galloping

Bounding

2 : 19   Trails of otter (greatly reduced in size).

Martes martes   Family: Mustelidae

Pine Marten

The male is termed Dog, the female, Bitch, and the young, Kitten.

OCCURRENCE It is found in the more remote parts of the country, such as north-west Scotland, the Peak District and the Lake District. Within these areas the species is sometimes common. The range now seems to be extending. The *Daily Telegraph* in January 1971 reported the Yorkshire Naturalists Trusts' recording 10–15 Pine Martens in Yorkshire, but the exact localities were not given.

HABITS The Pine Marten is a truly arboreal creature keeping as much as possible to the trees. It can, however, outrun a roe deer and is capable of catching a squirrel; the otter is the only British mammal that can outswim it.

Diurnal in habit, but not often seen as it tends to avoid man. A solitary species except in the breeding season. It keeps to regular runs, latrines and feeding places.

Food includes small birds, rats, field voles, wood mice, squirrels, rabbits, beetles, moths, mountain ash berries, blackberries, wild raspberries. Frogs and fish are also taken.

2 : 20   Pine marten standing.

TRACK The track consists of a large pad with five toes, radiating in an arch around the front of the pad. The claws do not show very clearly unless the ground is very soft. There is a subtle difference in the proportions between fore and hind foot; in the fore foot 1 : 1, in the hind foot 6 : 5.

SIGNS The food remains consist of bones and fur, usually found with the droppings. They are usually found on a vantage point where the surrounding country can be seen while feeding (e.g. on top of a hill). There is often a musty odour in the vicinity, but this is not as strong as that of the polecat. The droppings, or scats, are normally deposited in a regular latrine and are coiled. They are purple and dark mauve in colour. Fur, feathers and bones are often present in the scats. Most droppings contain a proportion of leaves and grass as well as other types of vegetation.

DWELLING PLACE This is sometimes an old squirrel drey or a crow's nest which has been modified and used as a resting place, but nests are also constructed in boulder and rock crevices. The home is known as a den.

Mustela putorius   Family: Mustelidae

Polecat

The male is termed Hob, the female, Jill, and the young, Kitten.

OCCURRENCE Since 1962 there has been an increase in the numbers and range of the Polecat (Walton, 1968). It has now been recorded from Anglesey where it had not been recorded since 1907. The range is extending into the Border counties and has increased most in south-west Wales. In places the Polecat is as common as it was 20–30 years ago. In Wales the species occurs along the rivers Teifi, Dgfi, Wnion, Conway, Wye, Caerleon, Severn and Dee. The status of this species in the Lake District is uncertain.

The Polecat has bred with Ferrets, and Polecat-Ferrets may be common in some areas.

HABITS Usually nocturnal, and not likely to be seen in the daytime. Prefers to keep to cover of woods and copses, but remains on the ground since it is rather a feeble climber. Farmland is favoured as there is a ready source of food. Solitary in habits, and uses regular paths and runways.

HABITAT Keeps to sheltered valleys, with plenty of cover disliking the bleak hill tops.

TRACK Five toes on each foot, only four are seen sometimes. The toes are set clear of the pad, which is rather indistinctly impressed in most cases. The fifth toe is set back next to the pad. Claws are long and distinct. The proportions of length to width on tracks is in the ratio 1 : 1 on the fore foot and 6 : 5 on the hind foot.

TRAIL When bounding the feet are placed in groups of four, as is typical of the *Mustelidae*. Average stride at this gait is 40–60 cms. When walking the feet are placed singularly astride the median line with a distance of about 23 cms. between each track.

SIGNS Food remains consist of animal fur and bones, sometimes near to droppings. When the droppings are fresh there is usually a strong musty odour accompanying them. The odour for which the polecat has earned ill repute is the foul smelling musk, emitted at will, from glands beneath the tail. This will sometimes be detected in places where the animal has been recently. The droppings are cylindrical, twisted

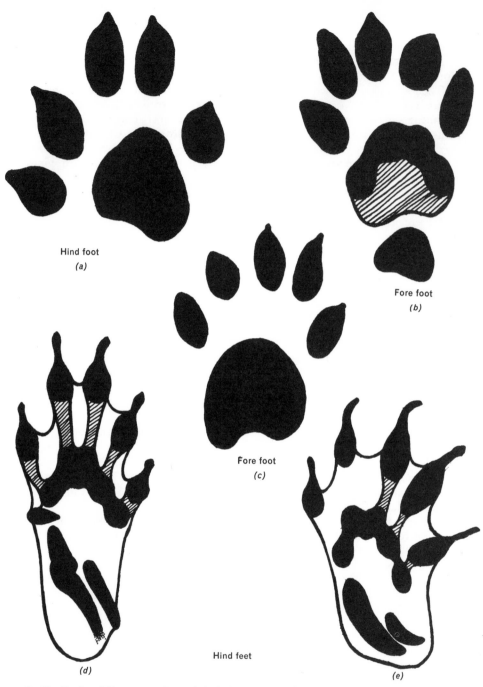

Hind foot
(a)

Fore foot
(b)

Fore foot
(c)

Hind feet

(d)

(e)

2 : 21   Tracks of Pine marten (natural size). See photograph, a, b, c, cast in very soft peat. d, e, the animal had jumped from a considerable height.

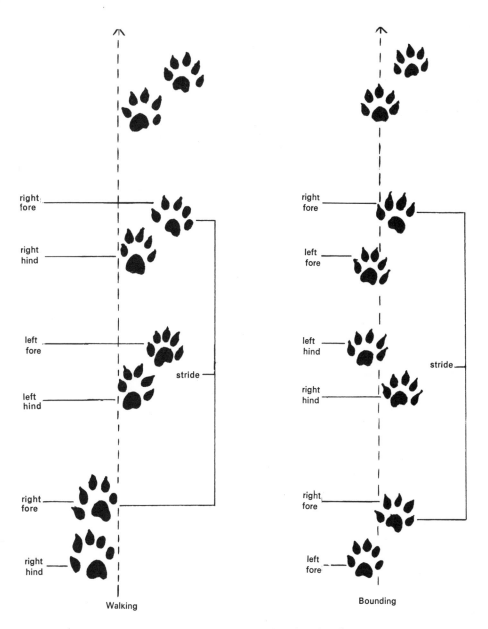

right fore

right hind

left fore

left hind

stride

right fore

right hind

Walking

right fore

left fore

left hind

right hind

stride

right fore

left fore

Bounding

2 : 22 Trail of Pine marten (greatly reduced).

TRAIL When bounding the feet touch the ground in groups of two, with a stride of 60–90 cms. between each pair. When running there is a lineal random placing of the feet.

61

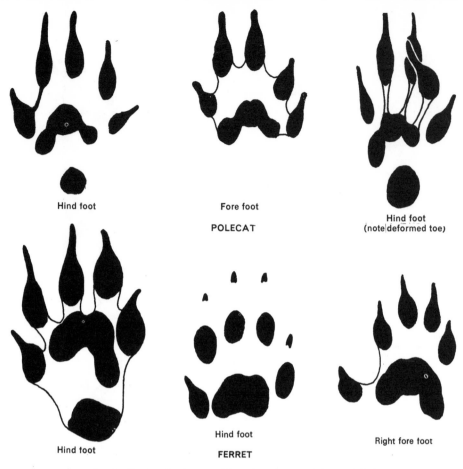

Hind foot

Fore foot

POLECAT

Hind foot
(note deformed toe)

Hind foot

Hind foot

Right fore foot

FERRET

2 : 23 Tracks of polecat and ferret in soft ground (natural size).

and tapering very much to one end, coiling slightly as they are dropped. These are variable in colour, and may contain fur, small bones and insect remains.

DWELLING PLACE The nest is often built in old rabbit burrows, the original occupants having first been eaten, and sometimes in rocky crevices. It is lined usually with grass and moss.

Mustela putorius   Family: Mustelidae

Ferret

Male of the species is the Hob, the female, the Jill, and the young, the Kitten.

OCCURRENCE A very wide distribution. This domesticated, close relative of the polecat has been escaping for many years from its captive state in this country and lives, often in close proximity to man, wherever there is cover and food. These albino beasts often exist in the same areas as their truly wild relatives and will cross-breed. Although the polecat has a limited distribution the cross-bred and albino forms are likely to turn up anywhere, and a tracker must be careful not to confuse them as their tracks and signs are similar. It must be remembered, however, that the ferret is essentially a domestic species.

HABITS Very much like those of the polecat in the wild. Will keep to cover which is within easy reach of a food source, often provided by man. In captivity the animal is penned, or even kept as a household pet, if tame enough, which has resulted in a loss of nocturnal activeness. Its domestic function is to be sent down rabbit holes, usually muzzled, to frighten the occupants out to the surface, where they are netted or shot. In the wild state this species does not climb readily, but it is not adverse to swimming.

HABITAT In domestication the animal is confined to the precincts of human habitation, but in the wild, scrub, copses and woods are haunted. Lowland areas are definitely preferred, although forests up to 600 metres in altitude are colonised.

TRACK On both fore and hind feet there is a semicircular pad, around which five toes are arched, four at some distance in front of the pad, and one set far back, level with the pad, and to the inside of the foot. The tracks have a length–width ratio of 1 : 1 (usually about 3.5 : 3.5 cms.), except in the case of a really fine hind track where a heel impression may show behind the pad making a total length of more than 5 cms.

TRAIL When walking at a relaxed pace there is a tendency for registration to take place, the average stride being 12–15 cms. the tracks forming no set pattern wide astride the median line. When moving at speed, the animal runs with an arched back, and also follows the usual carnivore gallop pattern, giving sets of four tracks 45 cms. apart.

SIGNS Feeding remains in captivity will not be important because of the controlled diet. The work of wild ferrets will be seen in the remains of small mammals, rabbits, hares, birds sometimes with the base of the skull bitten through. Amphibians, reptiles, even fish and eggs will be taken also. The droppings are about 3 cms. long, twisted within themselves (i.e. not coiled) and tapered at the end. They are generally black in colour and may contain the undigested remains of the meal. Specimens born in the wild have musk-producing anal glands which give rise to a strong smelling liquid telling of an annoyed or frightened animal at close range. Animals in captivity are sometimes without this characteristic, having had the glands cut out.

DWELLING PLACE In or near the abode of man.

Mustela erminea   Family: Mustelidae

Stoat

The male is called the Dog, the female, the Bitch, and the young, the Kitten.

OCCURRENCE This species is widely distributed over the British Isles. It is certainly less common than it used to be because of the persecution by gamekeepers, farmers, etc., who have depleted the population. In protected areas, and places where there is abundance of food, the stoat tends to multiply rapidly giving rise to localised regions where the animal is very common.

HABITS Predominantly nocturnal in activities, but specimens are often seen during the day. Tends to wander over a large area, but always settles in a region where food is easily obtainable (e.g. farms), and the greatest concentrations are never very far from human habitation. Most of the carnivores are of moderate intelligence, and the stoat is also possessed of an insatiable curiosity. It will explore burrows, ditches, buildings and even people where they present no danger. A stoat surprised by a human being will dive for cover in a hedge or hole, but if the observer waits long enough the animal's curiosity will get the better of it, and it will reappear for another look.

HABITAT Frequents hedgerows, paths, stone walls, ditches and copses. Although these animals will sometimes haunt highland moors they much prefer the open low-country with the sheltered nooks that man has provided in his modification of the countryside.

TRACK The track is typical of the Mustelidae family. There are on the fore foot three pads set at the back with five toes arched round at the top a considerable distance apart; it has a length of 2 cms. and a width of 2.2 cms. On the hind foot are four pads with the toes arched around the top, and there is a fifth pad set far back; it has a length of 4.2 cms. and a width of 2.5 cms. The claws generally show, and it is not unusual for a web to show between the toes.

TRAIL Normal gait is the characteristic 'gallop' of the Mustelidae with an arched back, the tracks being in groups of two where complete registration of hind over fore feet has taken place. There is a gap of about 20 cms. between each group. When moving at high speed the tracks are bunched in groups of four with a distance of some 30–50 cms. between them.

SIGNS The remnants of the carcases of birds, reptiles, any small mammals and hares or rabbits with the back of the skull bitten through are usually the work of a stoat. Eggs of chicken and game birds are taken when possible. The droppings are coiled and twisted within themselves and contain unchanged remains of the food (feathers, small bones, fur), and, when fresh, have a strong musty smell. Their colour varies with content. When alarmed the animal emits musty liquids from the anal glands. Food includes *Microtus* (the most important small rodent item for stoat and weasel, see Day, 1968), *Clethrionomys, Apodemus, Sorex, Rattus, Mus, Sciurus,* lagomorphs, *Talpa,* game birds, passerines and pigeons, earthworms and insects. Stoats and weasels have little or no effect on fish.

DWELLING PLACE Although the breeding nest will be in a niche in a dry stone wall, under a hedgerow or in a ditch, rabbit warrens are sometimes taken over, the owner having first been devoured. Like most of the carnivores, the stoat will sleep after a meal, and as it hunts and kills underground the burrow of its victim is often utilised as a temporary resting place.

Mustela nivalis   Family: Mustelidae

Weasel

The male is called the Dog, the female, the Bitch, and the young, the Kitten.

2 : 24   Stoat tracks.   2 : 25   Polecat ferret and latrine.

Plate 17 Common seals.

Plate 18 Atlantic seal (female). Note tracks.

Plate 19   Red squirrel.

Plate 20   Grey squirrel.

OCCURRENCE Fairly common within the areas where it occurs, and the distribution is wide on the mainland of England, Wales and Scotland. Absent from Ireland, the Isle of Man, Scillies, Orkneys, Shetlands, the Outer Hebrides and much of the Inner Hebrides. There is little information on the distribution of this species on the smaller off-shore islands of the Scottish coast.

HABITS No regular runways are constructed, but the runs of the voles and mice in the litter zone are often utilised. The sexes do not often mix, and the home ranges of both male and female are large (sometimes 3 to 9 acres in the case of males). The whole territory is hunted regularly. Sometimes a number of individuals will accumulate in one den and will hunt as a pack. Shelters are not always used permanently, and may well be the home of a recent victim. The animals probably do most of their hunting by night, but individuals are often seen abroad by day. They are small enough to enter mice and vole holes and often penetrate rodent-infested haystacks in farmyards, hence preserving rather than damaging the farmer's interests. The animals are agile climbers and capable swimmers.

HABITAT Common in most habitats, from lowland arable country to woods and open upland moors. Often farm buildings and the areas around them are inhabited. The most common occurrence coincides with the greatest concentrations of food (i.e. voles and mice). Specimens are known to occur in parks of extensively built-up areas.

TRACK Five toes on both fore and hind feet. The pads are small and elongated. There is a space between the toes and the pad, with five toes arched round the front of the pad, in the fore foot. On the hind foot two toes are set towards the back of the pad. The claw marks usually show and, although the size of the track will vary with the age and sex of the individual, an example of size may be given. Hind foot, length 1.5 cms.: width 1.3 cms.; fore foot, length 1.3 cms.: width 1 cm. The track is similar to, but smaller than, that of the stoat.

TRAIL The normal gait is the arched back gallop of the Mustelidae, a stride of from 25–30 cms. being taken. When bounding at speed, the tracks show in groups of four and there may be a distance of up to 30 cms. between each group.

SIGNS The food consists largely of small mammals. The indigestible parts, feet and tails for instance, will often be found outside the den along with the droppings, fur and bones. The droppings vary in shape and colour with contents, but usually contain the hair of voles and mice, as well as weasel fur, taken down while the animal has been grooming itself (a process on which much time is spent). A strong musk smell accompanies fresh droppings, and indeed musk is used to demarcate territories. The droppings are long, twisted and more pointed at the ends than those of the stoat.

DWELLING PLACE This is usually a small burrow; often one taken over from the

2 : 26 Attack on waterbird nest
and eggs; thought to be mink.

2 : 27 American mink.

2 : 28 Weasel and stoat droppings.

victim of a past kill. Occasionally niches in dry stone walls, and small caves may be utilised. The breeding nest is lined with fur, either from the weasel itself, or from prey. The feeding remains outside the holes will distinguish them from those of other small mammals.

Mustela vison   Family: Mustelidae

American Mink

OCCURRENCE Thompson (1968) gives a very detailed account of mink distribution. It appears that up to the end of September 1967 Mink had been recorded in every county in Great Britain apart from London and Middlesex. The highest numbers have been recorded in Hampshire, Sussex, Wiltshire, Devon, Gloucestershire, Lancashire, Yorkshire and Aberdeenshire. They are less common in the East Midlands, Wales and Scotland.

HABITS Tends to lead a solitary existence except in the breeding season. It is a very silent animal and, although it probably moves about by day, there is little chance of it being seen. Little is known about the movements of the feral specimens in this country, but they probably keep to regular paths and fairly well defined territories. This animal is a good swimmer and will usually make its home very close to a stream or river. It is thought that the males may travel long distances over land.

HABITAT Near to water at all times. Areas with plenty of cover and a reliable food source (sometimes man-made) are the most favoured.

TRACK The tracks consist of large pads each of which is composed of several lobes, with five toes arched around it some distance above. One toe on the fore foot is set back against the pad but as in the case of the hind foot it is more usual for only four toes to show. In soft conditions the webbing may be evident. The claws are long and tend to show as continuous lines from the toes. The size of the prints will vary with the specimen concerned.

TRAIL The normal gait is a gallop with arched back, so typical of Mustelidae movement. At an ambling pace the tracks occur in groups of four and are imperfectly registered. When moving at speed the tracks are not registered and form distinct groups of four. The distance between each group at this pace may be 40 cms. or more.

SIGNS It is difficult to distinguish the remnants of a mink's kill from that of other Mustelidae. Domestic birds are taken, but the wild food is very varied, Gerell (1967) recorded the following foods in Sweden: *Microtus agrestis*, *Arvicola terrestris*, *Rattus rattus*. Birds include mallard, coot. Fish: perch, burbot, salmon, grayling, trout, roach, rudd, bream, minnow, pike, and eel. Amphibians, crayfish and water beetles were also recorded from droppings analysis.

The droppings are loosely constructed, mucilaginous, evil-smelling and contain scales, bone, fur and shell. They are like otter spraints, but are smaller (2–3 cms.). It is uncertain if regular latrines are used.

DWELLING PLACE Burrows, often in the banks of rivers, are favoured as nesting sites. These usually have a strong musty smell, and droppings may be found outside.

Felis silvestris   Family: Felidae

Scottish Wild Cat

The male is termed Tom, the female, Puss, and the young, Kitten.

OCCURRENCE This species has been making a steady increase in its range from N.W. Scotland. In 1960 it was recorded as far south as Airdrie in Central Scotland. More recently (1972) it has been reported as far south as Northumberland, and although this needs confirmation it is encouraging to see this species increasing its range.

HABITS Solitary, avoiding man as completely as possible. Active mostly at night, but is abroad in the day as well. The isolated nature of its habitat renders any interference by man unlikely. Regular runs are followed, the cat ranging far and wide over a very large area to obtain its prey.

HABITAT Driven into remote areas by man, and lives in isolated woods and rocky places, usually high above sea-level. The open deer moors are also frequented, and if the cat is seen at all it is most likely to be seen ranging over one of these expanses.

TRACK The track consists of a large three-lobed pad, above which four toes are arched. The proportions in length to width of the hind and fore foot respectively are 7 : 6 and 6 : 5. The track is similar to that of the domestic cat, but is very much larger, and is longer than it is wide, whereas with the domestic cat this position tends to be reversed.

TRAIL When galloping, there is a partial registration of fore and hind feet, and the length of the stride is about 60 cms. When walking the feet do not register, and the stride is at about 32 cms.

SIGNS Feeding remains consist of hares, and other hill-top creatures, that is to say the uneatable remains of their carcases. In the rather bleak country the cat inhabits, food is scarce, so it is impossible for it to keep to regular feeding places; meals must generally be taken where the prey is caught. The droppings are put down at random, and the odour is of the usual musty type. These are twisted with tapered ends, containing insect remains and small bones. In colour they are dark grey with a slight tint of green.

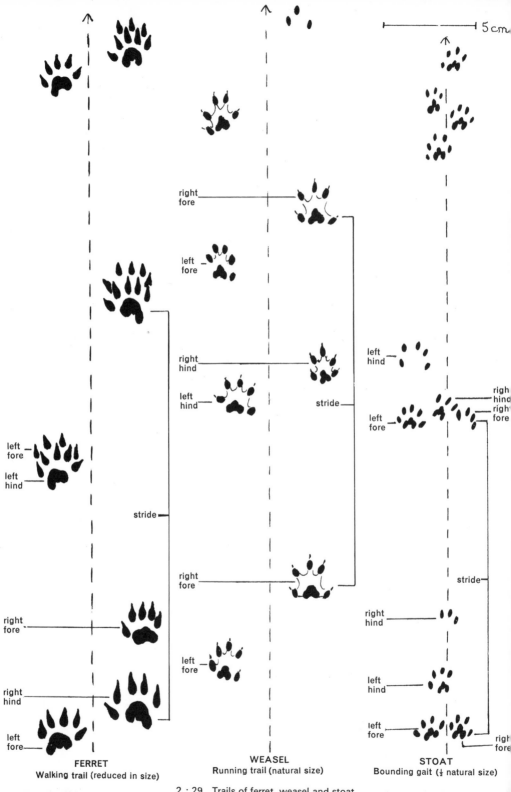

5 cm

right fore

left fore

right hind

left hind

stride

right fore

left fore

left fore

left hind

right fore

right hind

left fore

left hind

left fore

right fore

right fore

stride

right hind

right hind
right fore

stride

right hind

left hind

left fore

right fore

FERRET
Walking trail (reduced in size)

WEASEL
Running trail (natural size)

STOAT
Bounding gait (½ natural size)

2 : 29   Trails of ferret, weasel and stoat.

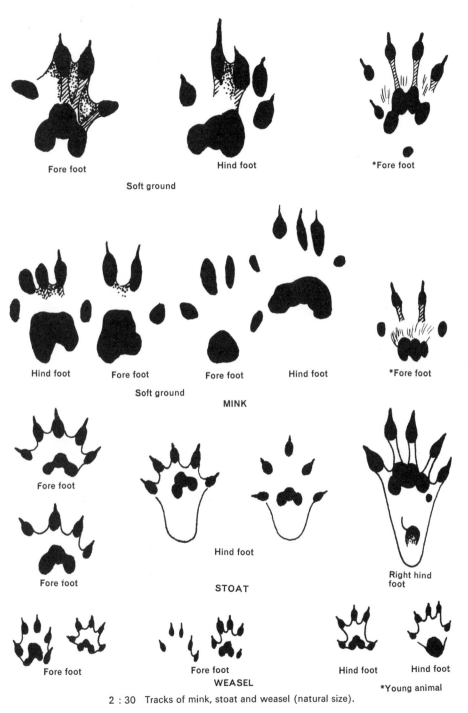

Fore foot

Hind foot

*Fore foot

Soft ground

Hind foot   Fore foot

Fore foot   Hind foot

*Fore foot

Soft ground

MINK

Fore foot

Fore foot

Fore foot

Hind foot

Right hind
foot

STOAT

Fore foot

Fore foot

Hind foot   Hind foot

WEASEL

*Young animal

2 : 30   Tracks of mink, stoat and weasel (natural size).

69

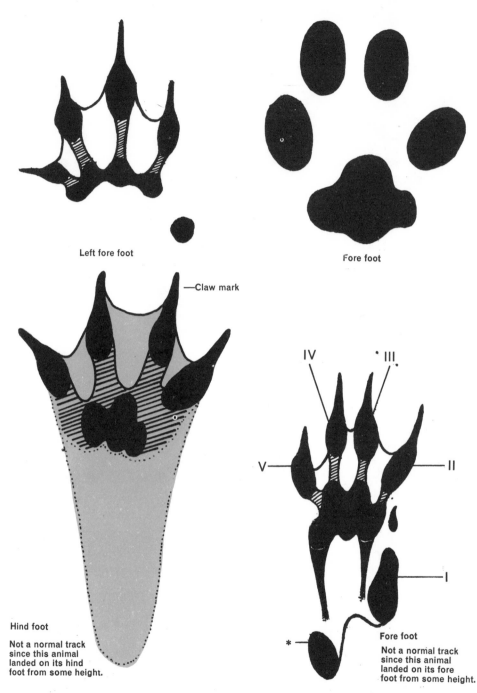

Left fore foot

Fore foot

—Claw mark

IV   • III .

V   II

I

Hind foot

Not a normal track
since this animal
landed on its hind
foot from some height.

*

Fore foot

Not a normal track
since this animal
landed on its fore
foot from some height.

2 : 31   Tracks of Wild cat (natural size). I, II, III, IV, V indicate the five toes, *being the pisiform bone
and pad beneath.

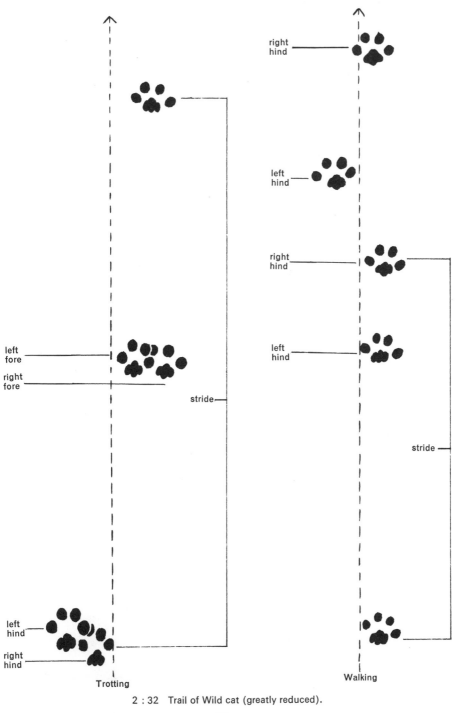

right hind

left hind

right hind

left hind

left fore

right fore

stride

stride

left hind

right hind

Trotting

Walking

2 : 32 Trail of Wild cat (greatly reduced).

71

2 : 33 Badger bundles. 2 : 34 Wasp nest opened by badger.

DWELLING PLACE The den is built in an isolated rock crevice, often inaccessible, and may sometimes be lined with grass or heather.

Felis domesticus   Family: Felidae

Domestic Cat

The male is termed Tom, the female, Puss, and the young, Kitten.

OCCURRENCE Common. Found everywhere in the proximity of humans. Although primarily associated with man, cats do wander and become independent of him, returning to a wild existence, fending completely for themselves.

HABITS Domestic cats are active by day, although they are equipped for the dark, possessing 'night-vision'. A stealthy animal, keeping concealed, as far as possible, when travelling. In the country will cross paths, but not follow them, preferring to make its own path, but does not have regular runs.

HABITAT Found in, and near to, man's homes and farms. It is often the farm cats which live in a wild, or semi-wild state, hunting around the farm, and often deserting to the countryside. Some take to the country completely, and may even become pests, preying on farm animals.

TRACK A three-lobed pad with four toes set clear of it in an arc. No claws show, as

2 : 35 Salmon eaten by otter. 2 : 36 Pine marten with red squirrel.

2 : 37 (*a*) Badger droppings. (*b*) Wild cat droppings. (*c*) Fox droppings. (*d*) Mink droppings.

2 : 38 Wild cat lair (occupied).

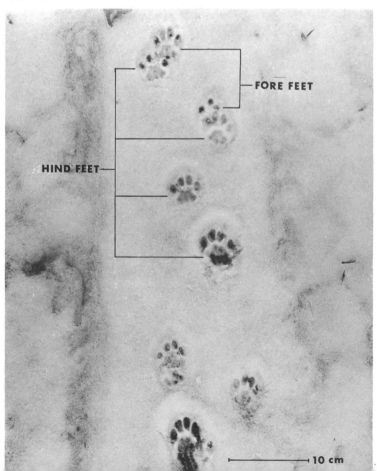

2 : 39 Cat tracks
and trail in snow.

FORE FEET

HIND FEET

10 cm

these are carried in a retracted position, when the animal is walking or running. The tracks are usually slightly wider than they are long, the ratio of length to width in the hind and fore feet respectively being something in the order 7 : 8 and 6 : 7.

TRAIL When walking the feet are placed on the median line widely spaced, and when trotting the feet register, with a wider stride. When stalking the feet are very close together, heel to toe in fact. As with the domestic dog no measurements are given as there is considerable variation in size with the different varieties.

SIGNS Few signs which can be positively identified as those of the cat will be found, other than droppings. Even these are usually buried, but when they are found, the droppings are sausage-shaped with pointed ends, and twisted within themselves, smell strongly, and vary greatly in colour with contents.

DWELLING PLACE Mostly in the homes and buildings of man, but the wild individuals may make dens in isolated areas.

DOMESTIC CAT (on soft ground)

2 : 40   Tracks of Domestic cat (natural size).

ORDER PINNIPEDIA

The Pinnepedia are represented by only two breeding species in the British Isles, the Grey and Common Seal. This carnivorous Order is distinguished in several ways, all connected with the aquatic existence. Many of the processes in the seal's life are carried out in the water, but as parturition and some sleep (the animals can sleep in the water as well) take place on dry land and complete alienation has not occurred, tracks and other signs may be found on isolated sandbanks, and coves where the animals are known to live.

The body is heavy and torpedo-shaped with only a short neck. The hind limbs are short and permanently turned backwards for use in swimming. The thigh bone is short, the tibia and fibula proportionately longer: five fully developed digits are present, the first and fifth being the longest, the centre toe the shortest. The digits are connected by a web. The feet extend well beyond the end of the body, to serve as a rudder in swimming, but are of little use in locomotion on land. The fore flipper is modified, but has all the bones of a mammalian hand. The upper arm is short, the lower a little longer, and the first finger, or thumb, is the longest of the digits. Almost the whole of the limb, except the hand itself, lies within the skin which covers the ribs. The fact that there is no collar bone means that the limb is comparatively free to move to and fro beneath the skin.

The forelimb has become specialised for its aquatic environment. It cannot be brought forward to support the body, and the action is rather like that of a looper caterpillar.

The breeding season will determine the times when there is the greatest likelihood of tracks and signs being found in any given area. To a certain extent the different distributions of the two species will act as a means of differentiation, but the difference in the months of parturition is also important. In the Common Seal this is about June and July; for the Grey Seal, October.

Although the importance of this Order is limited by a relatively small and obscure distribution, the species are so extremely unlike those of any other Order in this country, not just anatomically but in their tracks, as to make them extremely interesting to the tracker.

Phoca vitulina   Family: Phocidae

Common Seal

The male is termed Bull, the female, Cow, and the young, Pup.

OCCURRENCE The important colonies in the British Isles are found in the shallow areas of the Wash and East Anglian coast, the Shetlands and Orkneys, the Hebrides, the east and west coast of Scotland, and Northern Ireland. These are areas of concentration in the breeding season (June–July), but there is a more general distribution around the coast in other seasons. Fairly common; there are many recordings of isolated specimens in our larger estuaries, even the Thames.

HABITS Tends to spend a great deal of time in the water, usually in the shallows. It seems likely that most activity takes place during the day and that the resting period is at night, in areas such as the Wash, but in more isolated Scottish colonies this is probably not so. In the breeding season colonies form, but there is no social organisation. There is no territorial rivalry between the bulls, and the animals are

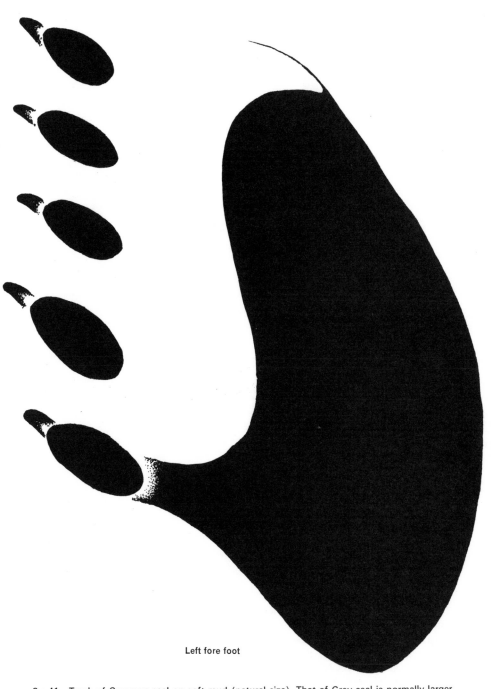

Left fore foot

2 : 41   Track of Common seal on soft mud (natural size). That of Grey seal is normally larger.
Note : Tracks will vary greatly in size.

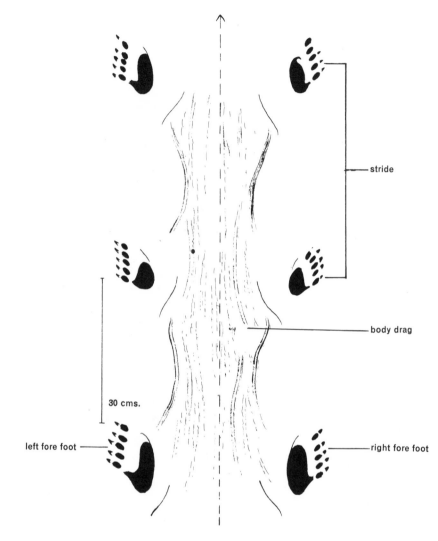

stride

body drag

30 cms.

left fore foot

right fore foot

2 : 42   Trail of seal (reduced).

probably monogamous. Usually there is an individual (a bull) which watches over the colony while it is at rest.

HABITAT In the lowland areas of southern England, sandbanks, mudbanks and estuaries are frequented. Animals come on to dry land as the water recedes. In rocky areas small coves with beaches are utilised, and obviously it is only in sandy or muddy conditions that tracks will be found. The animal never goes very far inland.

TRACK The tracks are very distinctive. The two front feet or flippers, although modified, still have five toes with well-developed claws, the rest of the hand showing little detail. The toe prints show in a line parallel with the direction of movement. The size of the track is variable with age and sex, but cannot be confused with any other Order. The Grey seal track is similar, but will be rather larger. The drag marks of the body will often show between the tracks.

TRAIL Flipper marks are in pairs, spaced widely from the median line (the distance will depend on the width of the body). In the case of the specimen shown the tracks lie 15 cms. to either side of the line. The distance between each pair varies with the individuals, but here it is about 30 cms. This distance will also vary with the speed; the back feet do not show, although the body drag between the tracks is usually obvious.

SIGNS The food consists mainly of fish and crustaceans, which are eaten in the water. Defecation also takes place mainly in the water and the only sign likely to be found is the moulted fur (July–September seems to be an important moulting period).

DWELLING PLACE No permanent shelter. Resting and parturition takes place on any suitable area of the inhabited coast. The animals may also sleep at sea.

Halichoerus grypus   Family: Phocidae

Grey or Atlantic Seal

OCCURRENCE Breeding colonies on the Pembrokeshire coast and Cardiganshire, the Scilly Isles and Cornish coast, Lundy, the Farne Islands, Inner and Outer Hebrides, the Orkneys, Shetlands and on the north and north-eastern Scottish coasts. Range slightly more extensive at other times of the year, but not so wide as that of the Common seal.

HABITS Social organisation in the breeding colonies only. At other times of the year resting places other than the breeding grounds are used. The bulls acquire territory in the breeding season as well as a varying number of cows. There is apparently no day–night rhythm, activity being controlled by the weather and the state of the tide. In the moulting season the sexes tend to segregate on the hauling out places.

HABITAT Usually the colonies are found on rocky shores, isolated islands and always near to an easy means of access to the sea. Specimens have been recorded up to a height of 85 metres above sea-level, and a small island may be totally occupied by a colony. Sandy, pebble or rocky beaches and coves are most commonly inhabited and records in estuaries are rare, except the unpolluted ones (e.g. Tweed).

TRACK (see Common seal). Similar to those of Common seal, but generally larger.

TRAIL As for 'Track'.

SIGNS As for Common seal. Animals normally excrete an oil, which leaves a pungent odour where they have been resting.

DWELLING PLACE Suitable places are utilised for resting and parturition on any part of the inhabited coast.

In addition to the species considered above there are a number of rare seal visitors to our shores. These species normally live in the Polar seas, but occasionally stray southwards and the following species have been recorded in Britain:

The Ringed seal (*Phoca hispida*). This is the smallest of the seals. It occurs off the

Greenland coast, in the Baltic Sea and the Gulf of Bothnia. A separate race exist in the Finnish lakes.

The Harp Seal (*Phoca groenlandica*). This is a gregarious species of the high arctic and has been recorded on drift ice far out to sea.

The Hooded Seal (*Cystophora cristata*). This species is mainly restricted to the North American arctic and sub-arctic, but it occasionally reaches British coasts.

The Bearded Seal (*Erignathus barbatus*). This species has a wide circum-arctic distribution and lives on the edge of the ice in coastal waters.

3 : 1 Common
dormouse.

Plate 21
Woodmice
quarrelling.

Plate 22
Bank vole.

Plate 23 Short-tailed Field vole.

Plate 24 Wood mouse with young, and one young of previous litter.

3 Lagomorpha and Rodentia

ORDER LAGOMORPHA

Distribution in the British Isles

Although represented by only three species in the British Isles this Order has a wide distribution and, even after the ravages of myxomatosis, the rabbit is found in most lowland areas. The Common hare has a fairly wide distribution also, and the Mountain hare occurs above 300 metres in the north of England and in Scotland so that few areas are totally without Lagomorphs. The Brown hare and rabbit seem to favour farmland and the greatest concentrations of numbers are usually found here. The Mountain hare normally lives in comparatively unmodified conditions, but will often seek shelter in plantations when the weather is hard. Generally speaking the species of this Order prefer open country with areas of shelter readily available.

Teeth

Like the Rodentia this Order is vegetarian and possesses well-developed chisel-like first incisors plus second upper incisors, a distinguishing feature of the group. Considerable damage is done to trees, especially by rabbits, which are generally treated as agricultural pests.

Limbs

The rabbit and hares belong to the Family Leporidae, in which the hind limb is rather longer than the fore and is used to give the body a powerful thrust forward when the animal is moving at speed. The tracks of this Order, when seen in soft ground, are distinctive, the hind feet forming long, slipper-shaped impressions. On harder ground only the toes and claws will show – usually only four on both the fore and hind feet. In fact the hares have four toes on the hind foot and five on the fore foot. The same is true of the rabbit (although the fifth toe is small, set high up on the foot and never shows). There are two distinct features which make it impossible for the Lagomorph tracks to be confused with those of any other Order: (1) even when the whole outline of the foot is distinct no pads will be seen and (2) the sole of the foot is completely covered in hair, a feature not occurring in any other Order. The main interest of this Order lies, perhaps, in that although the number of species is small, their distribution is wide, and the searcher is likely to be rewarded by the tracks of a member of this Order wherever he goes.

Oryctolagus cuniculus   Family: Leporidae

Rabbit

OCCURRENCE Formerly very common over the whole of the British Isles, especially in the west, excepting heavily built-up areas (although even here colonies occurred in parks). Myxomatosis has reduced density greatly and caused redistribution to some extent, but the species is now recovering and, in some areas at least, is becoming extremely common again.

HABITS Active at dusk and in the early morning, but in quiet areas diurnal activity also takes place. This species is gregarious with set runs, watering places and latrines. The paths are well marked in grassland and usually disappear through holes in hedgerows or thickets, where agglomerations of tunnels known as warrens are found.

HABITAT Cultivated land, woods, embankments, dune areas and hill country are favoured. Open terrain is often colonised, but the warrens are constructed under cover if possible. The rabbit is a proficient excavator, but prefers conditions where digging is easy.

TRACK In both fore and hind feet usually only four toes will show, and even in soft ground little detail other than the tips of the toes or just the claws is likely to be seen. The size of the print will vary with sex and age. As an example however: fore foot 2.5 (l) by 2 (w) cms.; hind foot 3 (l) by 2.2 (w) cms. In extremely soft conditions hair may show between the toes and on the sole of the foot. As with the hares the toes tend to point inwards.

TRAIL When bounding at speed the hind feet are placed close to the median line and opposite each other, with the fore feet placed one behind the other, after the hind feet, on the median line. At hopping speed the fore feet are again impressed close to the line, and the hind feet are drawn up close behind. When bounding the stride may be more than a metre in length, but at hopping gait is not likely to be much above 15 cms.

SIGNS Great damage may be done to crops, and the hedges and small trees near to the warrens may be severely clipped back and barked by the browsing rabbits. Much damage can be done to young trees in plantations and the species is therefore heavily persecuted. The droppings are round, usually black and moist when fresh, slightly flattened and under 1 cm. in diameter. Regular latrines are adopted by the

3 : 2 Rabbit droppings on a mound (note the fox droppings in the picture as well).

3 : 3 Damage done to trees by rabbits stripping the bark in hard weather. Height of stripping due to winter snow.

animals and are usually found on ant hills or mole hills out in the open, although tree stumps and rocks may be utilised.

DWELLING PLACE Burrows underground. These may consist of small dead end tunnels (stops) or extensive passages which have grown over a period of years. These are used for shelter and breeding, being extended outwards by the does digging fresh breeding chambers. Entrances will be either in banks or else concealed in thick vegetation.

Lepus capensis (= *L. europaeus*)   Family: Leporidae

Brown or Common Hare

The male is termed Buck, the female, Doe, and the young, Leveret.

OCCURRENCE This species is fairly widespread over the British Isles except in the vicinity of heavily built-up areas and in areas over 600 metres above sea-level (rather less in Scotland). It has been introduced into Ireland and some of the Scottish islands. In western Britain (Pembroke and Cornwall) the population becomes sparse.

HABITS Generally solitary but may form into groups under some circumstances. Day is spent lying up in 'form' (a shallow depression usually under cover). The animal moves along definite routes within a certain small area which is its own territory and is extremely well known to it. There may be several forms within this area. The main feeding times seem to be at dusk and sometimes at dawn, although the animal is probably abroad at night and may travel long distances. May be seen in the day, especially if they are disturbed in their form.

HABITAT Almost any open space, preferably with some tall vegetation under which to lie up, although this is not essential as can be seen in the case of hare colonies which have developed in large airports. Arable farmland, marshland and woodland are often occupied.

TRACK Five toes on hind foot and four on the front. The fifth toe on the hind foot is set far back and will not show except in very soft conditions. The tracks will vary with the individual, but will have inward pointing toes with no appreciable pad markings, although the hair on the sole of the foot may show if the ground is soft enough. If the whole hind foot from heel to claw is impressed it may be 150 mm. in length. More usually only the claw marks will show.

TRAIL When bounding at speed the tracks tend to splay out and there may be a distance of some 2 to 2.5 metres between each group. When bounding briskly the hind feet are impressed close to, and symmetrically opposite the median line, with the fore feet showing close behind. When hopping the hind feet are drawn up close behind the fore feet and short strides of about 20–25 cms. are taken.

SIGNS Can do considerable damage to crops, and like the rabbit this species does much harm in barking trees. Where both of these species exist together it is difficult to tell which is responsible for which damage. The droppings are about 1.25 cms. in diameter, are usually light in colour and slightly flattened, and not found in regular latrines. Hair may be found in the form during the spring and autumn moults.

DWELLING PLACE The form is usually only a shallow depression excavated under a small bush or some other cover. This is used as a simple shelter and as a nest for

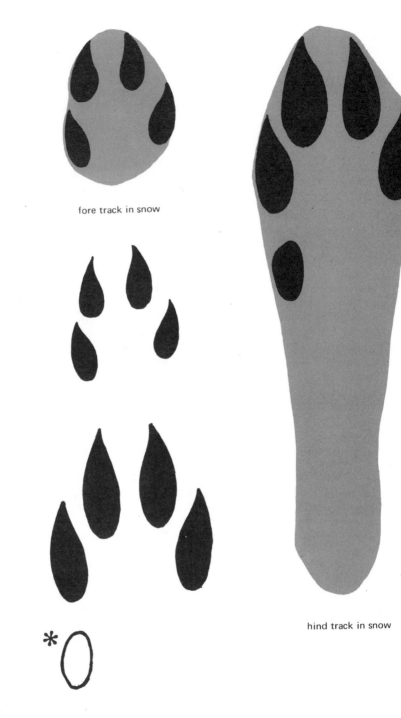

fore track in snow

hind track in snow

*

3 : 4 A Tracks of Brown
hare (natural size).

84

Mountain hare   Rabbit

3 : 4B   Tracks of Mountain
hare and rabbit (natural size).   85

3 : 5   Hare in form during daytime.

3 : 6   Hare's form (March).

the young, which are protected by camouflage. The young do not remain in the nest for very long; the female takes them out into the home territory, leaves them and pays occasional visits for feeding.

Lepus timidus   Family: Leporidae

Mountain or Blue Hare

The male is called the Buck, the female, Doe, and the young, Leveret.

OCCURRENCE The distribution is rather restricted, the animal occurring mainly

3 : 7   Brown hare's trail through field.

3 : 8   Mountain hare form.

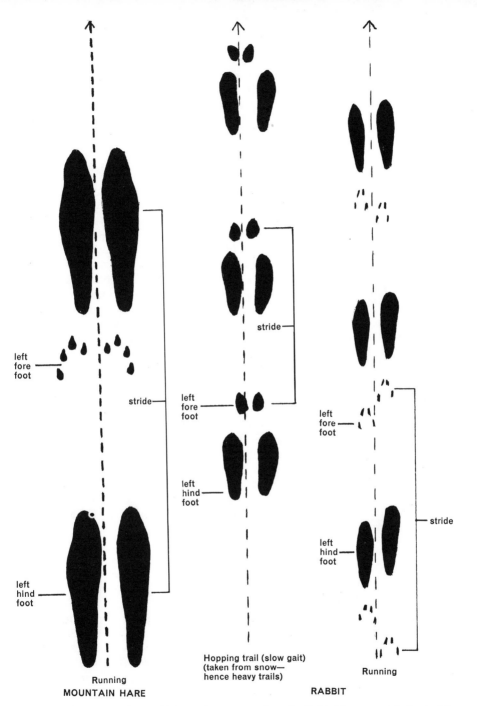

left
fore
foot

stride

left
hind
foot

Running
MOUNTAIN HARE

stride

left
fore
foot

left
hind
foot

Hopping trail (slow gait)
(taken from snow—
hence heavy trails)

left
fore
foot

left
hind
foot

stride

Running
RABBIT

3 : 9   Trails of rabbit and hares. When moving at a run the animal's hind feet appear in front of the
fore feet. When hopping the reverse is true.

in Highland Scotland and the Irish Mountains, but there are records in North Wales, and in the region of the Cheviots. There are probably pockets of this species as far south as the Peak District in England.

HABITS There is a tendency to be solitary and to avoid the territory of other individuals. There is a temporary pairing off in the mating season. The animal moves freely over the open terrain of the hill country and is not as timid of man as the other Lagomorphs, probably because of its isolated environment. Rather inquisitive by nature, even exploring human beings when they are at close quarters. When startled the hare will retreat to a shallow burrow, which is also used as a shelter.

HABITAT Mountain terrain, heather moors and craggy hill sides are colonised, largely at heights between 300 and 750 metres, but records have been taken of specimens living at lower altitudes. Open ground without any shelter is usually avoided as this would lay the animal open to attack from its predators. In very severe winters the hares will take cover in plantations and woods.

TRACK Considerably smaller than Common hare, the hind foot about 3 by 2 cms., the fore foot 3.5 by 3 cms. There are five toes on the hind foot and four on the front. In muddy ground the heel will rarely show, and only infrequently do the full five toes of the hind foot show, as the fifth is set well back. In very wet ground or snow the full extent of the foot will show, and generally speaking the hairs of the foot will distort the impression. Often only the claw marks, and not the pads of the toes will be visible.

TRAIL When hopping at speed the hind feet tend to come together close to the median line with the fore feet lying behind on the line. At this pace there is a stride of about 20–24 cms. When bounding at speed the tracks tend to splay out and a distance of some 2 metres may separate the groups. When hopping the hind feet are drawn up close behind the fore feet and a short stride of some 18 cms. is taken.

SIGNS The droppings are slightly larger than those of the rabbit, and will be scattered around close to the animal's sheltering place. In the spring when the white winter fur is being moulted small pieces of downy fur will show where the animal has recently been lying up, camouflaged by its white coat.

DWELLING PLACE The scrape is usually a niche under some boulders or a small burrow scraped out in a sheltered corner. This is the place where the animal takes cover, sleeps and shelters.

ORDER RODENTIA

Characteristics affecting tracks and signs

This Order is represented by the largest number of species in any occurring in the British Isles. Representatives occur in most habitats and some species are very common in the localities where conditions are suitable. It is the tracks and signs of the members of this group which are most commonly encountered in the field, although they may not be noticed because they are usually small. While the basic pattern of the feet does not vary (four toes on the fore feet, five on the hind, except in the coypu) there is considerable variation in size and in the pad structure on the sole of the foot. The morphological variations of the anatomical structure of this Order is not generally of sufficient importance to be considered in relation to the subject of this work. However, in some arboreal species the tail has developed into an instrument of balance (squirrels and dormice) and in yet others has even become prehensile (Harvest mouse).

The species of the Order are dealt with in the usual pattern of the book, but extra attention is given to signs, which are more extensive and diversified than in many Orders and provide important means of identification.

Sub-orders

Such a large Order is split into many sections, including three Sub-orders. The first of these is the Sciuromorpha, represented in Great Britain by only one family the Sciuridae (squirrels). The Sub-order Myomorpha is represented here by the Superfamilies Muroidea (voles, rats and mice) and Gliroidea (dormice). The other Sub-order, the Hystricomorpha, is represented by one of the Octodontoidae, the introduced coypu from South America.

Rodents and man

While all species in this Order are truly wild, some (particularly the rats and House mouse) tend to live in association with man. Generally speaking, however, the invasion of man's home and crops by members of this Order is not welcomed since considerable damage results. Great damage may be done to crops, to trees (by barking) and to fruit as well as the spoiling of stored food in warehouses and haystacks. The rats, carriers of disease which may affect man and his stock, may also cause quite severe structural damage. The well-developed and constantly growing incisors which enable the animals to gnaw so efficiently have enamel on one side only. This enables them to be kept razor-sharp.

The Rodents are all small to medium in size and are preyed upon by many carnivorous species (as well as man). They are, if not always gregarious, far from solitary.

This Order is at one and the same time the most common yet the most difficult to study completely. Some species occur almost everywhere (rats especially) while others like the Orkney vole have a very restricted distribution. Thus, although there are many broad similarities within the Order, the wide distribution presents a considerable challenge to a field worker. Species frequently overlap in their distribution, and in some small areas in southern England as many as eight species may be found in one habitat.

Clethrionomys glareolus   Family: Muridae (= Cricetidae)

Bank Vole

OCCURRENCE Widespread over nearly the whole of England, Wales and the lowlands of Scotland. Does not appear to occur above 600 metres. A small colony has recently been found in Ireland. See Classens, A. (1967) and Fairley, J. S. (1970) for further details of distribution.

HABITS Nocturnal to some extent, but certainly active by day in quiet areas only. Well-marked territories (the home range may be about 40 metres in diameter or a little more), but the males may travel long distances. Gregarious; sometimes high densities occur in small areas where circumstances are favourable. Moves about a great deal on the surface, but is also an active burrower. Extensive runs may be constructed in ground vegetation. Will occasionally climb.

HABITAT Commonly occurs in deciduous wood and scrubland. Banks and hedgerows with plenty of cover are inhabited. Common also in open terrain where small areas of cover are available (e.g. old quarries, broken-down brick walls, in fields).

TRACK There are five toes on the hind foot and four on the fore which is characteristic of the voles, as is the star-shaped pattern which the toes form. There are three central toes on the back foot which lie in a line, and there is a toe on either side of this line forming a virtual right angle. The claws do not often show, and the fore foot may be longer in proportion to its width than the hind leg (hind 13 mm. long, 13 mm. wide; fore 9 mm. long, 7 mm. wide). There are six prominent pad marks on the hind foot and five on the fore foot (Fig. 3 : 23).

TRAIL Normally moves at a running gait, but jumps sometimes, and may cover over 15 cms. at a bound. At running pace the tracks are not registered, and are slightly to either side of the median line. An average stride of about 8 cms. is taken.

SIGNS Omnivorous. Eats a high proportion of green plants, but also takes fleshy vegetation, fruits, fungi, roots and nuts. The nuts will be opened with very neat holes displaying small teeth marks, and the edge of the fungi will be nibbled and show the same marks. Numbers of berries or nut shells may be found in an old bird's nest, or under flat stones, and these may be the stores of a Bank vole. Much damage can be done to plantations by the barking of young trees, and as the animal is a good climber it may strip the tree to a considerable height.* Voles' work can be distinguished from that of squirrels by the size of teeth marks and the time of year the damage is done (in autumn and winter in the case of the vole and in summer by the squirrels). Snails form part of the diet, and a snail taken by a vole may be distinguished from that taken by a thrush in that the vole will nibble along the spiral of the shell, and the remnants of several will be found on a quiet path. The thrush will have broken the shells, and the smashed remains of many shells may be found near to a large stone. Tunnels in vegetation and food stores near to the nest are further indications of the animal's presence. The droppings are small and black and are usually deposited in a latrine slightly off the main run. Like those of the Field vole and mice they are too small to be of any value for identification purposes.

* There is no positive means of differentiating vole barking from that of the Wood mouse, except that the former will tend to be close to the ground, and the latter may extend to branches a considerable distance above ground level.

3 : 11 Bank vole's nest.

3 : 10 Entrance to a vole's run.

DWELLING PLACE A series of tunnels and runs in the ground and in ground vegetation, which are centred on the burrow where the grass nest is constructed.

Microtus agrestis   Family: Muridae (= Cricetidae)

Short-tailed Vole or Field Vole

OCCURRENCE Fairly widely distributed on the mainland and very common in some localities. Absent from Ireland, the Isle of Man, Scillies, Lundy, Lewis, Barra, Shetlands, Orkneys and some of the Inner Hebrides.

HABITS The peak of activity seems to come at night, but the animals are also active by day, and are frequently seen. Probably several individuals will inhabit a given piece of land, but a tunnel system in the litter zone will belong only to one. The range seems to be small, not more than 10 metres, but considerable damage may be done to grass and young trees at ground level (the animals do not normally climb).

HABITAT Rough grassland is preferred and networks of tunnels are made on and just below the surface of the ground. Under favourable conditions a plague of these rodents will cause considerable damage to pastures. Habitats far from ideal are also utilised and this species has been recorded in almost every circumstance (including marshland) up to a height of about 1,000 metres.

TRACK There are five toes on the hind foot and four on the fore, arranged in a star-shaped pattern characteristic of the voles. There is little difference in the size of the tracks (both are about 12 mm. long, and 10 mm. wide) and both have five pads on the fore and six on the hind foot. The claws usually show (Fig. 3 : 23).

TRAIL The normal gait is a running one, in which the body is held close to the ground. The tracks show in pairs, splayed out on either side of the median line and pointing slightly outwards. A stride of about 5 cms. is taken and registration does not usually take place. Scuff marks from the body and tail are not often seen.

SIGNS (see also *Clethrionomys*). Extensive runs are made in the litter zone of the habitat, but may be misleading since the tunnels may remain intact long after they have been abandoned. Evidence that the tunnels are in use comes from the heaps of cut grass stems and green droppings found in them. This species tends to feed more exclusively on grass than the Bank vole and usually turns to bark, roots, bulbs and fungi when conditions are abnormally hard.

DWELLING PLACE Tunnels in the litter zone supply shelter and highways for movement. The nest may be in these tunnels in which case they are usually at ground level, or in burrows excavated in the solid ground.

Microtus arvalis orcadensis   Family: Muridae (= Cricetidae)

Orkney or Common Vole

OCCURRENCE This has one of the most limited distributions of any British species, being found only on the larger islands of the Orkney group (with the exception of Hoy and Shapinsay). Common in several localities, and the population is very stable.

HABITS See *M. agrestis* (Field vole). Crepuscular and probably active during part, if not the whole of the night. Runs are constructed through the litter zone and connect with underground burrows.

HABITAT Most common in lowland areas (pastures and arable land), but also found in poorer and higher ground.

TRACK There are five toes on the hind feet and four on the fore feet arranged in a star-like pattern. The feet are similar in structure to those of *M. agrestis* but are larger, about 18 by 12 mm.

TRAIL The various gaits are similar to those of the other voles, but the stride is slightly larger, between 3.5 and 4.5 cms.

SIGNS In most respects similar to those of *M. agrestis*, but a much more restricted distribution makes comprehensive knowledge difficult.

DWELLING PLACE In some cases the litter zone and surface vegetation are utilised while in others the stones from ruined buildings are used for shelter. Under these conditions, particularly near ruined farms, the greatest concentrations of this species are known to occur.

Arvicola terrestris   Family: Muridae (= Cricetidae)

Water Vole

OCCURRENCE Found over most of England, Wales and Scotland with the exception of heavily built-up areas. The species occurs on the Isle of Wight, Anglesey, but on none of the other islands off Great Britain. In inhabited areas the density of population along a stretch of river is likely to be high.

HABITS Active mainly through the day, the most intensive period being in the evening up to late dusk. There is little activity at night. Well-marked territories exist, and these will be defended vigorously. Regular 'swims' exist, and paths may be seen in the grass by the water's edge. Hibernation does not take place, but food is stored below ground.

HABITAT In lowland: expanses of slow-moving water with a fairly constant régime are favoured (e.g. canals and ponds). In higher land: small streams are colonised up to 600 metres. Streams whose banks have a good deal of cover are favoured.

TRACK Four toes on the front, five on the hind. These are the largest vole tracks to be found, and are star-shaped. There are five pads on the fore foot, and six on the hind, but one of these is very much longer than the other five. Claws will usually show. The hind foot is proportionally longer than the fore foot (e.g. hind foot: length 2.9 cms., width 2.7 cms.; fore: 2.5 cms. by 2.3 cms.) (Fig. 3 : 23).

TRAIL The feet are placed close on either side of the median line, and the hind feet register partially over the fore. The stride varies, but as a specimen distance, 6 to 8 cms. between each pair of tracks seems fairly constant when the animal is running. The normal gait is a run, but bounds of up to 30 cms. may be made.

SIGNS The food of the vole is very varied. Reeds, rushes, roots and clover are taken. Water snails, fish, spawn, worms and on some occasions animals almost as large as itself may be killed and eaten. Prominent features in areas where voles are plentiful will be small boulders or patches of mud at the water's edge which have pieces of reed and water plant piled up on them, broken up and ready for eating. These places will be frequently used as latrines and little heaps of black droppings, cylindrical in shape and rounded at the ends will be found. These vary in size, but average about 9 mm. by 3 to 4 mm. Some damage is done by taking fish eggs, and by the tunnels undermining river banks. There is also the possibility that the bark

3 : 12   (a) Water vole eating a fish (it is uncertain if the animal killed the fish).

(b) Water vole nest in reeds away from the water. (This is unusual.)

(c) Water vole droppings and chopped grass remains on a stone in the middle of stream.

(d) Water vole garden.

of young willows may be nibbled, and potatoes and other root crops are certainly raided. Around holes in a bank covered with vegetation a 'vole garden' will often be seen. This is a circular area around the burrow where the vegetation has been cropped short by the animal stretching out from its hole and feeding on the plants.
DWELLING PLACE Complicated tunnel systems are made in the banks of rivers and streams, and these will have many exits both above and below the water line. The entrances on land are usually no more than a metre from the water's edge, but may be up to 10 metres. In the breeding season nests, in the form of large balls of reeds may be constructed in vegetation near the water, and may be up to 20 cms. in diameter (occasionally more). More usually the nests are made of reeds, water flags and coarse grass in the burrows.

Mesocricetus auratus   Family: Cricetidae

Golden hamster   A recent escape

OCCURRENCE The first records of Golden Hamsters living free in an urban environment in England were made in 1960 (Rowe, 1960). The first animals were living free in a pet shop and greengrocery store in Bath. In all fifty-two animals were taken.

Since then they have been reported in the following places: Finchley, Middlesex – twenty-one animals; Bootle, Lancashire – seventeen animals; Manchester, Lancashire – no numbers available, but known to be living in a series of five terrace houses; Bury St. Edmunds, Suffolk – in all 230 animals were captured alive or poisoned.
HABITS Hamsters, like other small mammals, live in extensive burrow systems and are mainly nocturnal. Little is known of their food habits in their native habitat but Bruce and Hindle (1934) believe that they are herbivorous. Hibernation seems to start in September and run through the winter months. Hamsters can withstand rather rigorous climatic changes and tend to hibernate only under very adverse conditions (Petzsch, 1950). It seems likely that field living populations could prove difficult to control and it is possible that a potential pest species has been introduced.

All preceding information from Rowe (1950, 1968).
TRACK The tracks are similar in size and shape to those of the Field and Bank Voles. The trail may be distinguished from these species by the tendency for lateral registration to take place on the hamster trail and the presence of claw marks. The length of the stride is also much greater being about 8.5 cms. at normal walking gait.
SIGNS No information is yet available.

Micromys minutus   Family: Muridae

Harvest Mouse

OCCURRENCE In England the greatest concentrations of this species are in the south and east, recordings becoming scarcer towards the Midlands and North. Isolated records have been made as far north as Aberdeenshire, but on the whole the animal is not common anywhere.
HABITS Usually described as diurnal, but in warm weather probably active at various times in the twenty-four hours. Hibernation does not occur, but there is less activity in cold weather. Rests in nests or burrows when not active. Territories probably exist, but nothing is known about their size and exact function. The

94

animal is a good climber and has a prehensile tail. The voice consists of faint, high-pitched squeaks.

HABITAT In summer months: cornfields, hedgerows, reed beds, long grass and even open fields. Breeding nest is constructed of reeds or corn leaves. In winter: takes to burrows just below the surface, although hay ricks may sometimes be utilised.

TRACK Very small, but may be distinguished from those of the shrews since the latter have five toes on both fore and hind feet. The claws show distinctly, and the hind foot is proportionately longer than the fore (e.g. hind: 1.3 cms. long, 1 cm. wide; fore: 8 mm. long, 8 mm. wide). There are six pads on the hind foot, two on the heel being elongated. Five pads occur on the fore foot, two together on the heel, three beneath the toes. The toes are widely spread on the front foot and on the hind they are arched slightly. The three central toes are not so obviously in line as they are in the House mouse.

TRAIL The normal gait on the ground is a run, but small bounds may also be taken. The hind foot registers on the fore, and a stride of about 3 to 4 cms. is made. The feet are slightly straddled on the median line, and the dragging tail will show as a thin wavy line.

SIGNS Grain, fruits, vegetables and insects are known to be taken. The food is laid by for winter, and stores will be found next to winter nests in the hay ricks. The droppings are very small and black and about 2 mm. in length. Damage is done to corn ears in the summer, especially in the vicinity of the nest. The animal has no noticeable smell.

DWELLING PLACE The summer breeding nest is a ball of cornblades and grass in the stems of the corn. Early in the year nests are made in hedgerows, later ones in the open fields. These are used only for a short time. The winter nests are either at ground level, or below the surface and are usually at the ends of tunnels.

Apodemus sylvaticus   Family: Muridae
Wood Mouse or Field Mouse

OCCURRENCE Common over the whole of the British Isles, except in highland areas. Found on most of the islands off our coast and many subspecies have been described. Locally the animal may occur in great concentrations.

HABITS Social structure revolves loosely round the family unit, but one home range will overlap another. Territories are generally small, but the males may roam over larger areas in the spring and summer. Activity largely nocturnal, with most intense periods at dawn and dusk in winter. May occasionally be seen outside hole in the daytime. Has complicated underground routeways, and definite paths within the territory. Usually silent, but a high-pitched squeak may be emitted at times. A good climber. Does not hibernate, and is active throughout the year.

HABITAT Most common small rodent in woodland living in the zone of broken-down and decomposing vegetation. Found also in hedgerows, fields, gardens and may be found in open grassland, especially where the Short-tailed vole is absent. Will inhabit areas with little ground cover.

TRACK The hind foot is very long (2 cms. long, 1.5 cms. wide) in proportion to the fore (length 1.3 cms., width 1.5 cms.). There are six pads on the hind foot, one large one situated below the toes. The fore foot has five pads. The toes splay widely on both fore and hind feet, and the claws show distinctly.

95

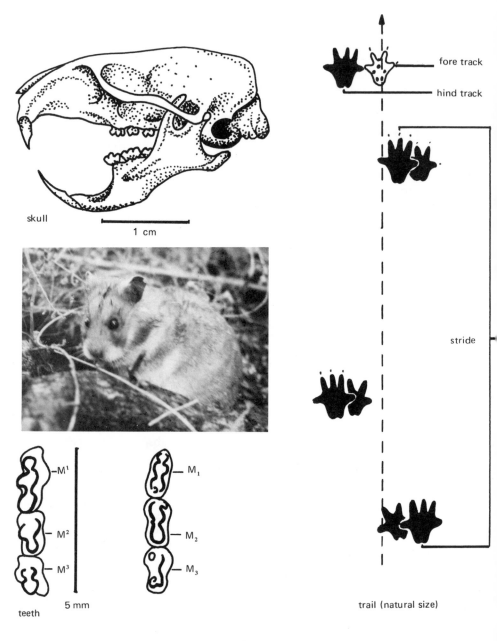

skull

1 cm

fore track

hind track

stride

M¹
M²
M³

M₁
M₂
M₃

5 mm

teeth

trail (natural size)

3 : 13 Golden hamster

Plate 25 Brown Rat in a warehouse.

Plate 26 Common dormouse. Note nest.

Plate 27   Coypu.

Plate 28   Muntjac
(Reeves).

TRAIL The normal gait is a run, but bounds of 15 cms. or more can be taken, and the animal has been reported to make vertical leaps of over half a metre. At running gait the hind feet partially register over the fore and astride of about 4 cms. is taken. Always moves rapidly; the tail is held high so that no drag marks will show. The feet are placed close on the median line.

SIGNS Seedlings, buds, fruits, nuts and snails are taken, and although branches may show signs of nibbling this is unusual as coarse material such as bark is not enjoyed. Nuts are usually opened with a slightly irregular but neat hole at one end. Berries may be eaten *in situ* on branches. Much damage done by eating sprouting wheat and newly-planted crops (damage to corn can be clearly seen where fields are bordered by hedgerows or woods, for here the stacks of corn will be destroyed by foraging individuals coming out from cover). Food is stored in hides underground, under logs, roots, in old nest and crevices in walls. The droppings are about 4 mm. in length, rounded in section, a very light brown when fresh, but turning almost black with age. Branches or old tree stumps are used as feeding places, and the remnants of shells and large quantities of droppings will be found there.

DWELLING PLACE Large tunnel systems in litter zone, but the nest itself is usually constructed of fine grass at the end of an underground burrow. This is used as a nursery, sleeping place and store.

Apodemus flavicollis   Family: Muridae

Yellow-necked Mouse

OCCURRENCE This species appears to be most common in the south of England. Matheson (1964) records this species in Breconshire, Denbighshire, Shropshire, Herefordshire and Radnorshire. Carmarthenshire (1954, 1962), Montgomeryshire (1961), Cheshire (1957). The species may occur in Lincolnshire and Northumberland, and has been recorded in Derbyshire. It occurs in small pockets within this range.

HABITS Little definite information here, but probably much the same as *A. sylvaticus* (Wood mouse). The two species will live together in the same area, but the larger Yellow Neck will tend to be aggressive. One slight difference in mode of life is that whereas *A. sylvaticus* will not visit human habitation very frequently the Yellow Neck will live quite happily in any building of the area it inhabits. A very good climber and possibly more agile than *A. sylvaticus*.

HABITAT Woods, hedges and shrubberies, much the same as the Wood mouse. Food stores, potting sheds, houses and other buildings will be frequented, and the species has been recorded up to 175 metres above sea-level.

TRACK A little larger than that of *A. sylvaticus* (e.g. hind foot 2 cms. long, 1.9 cms. wide; fore foot 1.3 cms. long, 1.5 cms. wide), but much heavier. The hind foot is broad in relation to its width compared with *A. sylvaticus*, and has six prominent pad markings, two of them set far back on the heel. The fore foot has five pads arranged in facing semicircles at the toe and heel level. The claw marks are prominent and will normally show.

TRAIL Almost the same as *A. sylvaticus*, as species move at identical gaits. The prints are heavier, however, and not registered. A stride of 4.5 to 5 cms. is average.

97

Muridae
Small star-shaped track with four toes. Five palm pads and rudimentary pad at the thumb. Genera : *Microtus, Clethrionomys, Micromys, Mus, Apodemus, Mesocricetus*
Size ranges from 8 to 13 mm. length.
Similar to above, but larger. Tracks star-shaped and four-toed. Outer toes almost at right-angles to mid-line. Genera : *Rattus, Arvicola.*

Gliridae
Four-toed, not star-shaped. Longer than wider, six palm pads. Genus : *Muscardinus.* Size : 10 mm. long.
Four toes, six pads outer toes not pointing outwards as in *Rattus* and *Arvicola.*
Genus : *Glis.* Size : about 16 mm. long.

Squiridae
Four-toed track with toes pointing forward. Four closely aligned pads on palm. Claw marks often absent and outline of track obscured.
Genus : *Squirrus.* Size : about 25 mm.

Capromyidae
Five-toed track, large. Fifth toe small. Claw marks blunt, but prominent. Hand-shaped track with five pads on the palm. No web present.
Genus : *Myocastor.*
Size : about 60 mm. long.

3:14 **FORE TRACKS: RODENTS**

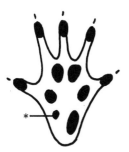

Muridae
The tracks range from small in the case of the mice, small voles and hamster to medium in the rats and water vole. The tracks are hand shaped and have six plantar pads. Claw marks show clearly. The tracks are distinguished from *Glis* and *Squirrus* by the pad arrangement.
Size : Small group, up to 20 mm. long.
      Medium group, from 30 mm. long.
* Not in *Arvicola* – only five pads present.

Gliridae
Common Dormouse. The track is five-toed and small, about 13 mm. The first toe is small and gives a 'club-footed' appearance. The four anterior pads are joined with two large separate pads behind.
Edible Dormouse. Track five-toed. Hand-shaped with claw marks clearly showing. Five strong plantar pads and one long one. The toe prints are distinct from the pads.
Size : about 30 mm. long, 25 mm. wide.

Squiridae
Five-toed track with strong claw marks. The toes are long. There are four oval plantar pads at the junction with the toes and one hind plantar pad.
Size : about 40 mm. long, 35 mm. wide.
* Metatarsal will only show in deep tracks.

3:15 HIND TRACKS: RODENTS
Note : The Coypu hind track has been omitted.

The tail is held high and no drag marks will be seen. The feet are placed rather widely on either side of the median line.

SIGNS Identical to *A. sylvaticus*. Much more restricted because of isolated pockets of Yellow Neck among the widespread covering of Wood mouse.

DWELLING PLACE Same as *A. sylvaticus*, except more often found in or near human habitation.

Mus musculus　　Family: Muridae

House Mouse

OCCURRENCE Common over the whole British Isles, both in rural areas and in large buildings, such as warehouses and stations, in built-up places. Many of the island races are distinct variants from those on the mainland.

HABITS Largely nocturnal, but not completely so. The amount of daytime activity will depend on the peacefulness of the habitat and the availability of food. Small home range from which little exploratory travel is undertaken. One male will usually occupy a territory with several females and defend it. In buildings there may be a greater degree of tolerance. In very high density conditions certain individuals will dominate, the surplus stock living in subordinance without territory or opportunity to breed. The voice is a high-pitched squeak, often heard in infested buildings.

HABITAT Open land, usually in arable countryside, and heath, walls and hedgerows. Field crops are inhabited as well as hay ricks, farms and town buildings. Those living in the open tend to move towards cover in winter (e.g. warehouses).

TRACK The hind foot has three central digits in a line and two others set at right angles to this. The foot is very long and narrow (1.7 cms. long, 1.2 cms. wide). The fore foot is broad in proportion to its length (1 by 1 cms.) There are five prominent pad marks on the fore foot. Claws show distinctly.

TRAIL Normal gait is a run with a stride of 4.5 cms. The feet are set wide on either side of the median line and no registration occurs. The undulating drag mark of the tail shows. Sometimes bounds, when strides of up to 45 cms. may be taken.

SIGNS Damage in buildings distinctive, food contaminated or nibbled showing small teeth marks. Half-eaten corn grains in stores common. Will eat almost any form of grain or stored food. The droppings are small and black, about 3 mm. long. Droppings reflect diet (e.g. if plaster, droppings are white and almost totally composed of plaster). In buildings rustlings and scrapings, as well as small holes in quiet corners may denote presence. A strong musty smell which is always present is a characteristic of this mouse.

DWELLING PLACE Temporary nests in hedgerows, but more likely to be constructed in dirty corners of neglected buildings. Will be made of any available material, from grass to fabrics, or even paper. In hay ricks where optimum conditions exist the animal will breed prolifically and communal nests may exist.

Rattus rattus　　Family: Muridae

Black Rat or Ship Rat

OCCURRENCE This was the only rat in the British Isles for 500 years when it was first introduced from the Near East. With the arrival of the Brown rat in the

100

3 : 16 Harvest mouse and nest.

3 : 17 Harvest mouse nest in stubble.

eighteenth century it seemed unable to compete and is now confined mainly to port towns, where it is probably supplemented in numbers by the importation of ship rats. Colonies still occur in the open on Lundy and the Channel Islands.

HABITS Lives almost entirely in the rafters and walls of buildings, particularly warehouses and other waterside buildings. Mainly nocturnal in activity. Where the Black and Brown rats share the same habitat the Brown rat is usually dominant. The general range of movement seems to be small, about 80 or 90 metres, although males may range further afield. Normally silent, but when wounded makes a crying noise or a scream. Regular runs are followed along rafters and pipes and these may be identified by black smears, where the rat has had to go under a cross-beam or round an obstacle (see also 'Signs'). The animal is a good swimmer and climber, and will tend to keep to cover.

HABITAT Climbs a great deal, and may inhabit trees (not recorded in this country). Will tend to go to the top of the building it inhabits if living in an urban environment.

TRACK The hind track shows three central toes in a line, with the first and fifth toes at right angles to these. Neither the fore nor the hind foot is long in proportion to its width (e.g. hind 2.1 cms. long, 2 cms. wide; fore 1.5 cms. long, 1.7 cms. wide). There are six pads on the sole of the hind foot and five conspicuous ones on the fore foot. The claw marks show distinctly. One distinguishing feature between

3 : 18 Water vole habitat.

3 : 19 Cones (a) complete (b) eaten by crossbill (c) eaten by squirrel.

Black and Brown rats is, that the tips of the toes of *R. rattus* tend to impress more deeply than those of its larger relative. Also the tracks of *R. rattus* are of a more delicate nature.

TRAIL The normal gait is a run. The hind feet register over the fore, and an average stride of 8 cms. is taken. The feet are close to the median line, and the drag of the long tail shows in a heavy, distinct and almost continuous line. Bounds of up to 50 cms. may be made when travelling at speed.

SIGNS Will eat almost anything, although it is in granaries and other food storehouses that its activities are the most often seen, and are the most damaging. Teeth marks and contamination of food will signify the presence of a rat, just as gnawed wood-work and piping will. 'Smears' are commonly found on the regular pathways. These are the difficult passing places, where the animal with its greasy fur has brushed against the wall and caused a black mark. In the case of *R. rattus* a special loop smear, a semicircular mark where the animal has had to swing under a cross-beam or pipe, is commonly found. The droppings are narrow and curved (10 by 2 to 3 cms.) and vary in colour with content. They will be dropped anywhere, often on the feeding ground, hence causing the contamination of large quantities of food.

DWELLING PLACE The nests are constructed of any soft material available and will be located in rafters and behind pipes in the roofs of buildings. This is in contrast to the Brown rat, which usually builds near to, or on, the ground.

Rattus norvegicus   Family: Muridae

Brown Rat or Norway Rat

OCCURRENCE First introduced in the eighteenth century and has since spread widely over the British Isles, displacing *R. rattus* (Black rat). Occurs mainly near man-made installations, both in the town and country.

HABITS In a restricted environment the range of movement is usually not more than 30 metres. Shelters in burrows, and in farmland. Extensive tunnel and run systems

3 : 21   Damage by rats to hayrick.

3 : 20   Rat runs and burrows.

may be built up in the hay ricks and vegetation. Largely nocturnal, although there is also a peak of activity at dusk. Large colonies may occur in a particularly favourable environment (e.g. hay ricks). Large-scale migrations occur when major environmental changes take place (e.g. dismemberment of the hay rick). A good swimmer, also an active burrower. Tends to be less retiring than *R. rattus.*

HABITAT Mostly associated with town buildings, farms, sewers, hay ricks and rubbish tips. May also occupy walls and river banks, as well as fields and woodland, especially where there are rabbits.

TRACK There are three central toes in a line on the hind foot, but the first and fifth toes are not at right angles to them. The fore foot is broad in relation to its length while the whole track is much heavier than that of *R. rattus* and is larger (hind foot: 3.5 cms. long, 3 cms. wide; fore foot: 2 cms. long, 2.8 cms. wide). There are six prominent pads on the hind foot and five on the fore. The claws usually show, and the tips of the toes impress deeply.

TRAIL When running the feet do not quite register, and are slightly straddled across the median line. The feet point slightly outwards, and a stride of 9–10 cms. is taken. When in a hurry can bound, and may take strides of up to 60 cms. When bounding the feet show in pairs, alternating hind and fore. The tail drag may show, but it is extremely rare since the tail is normally carried off the ground. It has been recorded that rats may 'kangaroo-hop' when carrying something large. Brown, L. E. (1966) has used tracking plates in her study on Home Range and movement in small mammals. The animals were toe-clipped to allow individual recognition of the animals so marked. 'The tracking plates were strips of paper-backed metal foil overlaid with a fine talc suspension held in a silicone water repellent medium. The plates were placed for protection in waxed cartons. Large numbers were used, especially in areas of particular interest. . .' The cartons were held in place by metal skewers and the entrance was protected by a plastic hood.

SIGNS (see also *R. rattus* 'Signs'). Damage to food in warehouses is extensive in places. Pipes and boards are chewed through and extensive tunnel systems may be built under paving stones. Most of the gnawing damage done in buildings is by the Brown rat. Hay ricks can be badly damaged, and rats living in open country will take almost any vertebrate or invertebrate food they can get, and even House mice are eaten. Insects and vegetable matter are also taken. Droppings are large and cylindrical (17 by 6 mm.) and will vary greatly with content. Runs in farmyards and across fields will often be found.

DWELLING PLACE Nest is constructed in crevices, under floorboards, in hay ricks. Will tend to be at ground level, whereas *R. rattus* will build above ground level. Extensive tunnel and run systems supplement the nest.

Muscardinus avellanarius   Family: Gliridae (= Muscardinidae)

Dormouse

OCCURRENCE Nowhere common. Absent from Scotland and Ireland, and seems to be in overall decline.

HABITS Almost completely nocturnal, tending to move above ground level in grass and bushes. Several nests may be constructed by an individual in one year, usually fairly close to each other. Occasionally colonial tendencies are shown by this species, several individuals building their nests in a small area. It hibernates, but

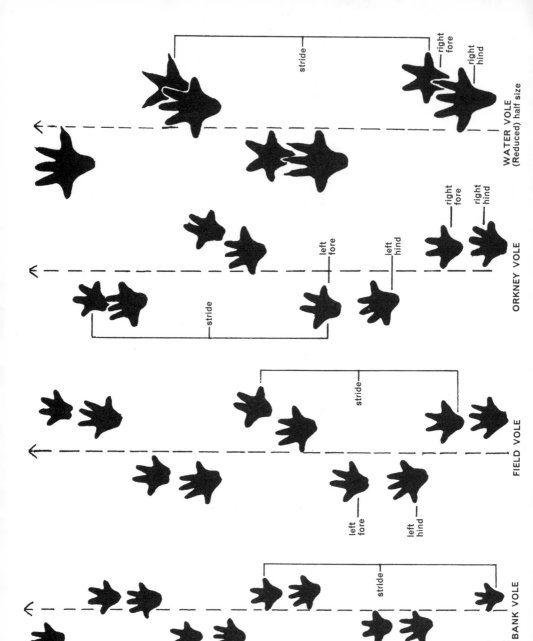

WATER VOLE
(Reduced) half size
right fore
right hind
stride

ORKNEY VOLE
right fore
right hind
left fore
left hind
stride

FIELD VOLE
stride
left fore
left hind

BANK VOLE
stride
left fore
left hind

3 : 22A   Vole trails (natural size).

104

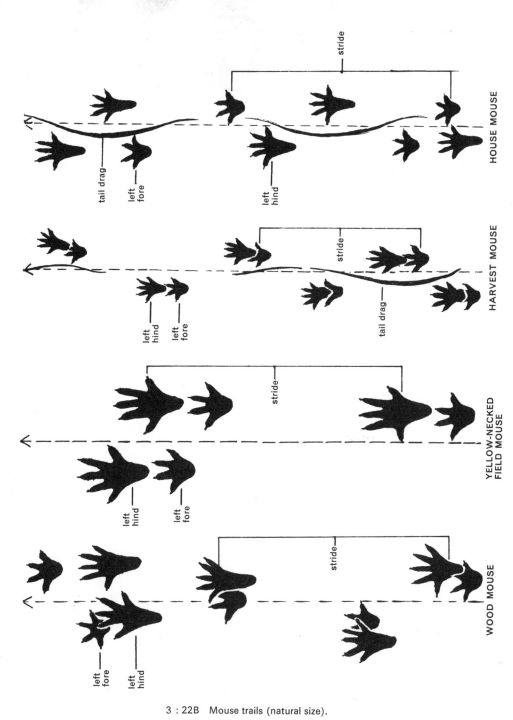

stride

HOUSE MOUSE

tail drag

left
fore

left
hind

HARVEST MOUSE

stride

left
hind

left
fore

tail drag

YELLOW-NECKED
FIELD MOUSE

stride

left
hind

left
fore

WOOD MOUSE

stride

left
fore

left
hind

3 : 22B   Mouse trails (natural size).

105

right hind	right fore	left hind	left fore	right hind	right fore
Harvest mouse		Common dormouse		House mouse	

left hind	right fore	right hind	right fore
Yellow-necked mouse		Wood mouse	

MICE

left hind	right fore	left hind	right fore
Bank vole		Orkney vole	

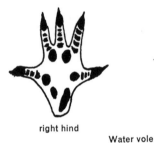 

right hind	right fore	left hind	right fore
Water vole		Field vole	

VOLES

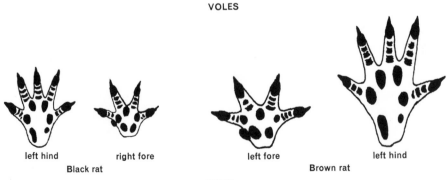

left hind	right fore	left fore	left hind
Black rat		Brown rat	

RATS

3 : 23 Tracks of Common dormouse, mice, voles and rats (natural size).

may be active for short periods in mild spells during the winter months. It is an excellent climber and a good swimmer, but does not dig. Little is known about territories, but evidence suggests that the animals wander extensively within a large radius.

HABITAT Prefers undergrowth in well-established woods, especially where trees with edible fruits are found, e.g. beech, hazel, sweet chestnut. Forages on the ground at night, and usually hibernates at ground level.

TRACK The hind foot has four long digits and long claws, on the inside a short stub toe minus claw. It is long and broad (1.5 cms. long, 1.1 cms. wide). The fore foot is unlike the tracks of other small rodents (i.e. mice, etc.) in that the length is greater than the width (1 cm. long by 8 mm. wide). On both feet there are very prominent pads which give positive identification.

TRAIL Normal gait a walk but does run. Feet set close to the median line. Tracks sometimes register. The tail drag shows, but more 'fluffy' than mice.

SIGNS Large areas of vegetation, normally above ground level, are stripped and fruit of various kinds may be damaged or completely removed. An extremely good indication of this species' presence is a large area of honeysuckle stripped of foliage and bark for the animals are partial to this form of bush. Droppings are not commonly found and give little help as positive means of identification.

DWELLING PLACE The nest is made of vegetable matter, mainly pieces of bark, and may be found either in reeds and other vegetation close to the ground or else in thick undergrowth, especially in well-developed honeysuckle-bushes. Occasionally holes in the boles of trees may be utilised, and since the animal is a good climber there is no reason to suppose that it does not often construct its nest well above ground level.

Glis glis   Family: Gliridae (= Muscardinidae)

Edible Dormouse

OCCURRENCE Introduced into Tring Park, Hertfordshire in 1902. It has since spread slowly, and now occurs sporadically over the surrounding Chiltern countryside for a radius of about 25 miles. It is nowhere very common, and although successfully established shows no sign of becoming widespread.

HABITS Largely nocturnal; gregarious, in some cases living in small colonies. Tends to favour houses in this country, as it is a hibernating species, and looks for somewhere warm to go in winter (although roofs and barns may suddenly be occupied for a year and used for breeding). Normally not very active, although an agile climber. No regular runs exist on the ground, and the home range is not usually more than 100 metres in diameter, although in autumn when searching for somewhere to hibernate, may wander for distances of more than a kilometre. Sleeps in tree holes during day. Voice is a series of low squeaks or nasal snufflings or grunts, or when disturbed a spitting purr. May be disturbing to humans when moving about in the rafters of a house it has occupied.

HABITAT Mainly deciduous woodland, but seems to prefer buildings in this country. Almost all specimens are found in barns, lofts or wall cavities of houses, especially in autumn.

TRACK The track is rather similar to that of the squirrel, with a large rectangular pad on the front foot, and the tips of four toes showing. These do not curve round,

107

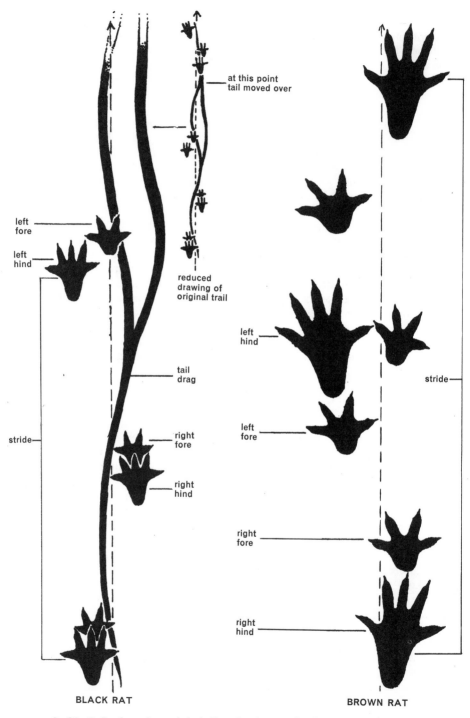

at this point
tail moved over

reduced
drawing of
original trail

left
fore

left
hind

tail
drag

stride

right
fore

right
hind

left
hind

left
fore

stride

right
fore

right
hind

BLACK RAT

BROWN RAT

3 : 24 Trails of rats (natural size). Note the absence of trail drag in the Brown rat.

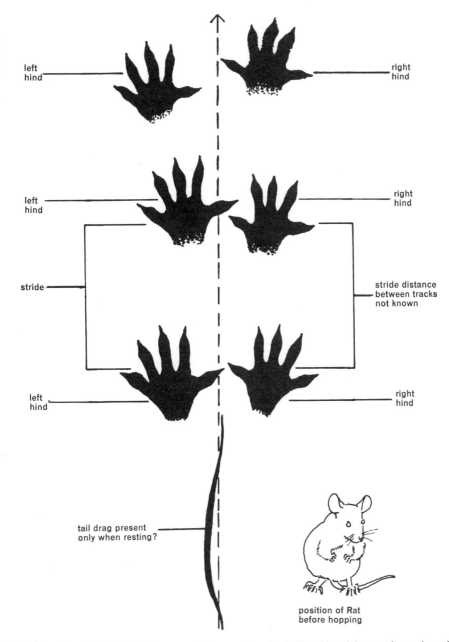

left hind · · · right hind

left hind · · · right hind

stride · · · stride distance between tracks not known

left hind · · · right hind

tail drag present only when resting?

position of Rat before hopping

3 : 25 Hopping gait of rat. It has been recorded on good authority that this gait is sometimes adopted when carrying something large, but not heavy. The authors, however, have not seen this. The trail shown therefore is only a suggested result of this type of gait. When actually hopping the tail would probably be held clear of the ground, since this would give balance. The tracks would probably be close together, and there might even be partial registration.

but are located more at the front of the pad than in the squirrels. The hind foot has a thumb-like fifth toe and three toes in a line. The prints of this species can easily be distinguished on closer inspection since they are smaller (e.g. hind: 3 cms. by 2.5 cms.; fore: 2 cms. by 2.2 cms.). The claws do not often show, and the pad structure is more complicated; six on the fore foot and two composite ones on the hind. Further, the bushy tail drags, leaving scuff marks.

TRAIL When walking, the feet tend to turn outwards very slightly and the hind foot will register over the fore. An average stride of 7 cms. is taken, the bushy tail drags and makes extensive scuff marks, and the feet are set wide astride the median line. When moving at speed the animal runs and bounds. When bounding the tracks will be in groups of four with a gap of about 30 cms. between each group. Tail marks will not often show at this gait.

SIGNS Eats all kinds of fruit, nuts, insects and the bark of certain trees (e.g. willow and plum). Food stores seem to be exceptional. Most important signs around human habitation (e.g. chewed fruit peel and nibbled apples). Nuts are not nibbled open with a neat hole as in the case of the mice, but usually have a large jagged hole in them. Favourite feeding places may be tree stumps or even window-sills. May do considerable damage to stored food, especially apples. The droppings are irregular and vary greatly in size and colour.

DWELLING PLACE Nest may be made in tree holes and will consist of various types of soft vegetable matter. In this country it is more often in an attic or stable, and will be made of any available soft material (e.g. cloth). The nest will be constructed in a warm, concealed niche or corner.

Sciurus vulgaris   Family: Sciuridae

Red Squirrel

OCCURRENCE Common over much of Ireland and present over much of Wales and Scotland, where it may be locally common. Rare or absent in most parts of England where it has been generally displaced by the Grey squirrel. It still occurs in East Anglia (Thetford), in some northern and western counties, the Isle of Wight and Arran, and also Anglesey. There appears to have been a reduction in numbers in Scotland in the eighteenth century, but introduced stock supplemented the numbers. The stock in Ireland may be introduced. In the early part of this century there was a decrease in numbers, and in the areas occupied by the Grey squirrel this deficit has not been made good.

HABITS No evidence that territories exist. Diurnal. There is no true hibernation, but bad weather inhibits activity. The animal is very agile in trees and spends most of its time there, visits to the ground being made to forage for food. Trails in the grass, linking the bases of trees may be found. The animal is also an able swimmer.

HABITAT Occupies mainly the coniferous woods outside the range of the *Sciurus carolinensis* (Grey squirrel). Will inhabit mixed woods and even deciduous areas or sparsely wooded country, but by nature is shy and will remain in seclusion if possible. This species is declining in terms of the areas it occupies, and even where *S. carolinensis* is not found it does not seem to be doing very well.

TRACK Similar to that of *S. carolinensis* in general shape, although the pads are more delicate, and there is less likelihood of the whole foot showing. The total area of the track may be greater than that of *S. carolinensis*, but it is more clearly defined, the claws usually showing.

TRAIL The normal gait is a series of hops about a metre in length, sets of four tracks show distinctly with the feet straddled slightly. At a slower, browsing pace a stride of about 45 cms. is taken. The tail is held high so that scuff marks do not normally show. Jumps of more than 4 metres may be made.

SIGNS (see also *S. carolinensis*). Less damaging to vegetation than the *S. carolinensis*. Scratch marks on bark, usually three parallel lines, indicate where the animal has climbed a tree. If used regularly the bark may become chipped and roughened. Food is usually eaten in the trees, although it is collected on the ground. The droppings are similar to those of the *S. carolinensis*. Pine cones found with the scales gnawed off are usually the work of this species. The food is stored in small hollows and holes when it is particularly abundant, and it is probably relocated by smell. Runs may exist in the grass, and may be distinguished from those of rabbit in that they lead from tree bases.

DWELLING PLACE The drey (nest) is usually located in coniferous trees, and is often spherical in shape. Tittenson (1969) lists grass, moss, pine cones, needles, stripped or flaked bark, eaten cones, etc., as the most common construction materials, with eaten buds, ferns, whole cones, leaves and stems and feathers being used to a lesser extent. One drey was separated into its component items, which showed the following proportions by weight.

Grass	*Moss*	*Pine needles*	*Other items*
88 grms.	29 grms.	26 grms.	13 grms.
(57%)	(19%)	(16%)	(8%)

Tittenson recorded 98% of the dreys as adjacent to the main trunk, either in a fork in the trunk or in large side branches. The other 2% were only a short distance along a side branch from the trunk.

It is important to remember that the dreys of both species of squirrel may be confused with clumps of ivy, so careful inspection is required.

Sciurus carolinensis　　　Family:　Sciuridae

Grey Squirrel

OCCURRENCE Introduced into the British Isles, and allowed to escape between 1876 and 1929 from about 30 centres. It has spread rapidly since then and is now found over much of England and Wales, but has not been reported in Cumberland, the Isles of Wight and Man, Anglesey and the Channel Islands. Few reports in Northumberland, Westmorland, Caernarvonshire, Cornwall and Norfolk. The animal is fairly common in Ireland, but is restricted mostly to the Central Lowlands and the glens in Scotland. In places the population may be very dense.

HABITS No evidence of territories and the home range tends to be small. Females will drive intruders from the nest tree, and young animals, males and non-breeding females will share the same nest. Feeding may be communal in areas of high density. Diurnal. Tends to keep to trees, coming to ground only to forage and feed, but is a good swimmer. A very able climber. No pathways exist on the ground, but

111

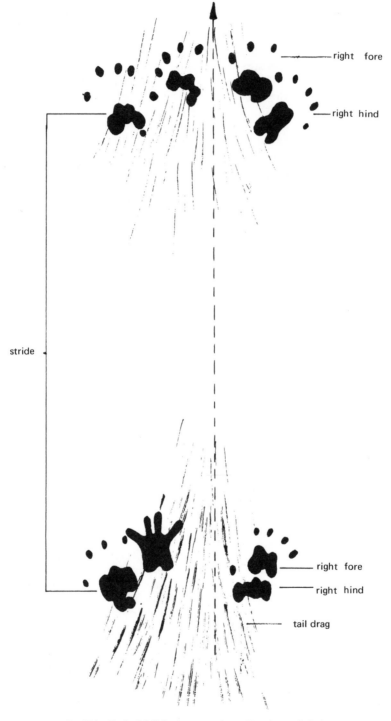

right fore

right hind

stride

right fore

right hind

tail drag

3 : 26A Trail of Edible dormouse bounding (natural size)

Plate 29 Red deer stag with hinds.

Plate 30 Sika deer herd.

Plate 31   Fallow deer bucks.

Plate 32   Chinese Water deer.

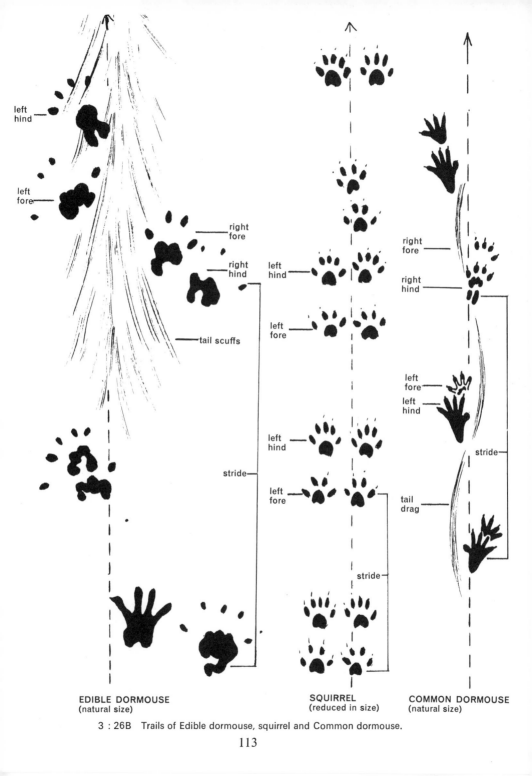

left
hind

left
fore

right
fore

right
hind

tail scuffs

stride

EDIBLE DORMOUSE
(natural size)

left
hind

left
fore

left
hind

left
fore

stride

SQUIRREL
(reduced in size)

right
fore

right
hind

left
fore

left
hind

stride

tail
drag

COMMON DORMOUSE
(natural size)

3 : 26B   Trails of Edible dormouse, squirrel and Common dormouse.

113

regular routes and approaches are followed in the trees. The voice is shrill and chattering, and will often be heard, especially when the animal is annoyed.

HABITAT Anywhere where trees are to be found, from extensive mixed woodland to isolated clumps of standards. Coniferous plantations will be colonised if seed-bearing hardwoods exist near by. Seems to prefer low altitudes.

TRACK When the whole of the hind foot shows it is rather hand-like, with the first toe on the inside of the foot occupying the same position as a thumb. On harder ground the circular toe tips will show around a large semicircular pad. On the fore foot there are four toes set around an almost rectangular pad. The claws show distinctly in most cases.

TRAIL The normal gait is a series of hops rather more than a metre in length. Sets of four tracks will show distinctly with the feet straddled slightly. At a more leisurely pace, when browsing for instance, a stride of about 50 cms. is taken. The tail is held high, and scuff marks do not show. Moves very quickly in the trees and jumps of up to 4 metres may be made from branch to branch.

SIGNS Food consists of many things. Acorns are the most popular but hazel nuts and cones as well as almost every form of hard fruit are taken. Bulbs, roots, shoots and buds are all eaten, as well as soft fruit, fungi, grain and catkins, insects and occasionally larger animals. Cones are split, and nuts usually split open, birds' eggs are also taken. There is often a favourite feeding place, such as a tree stump or branch, on which the remnants of hips, nuts and berries may be found. Piles of such remains may be found on the floor underneath a branch. Fungi eaten by the squirrel will be recognised by the large teeth marks on the cap. In summer trees are barked, often by an animal sitting on a branch, and very deep wounds are inflicted to get at the inner soft, sappy bark. Sycamores are the most commonly attacked and are often killed. The animal is, therefore, a serious pest. Food is buried in shallow troughs and is relocated by smell. Deep scratch marks will be found in the bark of trees, especially those leading to the drey. The droppings vary in shape and colour, but may be circular and black like a rabbit (only smaller, about 8 mm. diameter) or rat-like, but larger. Grey squirrels gnaw patches of bark on trees. At the same time they scent mark them with urine, and this often gives rise to a dark, strong smelling area below the gnawed patch. There is no satisfactory explanation for this at the moment since this behaviour occurs at activity peaks throughout the year (Taylor, 1968).

DWELLING PLACE The 'drey' consists of twigs and other coarse vegetation for a framework, and of moss, grass or even animal fur for a lining. It is constructed at almost any height between 2 and 15 metres in large forks of the tree. In summer leafy platforms on the extremities of trees may be made. The drey is circular and usually about the size of a large football, although this will vary greatly. Bushes and holes in trees may also be used for nesting, and almost every species of tree is frequented. The winter dreys are situated on a fork formed by a main branch with the trunk, but the summer drey tends to be on small branches away from the main trunk. The dreys tend to be located somewhere near the mid-point of the height of the tree.

Hazel nuts attacked by squirrels can be distinguished from those taken by mice and voles by the irregular outline of the hole and if the shell is broken into two halves.

114

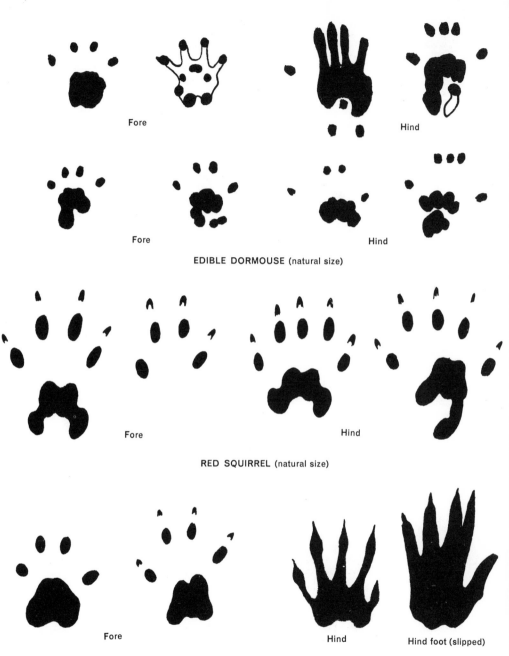

Fore

Hind

Fore

Hind

EDIBLE DORMOUSE (natural size)

Fore

Hind

RED SQUIRREL (natural size)

Fore

Hind

Hind foot (slipped)

GREY SQUIRREL (natural size)

3 : 27 Tracks of Edible dormouse, Red squirrel and Grey squirrel (natural size).

3 : 28A Fungi eaten by squirrels. (Note broken condition.)

3 : 28B Fungi eaten by slugs.

Nuts found wedged into bark crevices and split are not the work of squirrels but of woodpeckers. They wedge the nut into the bark so that they are able to open the nut and retrieve the contents.

Myocastor coypus   Family: Capromyidae

Coypu (Nutria)

OCCURRENCE The distribution of this species was originally controlled by the coincidence of Nutria farms with suitable habitat conditions (i.e. water and marshland). This South American species started escaping from farms in the 1930's and first became established in the Norfolk Broads area. It has since radiated out from here following the many watercourses, but is still largely confined to East Anglia (with the exception of a small colony in Buckinghamshire). Despite intensive extermination efforts there seems little chance of the species being destroyed.

HABITS Active mainly at dusk, but also at night. In the wild this species is abroad by day only in cold, overcast conditions. Well marked paths, which lead through the riverside vegetation, are used and usually give easy access back to the river. When swimming the animal sometimes 'hums' and in extreme distress gnashes its teeth so that pieces may actually break off. Several families group together, and range is restricted by availability of water.

HABITAT The marshes, reeds and river banks of the Norfolk Broads and similar conditions on the various contributory rivers.

TRACK Five toes show on the hind track and five on the fore. There is great variation in size depending on the age and sex of animal. The hind track is much longer than the fore (e.g. hind 12 by 7 cms.; fore 6 by 6 cms.) and shows webbing only between the four outside toes. There is no webbing at all on the front foot. Prominent points on the pads, the tips of toes and the long nails show more deeply impressed than the general outline of the track.

TRAIL Tends to move with slow crouching walk on land. The feet are placed surprisingly close to the median line and the hind feet register over the fore. The tail is dragged along the ground and leaves a continuous mark, usually to one side

116

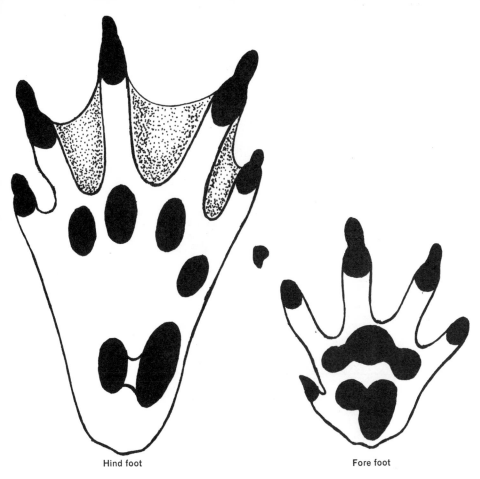

Hind foot   Fore foot

3 : 29   Tracks of coypu (natural size).

of the median line. Again the length of stride will depend on the individual, but as an example the specimen in the text is walking at a slow gait with a stride of 21 cms. The animal can move at speed with a series of short hops and bounds.

SIGNS As a vegetarian feeding on the reeds, sedges and water-borne plants of its habitat few feeding remains will be found. On rare occasions freshwater mussels will be taken and groups of animals grazing on grass may often be seen at dusk. Some damage is done in sugar beet and ground vegetable-producing areas. It is not so much that the animal eats aquatic vegetation but that it tramples down great areas, upsets the ecological balance and destroys valuable thatching material which makes it an object of persecution. It also makes large but not deep burrows in banks. The droppings are spindle-shaped and have a ridged surface; they vary in colour and may be from 2 to 4 cms. in length.

DWELLING PLACE Burrows are made in river banks, but these are usually only short refuge places. The true nests are mounds of marsh plants made on dry land and slightly away from the water.

117

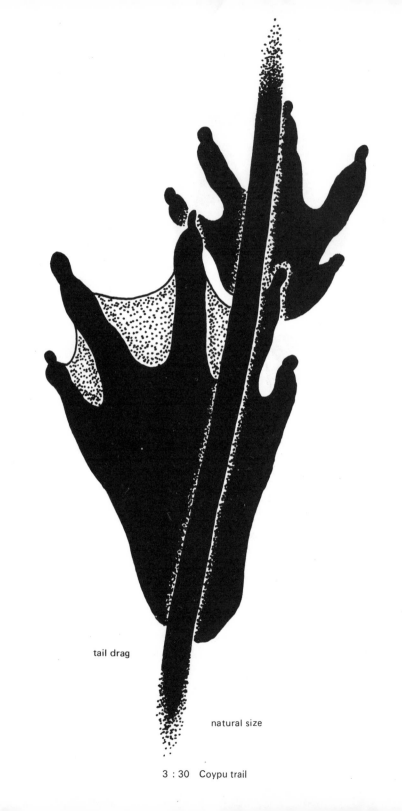

tail drag

natural size

3 : 30 Coypu trail

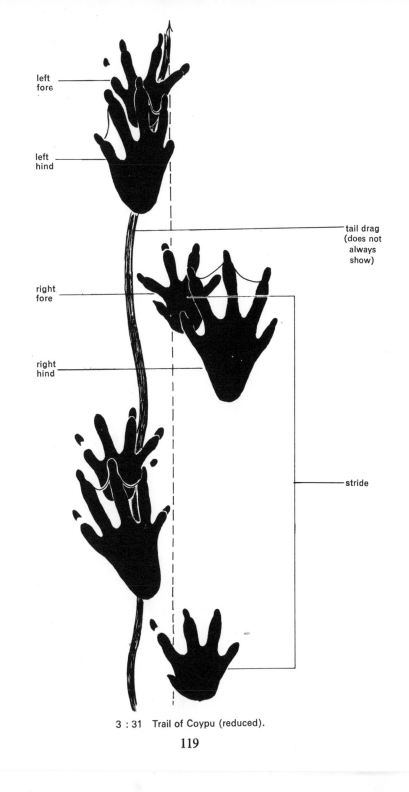

left
fore

left
hind

tail drag
(does not
always
show)

right
fore

right
hind

stride

3 : 31   Trail of Coypu (reduced).

119

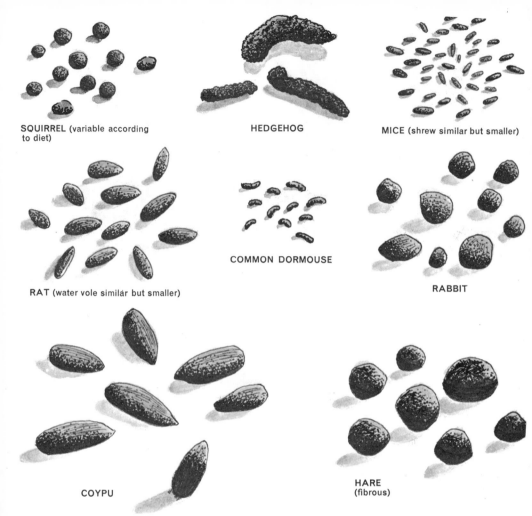

SQUIRREL (variable according
to diet)

HEDGEHOG

MICE (shrew similar but smaller)

RAT (water vole similar but smaller)

COMMON DORMOUSE

RABBIT

COYPU

HARE
(fibrous)

3 : 32   Droppings of rodents, lagomorphs and hedgehog (natural size).

3 : 33   Edible dormice eating apple.

3 : 34   Mountain hare in winter coat.

3 : 35   Coypu damage.
A Turnip.
B Sugar beet fields.
C River bank.

4 Artiodactyla, Perissodactyla and Marsupialia

ORDER ARTIODACTYLA

This Order is, along with the Perissodactyla, the most highly specialised of all land mammal Orders. It is one of the most challenging to study for, although many of its domestic species will be met with almost anywhere in the country, some of the deer species have very limited distributions and this, in conjunction with their shyness and solitary habits, presents a difficult task to the tracker. Little general comment need be made on this Order for, despite the apparent similarity of tracks in many species, there is in fact a great variety in form on which a reliable means of identification may be based, as the contents of this chapter will show.

The specialised limb

The rather specialised limb is the distinctive feature of the morphology of this Order, and it may be briefly considered here. There has been a reduction in the number of toes (one disappearing altogether) and the third and fourth digit have developed to an equal extent so that these form the main part of the track. The second and fifth digit still exist, but at a varying distance above the third and fourth on the back of the limb. The relative change in position of the dew claws in different species means that in some cases these will show under any circumstances (reindeer, pig), in others only under soft conditions (muntjac) and in some (cow) not at all.

The families of the Order

Three families represent this Order: the Cervidae or deer (our only wild artiodactyls); the Bovidae – sheep, goats and cattle; and the Suidae or pigs.

Deer

The Cervidae is the largest family and, although there are probably a dozen species in the parks of England, only the four which have recently escaped and have become

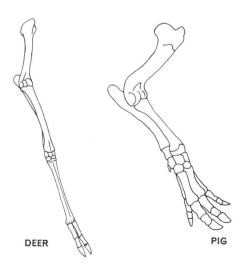

4 : 1   Illustration to show the way in which Artiodactyl limbs have been modified in different species.

DEER   PIG

established, or are likely to become established, have been dealt with here. In Scotland the reindeer has been reintroduced after its extinction in the twelfth century, and although it is still controlled, if the herd breeds successfully it may soon be released to roam over a wider area of the Cairngorms. Two species of deer, (excluding the reindeer), may be considered as indigenous in this country, the Red deer and the Roe deer. All of the other species have been introduced, largely from the latter part of the nineteenth century onwards and, although not usually considered as worthy of attention equivalent to our 'native' species, they are becoming more common and must be given full attention in a work of this sort.

Each species is dealt with in the accepted pattern of the book, except that an additional illustration of the shed antlers (excepting those of Chinese Water deer) is given with all species, although antlers will not be found very often (e.g. see Figs. 4 : 10, 4 : 11, 4 : 12, 4 : 13, 4 : 23, 4 : 24, 4 : 25, 4 : 27). With these illustrations are smaller ones showing other years in antler growth.

In the case of the Muntjacs both species are dealt with together as there is insufficient difference in their tracks and signs to devote a separate section to each of them. As a general rule species only have been dealt with in this volume, but in the case of the Siberian Roe (a subspecies of the Roe) variations in antlers warrant a separate illustration. A full section in the text has not been given over to this.

Sheep, goats and cattle

The sheep, goats and cattle are treated in the standard fashion, except that distribution maps are omitted. The distribution of these animals has been so modified by man that it would be of little value to map their occurrence which is very wide. There are some occasions when the dew claws of these species will show, but this is not common as vestigial toes are fairly high up on the limb.

Pigs

Again no distribution map is given in the case of the pig, our domesticated and only member of the Suidae. Here the dew claws show frequently, often in almost every track, as they are so low on the limb.

4 : 2   Skull of Roe deer showing antlers.

4 : 3   Skull of Chinese Water deer showing absence of antlers but great development of canines.

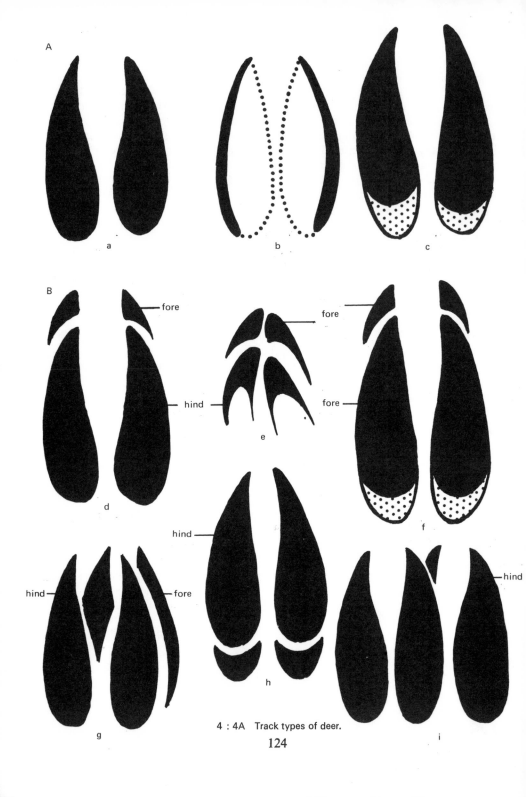

A

a

b

c

B

fore

hind

d

fore

hind

e

fore

fore

f

hind

fore

g

hind

h

hind

i

4 : 4A   Track types of deer.

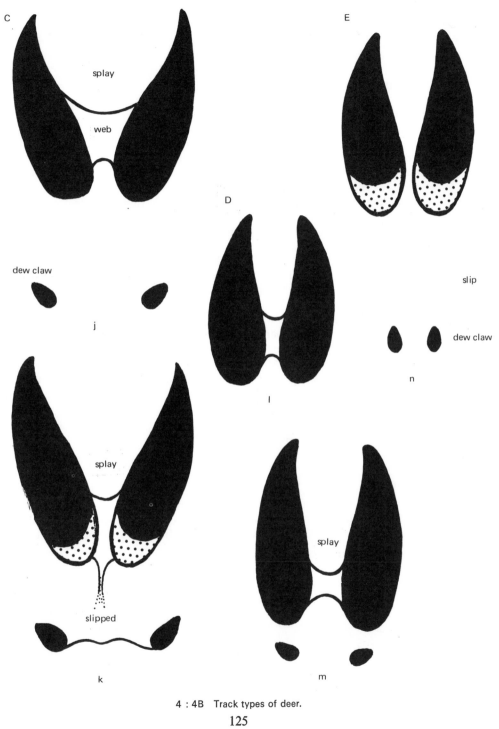

4 : 4B   Track types of deer.

Guide to track types

A. Normal-single track, i.e. two cleaves. Three types:
   - *a.* Perfect tracks – two simple cleave marks.
   - *b.* Hard ground – extreme edges showing and sometimes inside edge.
   - *c.* Slipped – exaggerating the length of the track.

B. Registered – double track formed from more than one set of cleaves:
   - *d.* Perfect register – hind track over the fore.
   - *e.* Hard ground – only tips show.
   - *f.* Hind track slipped – gives false length.
   - *g.* Partial register – the fore track shows to varying degrees.
   - *h.* Over-register – the hind foot oversteps fore foot so that the back end of the fore track is exposed behind the hind track.
   - *i.* Lateral register – hind track side steps fore track so that three cleaves tend to show.

C. Splayed running track – dew claws generally visible and the webbing may show. Two to three main types:
   - *j.* Normal running track – dew claws show, cleaves wide apart and webbing showing. On hard ground only the extreme edges of the cleave show.
   - *k.* Slipped – similar to *j* but the lengths are exaggerated.

D. Splayed track – cleaves parallel, web shows. Two types:
   - *l.* Perfect splay – web only shows.
   - *m.* As in *l.* but track further apart and as well as the web showing, the dew claws show close behind the cleaves.

E. Slipped – Found on steep slopes. The cleaves are exaggerated in length and the dew claws show. The dew claws are some distance behind the cleaves but are very close together.

*Muntiacus muntjak   Family: Cervidae

Indian Muntjac   Muntjacs (Barking deer)

Muntiacus reevesi

Chinese Muntjac

OCCURRENCE The Chinese and Indian muntjacs were introduced at Woburn in the late nineteenth century. Since then there have been many escapes, and the deer have become firmly established, particularly in the Midlands and South. Although

* Possibly extinct now in this country as a wild animal.

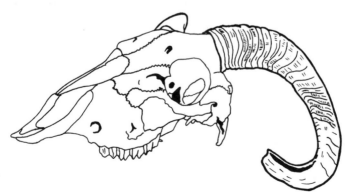

4 : 5 Skull of sheep showing the horns, which are not shed annually. Compare with Fig. 4 : 2. In the deer the antlers are lost each year.

these animals occur near to built-up areas they are not often seen, and nowhere can they be called common. The winter of 1962 took a heavy toll and numbers of both species died of starvation.

HABITS Both species tend to be solitary, or move in pairs. They are diurnal and if they are known to exist in a particular area can sometimes be observed grazing in small woodland clearings. They remain concealed either by lying up through the day or else travelling through tall vegetation. They make very little noise generally

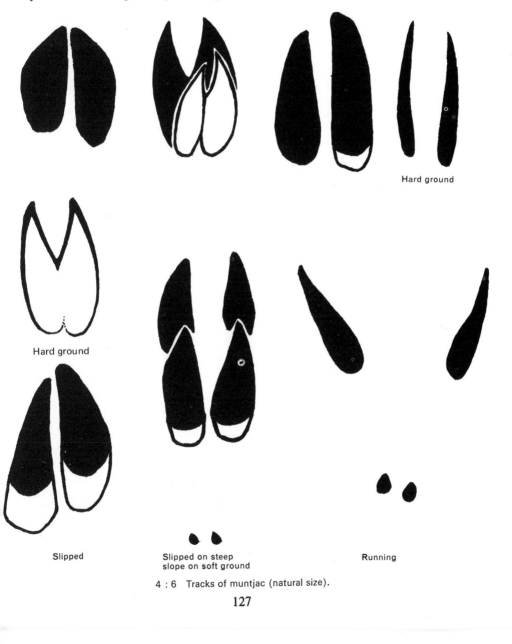

Hard ground

Hard ground

Slipped

Slipped on steep
slope on soft ground

Running

4 : 6   Tracks of muntjac (natural size).

4 : 7 Muntjac droppings.   4 : 8 Muntjac run (tunnel).

but bark when frightened or annoyed. Regular routes and feeding places may be used, and long journeys may be undertaken in the summer.

HABITAT Woodland, with thick undergrowth of ferns and bushes in which they may remain concealed. Watering places are usually at points where the streams are well screened by vegetation.

TRACK The size of the track will vary, but it will usually be under 3 cms. in length, pointed and narrow. (Slips and distortions are frequent). In both species the tracks will be similar, and it will be necessary to see the antlers if the species present in an area is to be identified. The characteristic feature of a muntjac track is that the two halves of the foot are uneven in size. When jumping the feet splay and the dew claws often show.

TRAIL The illustrations can be relied on to give an indication of the differences in stride size, but generally speaking if the deer is walking then the prints are perfectly registered on either side of the median line with a distance of about 30 cms. between each. When trotting the prints either partially register or are just apart.

SIGNS Little damage is done to man's crops, as wild herbage only is grazed upon. The trees on a regular run are worn by passing bodies, and there is often a musky smell from the scent deposited by the males. This is strongest in the breeding season (October to March). The shed antlers give the only easy means of distinguishing between the two species and even here size can be confusing. Trampled vegetation in concealed spots will indicate resting places. The droppings are small, rounded, slightly elongated black pellets about 1 cm. in length, and if the animals are not disturbed, are deposited in regular places.

DWELLING PLACE Like other deer a concealed area of flattened vegetation in which the animal will rest, give birth to its young and hide itself by remaining absolutely still and relying on the colour of its coat for protection.

Cervus elaphus   Family: Cervidae

Red Deer

The male is termed Stag, the female, Hind, and the young, Calf.

OCCURRENCE This species is indigenous and occurs both in the form of wild herds and as a park animal. True indigenous wild herds occur in Scotland, Devon, Somerset, the Lake District and parts of Ireland. The animal is kept in many parks and wild herds have grown from the escapes of this stock (e.g. Thetford Chase, Ashdown Forest, Scottish Lowlands). Distribution is wide over the British Isles with the exception of Wales.

HABITS Diurnal and gregarious. Herds tend to be large and to have one leader in the

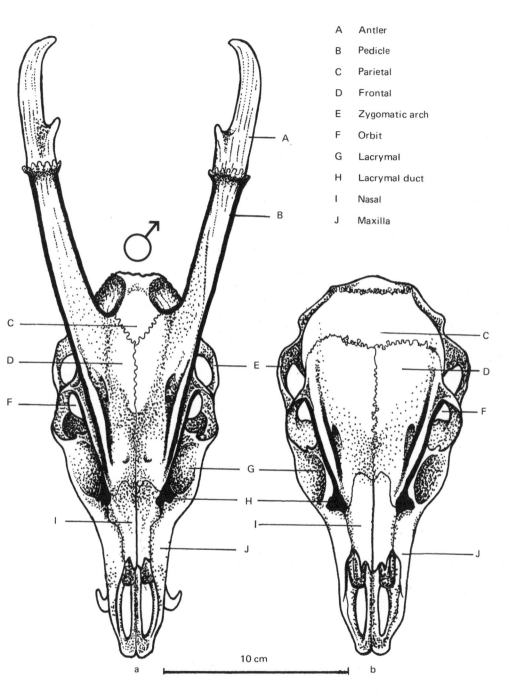

A	Antler
B	Pedicle
C	Parietal
D	Frontal
E	Zygomatic arch
F	Orbit
G	Lacrymal
H	Lacrymal duct
I	Nasal
J	Maxilla

10 cm

a   b

4 : 9 Muntjac skull; male and female.

129

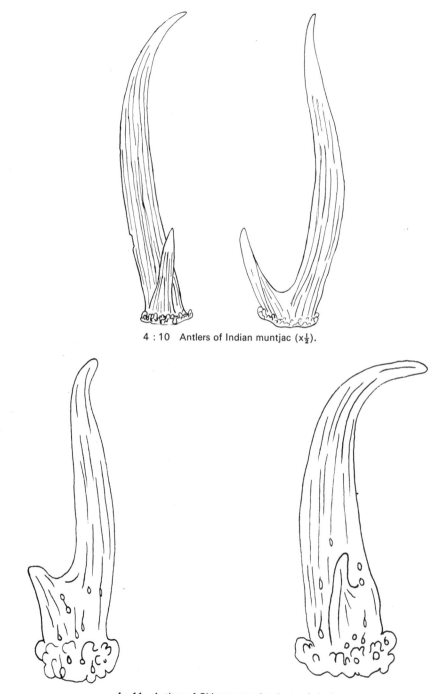

4 : 10   Antlers of Indian muntjac (x$\frac{1}{2}$).

4 : 11   Antlers of Chinese muntjac (natural size).

130

rutting season, mid-September–end October, but in winter the stags and hinds live apart, the very old males living a solitary existence. The animals graze at dawn and dusk, spending the day resting in woods or on hills. They migrate to more sheltered conditions in winter. A highly-developed social code exists and in the winter families occupy set territories in the lowland pastures. The famous stag roar may be heard across the moors in the rutting season.

HABITAT In woods and on moorland. In the highlands there is a seasonal movement between the two (forest in winter; moors in summer). In Scotland mountainous terrain is also inhabited, although the animals often take to the poorer terrains to avoid man.

TRACK The tracks are large and not very long in proportion to their width (e.g. length 8 cms.; width 7 cms.). They are rounded with heavy ridging around much of the perimeter of each toe, which impresses strongly. The inner walls of the toes are concave. The feet tend to splay out fairly easily, but the ground must be soft before the dew claws will show.

TRAIL When walking the tracks rarely register perfectly, unlike the other species of deer, and tend to be slightly to either side of the median line. When trotting the feet do not register, but are put down heel to toe, and almost in a straight line on the median line itself. When galloping the feet show in groups of four, with the toes spread and the dew claws sometimes showing. There is a distance of between 2 and 3 metres between each group.

SIGNS Feeds on grass and moss, and various forms of fruit from trees in woodland habitat. Heather is eaten on the moors. Damage is done to trees by clipping back shoots and buds and by stripping bark (up to a height of almost 3 metres). In bad

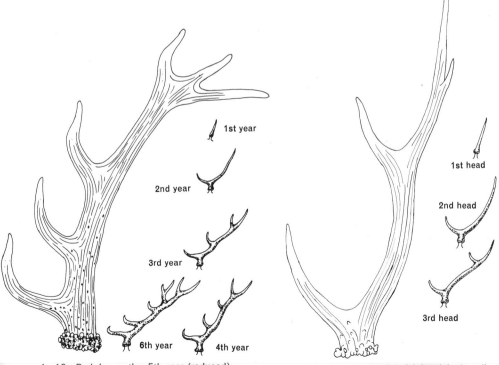

4 : 12   Red deer antler, 5th year (reduced).   4 : 13   Sika deer antler, 4th head (reduced).

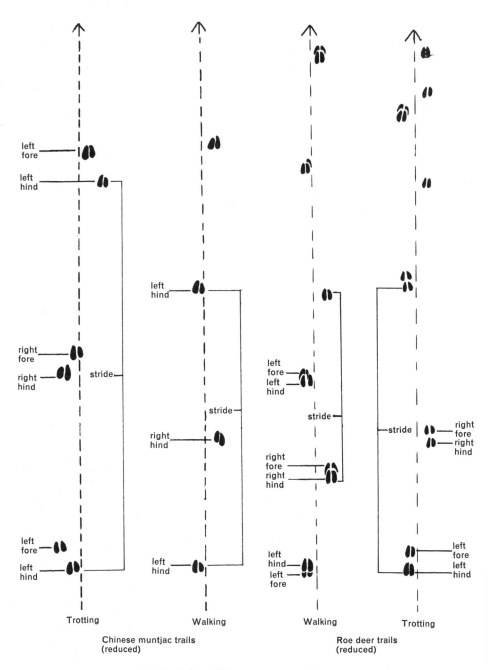

4 : 14   Trails of Chinese muntjac and Roe deer.

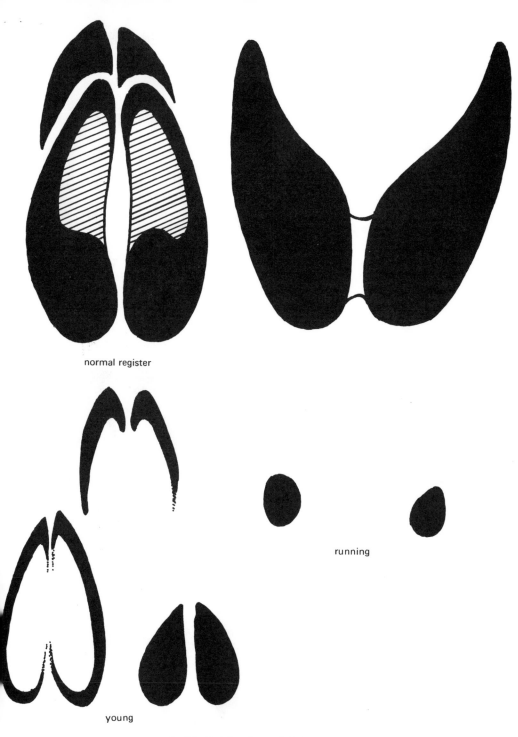

normal register

running

young

4 : 15   Red deer (natural size).

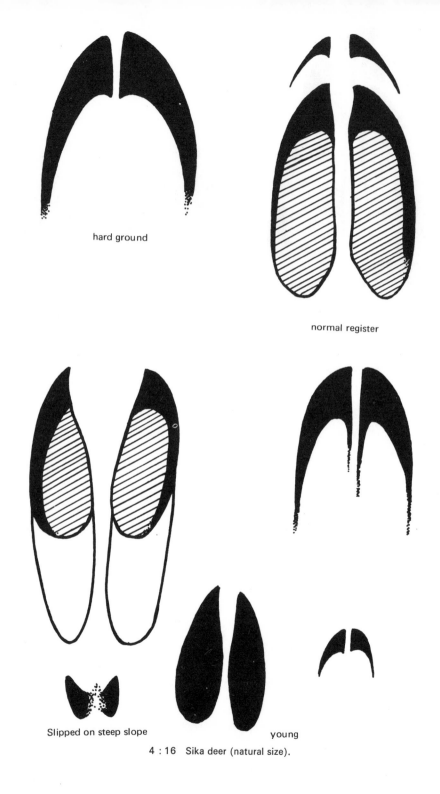

hard ground

normal register

Slipped on steep slope   young

4 : 16   Sika deer (natural size).

winters crops will be raided, but generally speaking not a great deal of damage is done to the human economy. The droppings are about 2 cms. long, in the case of females elliptical in shape; in males pointed at one end and flattened at the other. They are dropped in groups and vary greatly in colour from light brown to black. In the rutting season (September–October) the stag droppings are like miniature cow pats about 5 to 7.5 cms. across. The depressions in peat or mud in a deer-inhabitated area may denote wallowing places, and frayed and worn branches near the ground show where the stag has been attempting to rub the velvet from his antlers (between mid-July and the end of August). The antlers are shed between mid-February and the end of March.

DWELLING PLACE These will be sheltered areas of vegetation in the woodland habitat, which have been trampled to form lying-up places. Depressions in heather, often on a vantage point, may be summer resting places.

Cervus nippon   Family: Cervidae

Sika Deer

The male is called the Stag, the female, the Hind, and the young, Calf.

OCCURRENCE Common in several areas of the British Isles. This species was introduced into various parks in the latter part of the last century and established herds in suitable places through numerous escapes. These occur in south and south-east England (especially common in the New Forest), Devon and Somerset, northern England, much of the North-west Highlands of Scotland and parts of eastern Ireland.

HABITS Often said to be active mostly at night, lying up in cover through the day. While it is true that the deer do not become active until dusk small groups may often be seen wandering through the day. The animals are not socially inclined, the stags living alone, and the does in groups of two or three except in the breeding season when they too are solitary. Regular paths are followed and apparently regular routines are adopted.

HABITAT The preference seems to be for unfrequented woodland, with thick undergrowth. The animals lie up in this through the day, but open heath and gorse land near to the trees are frequented by night and here the animals browse. Occasionally, at night, individuals will visit fields planted with root crops.

TRACK The tracks are large, about 8 by 5 cms. in a large specimen, but there is great variation. The cleaves are rounded at the tips and broad, their raised edges showing distinctly on the perimeter. The toes tend to splay in soft ground making the tracks appear much broader than they are.

TRAIL When walking the tracks register, the feet being slightly straddled across the median line. The length of stride is about 1 metre at this pace. When trotting at high speed registration does not take place and there is a gap of more than 1 metre between each group of tracks.

SIGNS Feeding remains are not commonly found except the usual stripping of bark from trees, and young cut back shoots. The deer are accused of doing extensive damage in some areas to young trees and crops. The droppings are small, black and currant-like and are often cast in regular latrines, although random dispersal also occurs. The antlers are cast in early April, and may well be found in areas where the

135

deer is common. These antlers are rather similar to, but very much smaller than those of Red deer. The velvet may be found on wire or low branches from early July until late September. The lying-up places and paths in thick undergrowth will show that the deer are present, but as these are not distinguishable from those of several other species tracks and droppings will have to be used for positive identification.

DWELLING PLACE The animal has no permanent shelter, even when new born, although the same lying-up place may be used every day.

Dama dama   Family: Cervidae

Fallow Deer

The male is termed Buck, the female, Doe, and the young, Fawn.

OCCURRENCE This species is widely distributed over most of the British Isles. It was probably introduced as there is no fossil evidence of its being a native animal, but it was certainly established by the twelfth century. There are herds in private and public parks and wild stock occur in several of our forested areas (e.g. New Forest, Epping Forest and Rockingham Forest). Common in many southern counties, but less so in Wales and Scotland, and, although occurring widely in Ireland the population is nowhere very dense.

HABITS The feral herds are usually small and tend to be diurnal. A silent animal except in alarm when a sharp bark is emitted. Regular paths and grazing areas are adopted, and when travelling the members of the herd will move in single file. This species relies more on concealing itself than on speed for protection. Herds may be seen grazing at dawn or dusk in clearings and fields around the edge of woodland. The older individuals tend to move alone by night.

HABITAT Large areas of woodland (other than purely coniferous) with heavy undergrowth if possible. Sometimes large expanses of bracken in forest clearings are frequented.

TRACK The track is long and slender (e.g. 6.5 by 4 cms.) and is tapered. The outer ridges and the heel impress more heavily than the rest of the foot, and in hard ground often only these outer lines will show. The inner walls of the toes are concave and one toe is usually slightly broader than the other. The dew claws will show only in very soft conditions, and splaying is rare.

TRAIL When walking the feet register close on the median line. When trotting the stride is slightly longer and the tracks do not register perfectly. When galloping at speed the tracks show in groups of four with a gap of about 110 cms. between each group. Often the trail will be confused, especially with a large male, and the clear-cut groups will be obliterated.

SIGNS Feeds mainly in and around woods. Grass and tree fruits are taken, and barking may cause considerable damage. Farm crops will be eaten in a severe winter. Droppings may be found in a heap, or in a string if the animal is moving and no regular latrine is used. The droppings are sometimes faceted and jointed, about 1.5 cms. in length and black in colour. They are pointed at one end and are concave or flat at the other depending on which sex dropped them (male concave: female flat). The antlers are shed in April or May and are perhaps the most likely of all species to be found. In the mating season trees are frayed by the bucks

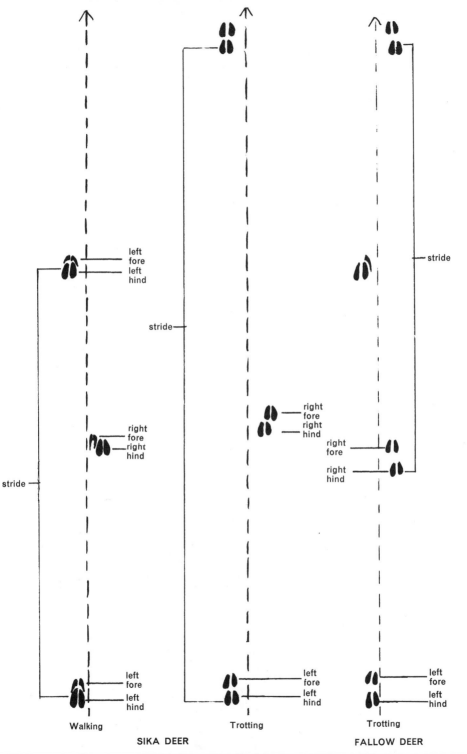

left
fore
left
hind

stride

right
fore
right
hind

right
fore
right
hind

stride

right
fore

right
hind

stride

left
fore
left
hind

left
fore
left
hind

left
fore
left
hind

Walking

Trotting

Trotting

SIKA DEER

FALLOW DEER

4 : 17   Trails of Sika and Fallow deer (reduced).

4 : 18 Sika deer tracks.   4 : 19 Reindeer tracks.

to mark territories and their musky scent deposited to demarcate their boundary. Ring paths around trees may be found and also ruts dug by the bucks' antlers.
DWELLING PLACE Resting places are usually denoted by areas of flattened vegetation in concealed areas.

Capreolus capreolus   Family: Cervidae

Roe Deer

The male is termed Buck, the female, Doe, and the young, Kid.
OCCURRENCE This species is not common over the whole of the British Isles, and occurs only in areas where there is suitable cover. Where the animals are found there is usually a considerable concentration of numbers. The Roe is no longer common in the Midlands or in Wales, and is believed to be completely extinct in Ireland. The greatest concentrations are in southern England, the Grampians and the north-west Highlands of Scotland.

4 : 20 Fallow deer tracks.   4 : 21 Roe deer tracks.

Normal

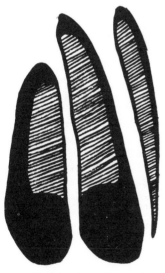

Registered on soft ground

4 : 22 Fallow deer tracks (natural size).   running track slipped   unusually large

HABITS Tends to be solitary, and is largely nocturnal, being rarely seen even in areas where it is known to be common. The deer will avoid human beings at all times by going into cover and 'lying low'. Despite its shyness this species is very inquisitive and will readily investigate anything unusual in its environment, provided

4 : 23 Antler of Roe deer (x⅔) showing abnormal growth. This abnormal growth is not confined to the Roe but is found in other species of deer. It may be the result of damaged reproductive organs, malnutrition, illness or even frost-bite.

this does not entail exposing itself. When feeding (near dawn or dusk) the deer will come out to the edge of cover (e.g. on to a forest path or the outskirts of the trees).
HABITAT Prefers to keep to woodland where there is plenty of cover and the animal may move without making its presence known. The woodlands most favoured are those traversed by rivers, which give drinking water and some secluded open spaces.
TRACK The slot is fairly delicate, being 3 to 4 cms. wide and 4 to 5 cms. long. The cleaves tend to converge and to narrow towards the front of the track, and splay out on soft ground or when the animal is moving at speed. The dew claws show on soft ground, and tend to be uneven in size as are the cleaves.
TRAIL When walking the tracks are in groups of two close to the median line. Registration takes place, and there is a distance of about 35 to 40 cms. between each group. When trotting the tracks do not quite register, and when bounding at speed the tracks come in groups of four, are often splayed out and show the dew claws. The distance between them is more than 2 metres.
SIGNS The feeding remains are few, except for some bark stripping, especially on young conifers (e.g. Forestry Commission plantations) up to a height of about 100 cms. Bushes are also eaten. The droppings are oval in shape, are usually black and about 1.5 to 2 cms. long. There is often a regular latrine. During the rutting season scrape marks, made by the male as part of the courting ritual, will be found in the ground. 'Rutting rings' show where the buck has run in a circle after the doe. The antlers are shed November–December. Areas of worn bark low on the boles of trees signifies rubbing to remove antler velvet. Where the animals have been resting or

140

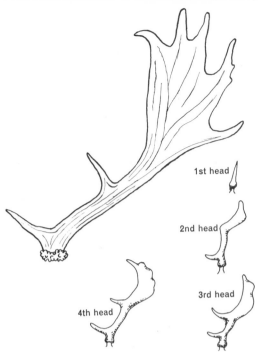

1st head

2nd head

3rd head

4th head

4 : 24 Fallow deer antler, 6th head (reduced).

4 : 25 A cast Fallow deer antler.

grazing very recently there is sometimes a slightly musky odour. Depressions in the low grass or vegetation are the signs of the lying-up places of deer.

DWELLING PLACE No fixed home, but the deer will lie in low vegetation with which they merge and are camouflaged. The young are dropped in the open, and remain protected by the habit of keeping still in surroundings with which they blend completely.

Capreolus capreolus pygargus   Family: Cervidae

Siberian Roe

Although it is doubtful if there are any feral specimens left of this animal (it escaped from Woburn and established small colonies) a brief mention can be made of it here. It is a subspecies, rather larger than the British roe and it is on this fact that most of the differences depend. The antlers of the Siberian roe are very slender, have a very rough surface and the tines set high.

Hydropotes inermis   Family: Cervidae

Chinese Water Deer

OCCURRENCE This species was first introduced into Woburn Park in 1900 and has since escaped and established feral herds over much of Bedfordshire, Hertfordshire and Buckinghamshire. Some stock has been introduced into parts of Hampshire

141

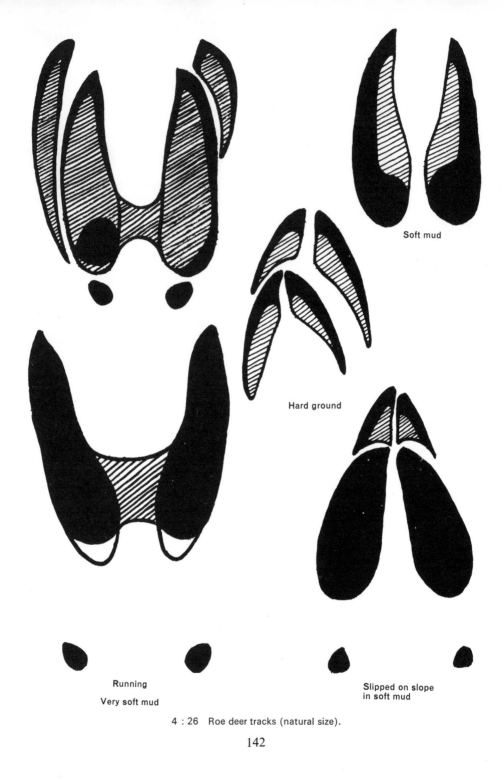

Soft mud

Hard ground

Running

Very soft mud

Slipped on slope
in soft mud

4 : 26   Roe deer tracks (natural size).

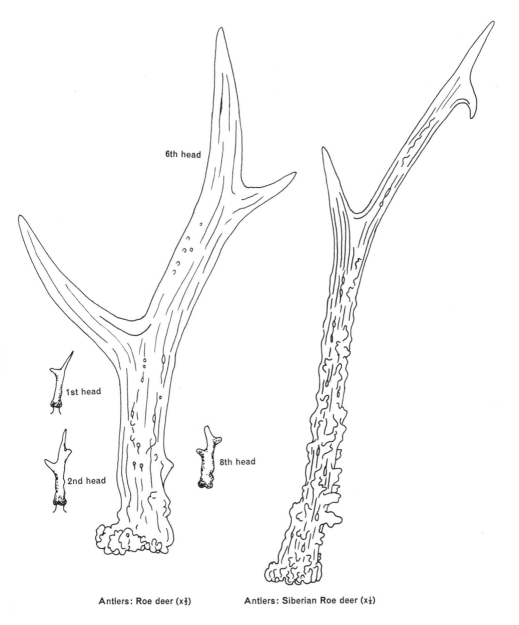

6th head

1st head

2nd head

8th head

Antlers: Roe deer (x⅔)   Antlers: Siberian Roe deer (x½)

4 : 27   Antlers of Roe deer and Siberian Roe deer.

143

and Shropshire, but no other areas have been colonised. The population is nowhere dense.

HABITS Not much is known of the habits of the wild species in this country, but it is thought to be active both by day and night, grazing at dawn and dusk on grass and root crops. The animals are solitary and generally silent except when alarmed and in the rutting season when they make shrill whistling sounds. They spend much of the day under cover. Regular routes and set territories are probably adopted, and traces of paths may be found in woodland undergrowth or reed beds.

HABITAT In Britain the animal has adapted itself to open grassland and woodland, but where possible will inhabit areas where large expanses of water and marshy conditions can be found. Reservoirs are the most favoured, and it is on their margins, among the reed banks, that most of the tracks, droppings and other signs will be encountered.

TRACK The track is distinctive. It is long, pointed and narrow (e.g. length 5 cms., width 3 cms.). The backs of the cleaves do not impress very heavily, as in other deer, although there is a raised ridge in evidence on the outer edge of the toes. The inside wall of the toes is flat or convex, a distinctive feature. When impressed deeply a web-like structure will show between the toes. When moving at speed the toes splay widely and the dew claws show distinctly.

TRAIL The tracks are usually slightly to either side of the median line, and at walking gait are almost perfectly registered with a distance of between 30–40 cms. between each print. When trotting the prints register imperfectly, and at the gallop groups of four prints, spread and with the dew claws showing, will be seen.

SIGNS Food consists of grass and crops of various types, taken in grazing grounds around the edges of the cover. It is uncertain if the animal damages trees (probably not!) and in any case it is not widely spread enough to cause any real nuisance. The droppings are cigar-shaped, non-adherent and black. They are about 1.5 by 5 cms. and are dropped in small heaps, although it is uncertain if regular latrines are used. Neither sex has antlers, but both have tusks in the upper jaw (large in the males) which are used for defence. The presence of this species in an area of marsh will sometimes be given away by the strong musty smell deposited by the males to attract females, and to mark out territorial boundaries.

DWELLING PLACE Little is known about the resting habits of the animal in this country, but lying-up areas are probably signified by flattened areas of reed, or undergrowth in woodland.

Rangifer tarandus   Family: Cervidae

Reindeer

OCCURRENCE This species was originally indigenous, but became extinct during the twelfth century. The reindeer are restricted at the moment to a small area (5000 acres) in the Cairngorms, but have been allowed to expand beyond the boundary of the original small pen with a six-foot double fence into which they were put when

4 : 28   Fallow deer droppings.   4 : 29   Sika deer droppings.

4 : 30   Red deer pre-rut droppings.   4 : 31   Reindeer droppings.

they were reintroduced in 1952. Although the grazing rights have been extended the deer show no great interest in wandering. The herd is normally checked daily, but they cannot be closely watched.

HABITS The animals tend to form into herds, and do not follow any particular paths except those leading to watering places and salt licks. Silent and diurnal the reindeer may sometimes be seen grazing on the open moor. They merge well into their surroundings when lying up in the heather. Unlike the reindeer of the Arctic these animals do not move down to shelter in bad weather, but move higher up to drier places in the mountains.

HABITAT The open moorland of the Cairngorms. Large patches of open land traversed by frequent streams and areas of woodland where the various lichens, the food of the deer, are to be found.

TRACK The track is large, rounded and very broad with a wide gap between the convex-shaped toes. Examples of dimensions are: length 9 cms., width 10 cms. The feet are broad to enable the animal to walk with ease on the snowfields of its Arctic habitat. The toes spread easily, and the dew claws, which are set low down on the limb, will show even on firm ground.

TRAIL: When walking the tracks register almost perfectly, are close to the median line and do not point out very obviously. The length of stride will vary with the individual, but in a first year male about 40 cms. is an average figure. When trotting the tracks register imperfectly, spread a little, point outwards and may show the dew claws. At the gallop the tracks are in groups of four.

SIGNS The food consists almost exclusively of lichen, and even under snow the animals can find their own fodder. They do not, therefore, damage trees in any way. The droppings are very variable and may be anything from 1.5 to 2.5 cms. in diameter, and from greeny-brown to black in colour. They are usually bottle-shaped, however, one end being flat or concave, the other pointed. They are non-adherent and are deposited in small heaps, although no regular latrine is adopted. Both sexes have antlers, a unique occurrence among the deer, and these are long, slender and palmate, and have many points. At the moment these signs will be found only in a particular region of the Cairngorms, where Roe deer are found also; there is, however, no possibility of confusing the signs of the two.

DWELLING PLACE In bad weather, reindeer *may* lie: they show great indifference.

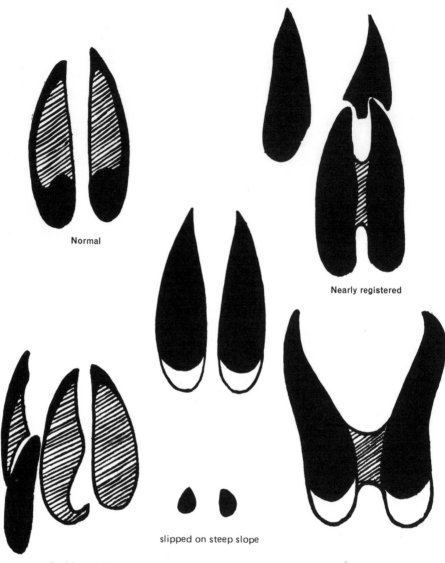

Normal

Nearly registered

slipped on steep slope

Double register

Running

On soft ground

4 : 32   Track of Chinese Water deer (natural size).

146

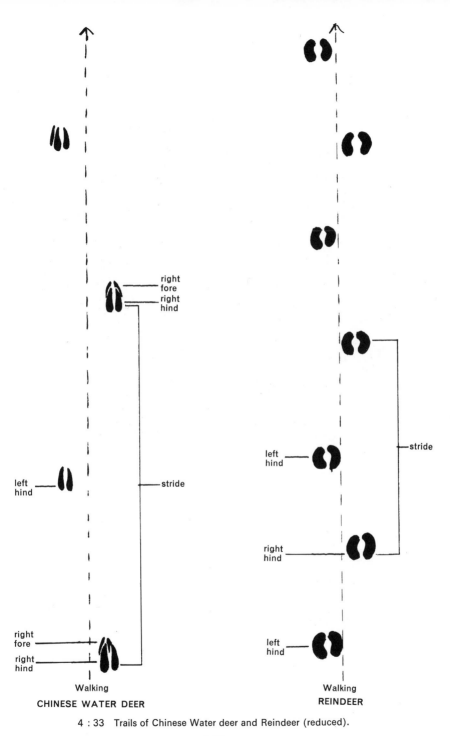

right
fore
right
hind

left
hind

stride

right
fore
right
hind

Walking
CHINESE WATER DEER

left
hind

stride

left
hind

right
hind

left
hind

Walking
REINDEER

4 : 33   Trails of Chinese Water deer and Reindeer (reduced).

147

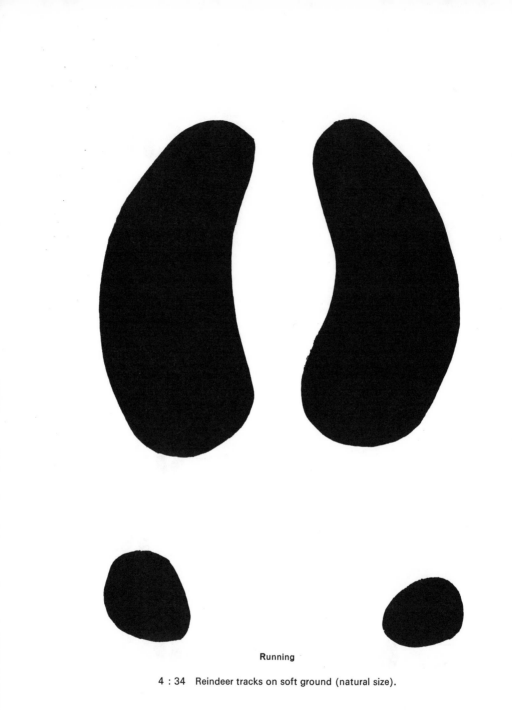

Running

4 : 34   Reindeer tracks on soft ground (natural size).

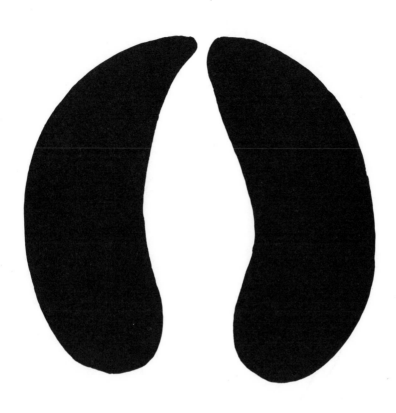

4 : 35   Reindeer tracks on soft ground (natural size).

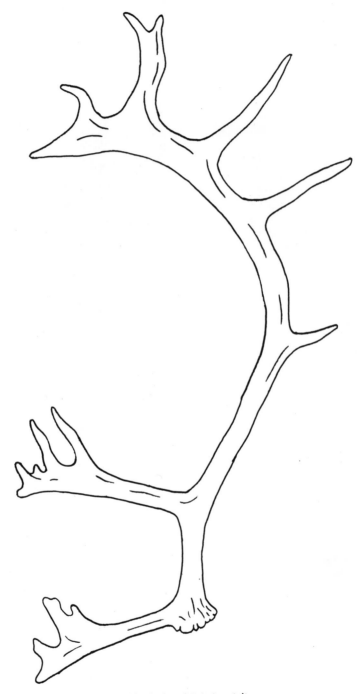

4 : 36   Antler of Reindeer (x$\frac{1}{5}$).

150

4 : 37 Bull reindeer.

4 : 38 Reindeer skull.

Ovis aries

Sheep   Family: Bovidae

The male is termed Ram, the female, Ewe, and the young, Lamb.

OCCURRENCE The sheep in this country are very widely distributed, and many breeds exist in the British Isles. Apart from being kept in areas where no other form of livestock can survive successfully (highland in Ireland, the Welsh Uplands, the northern Pennines, the Lake District, southern Uplands, Grampians, the North-west Highlands and the isolated islands) they are bred for special purposes under favourable conditions (e.g. for meat on Romney Marsh; for wool in the Tweed Basin). These are the least controlled of all the domestic Artiodactyls and roam freely over large areas of moorland, especially the black-faced variety of hill sheep, which is well suited to the difficult conditions of the north-west Highlands of Scotland.

HABITS Very much a herd animal. Largely active by day and not very far-ranging on the rich lowland pastures. On the poorer hill pastures, such as those of Scotland, the animals are marked and allowed to wander over large areas. Regular paths and patterns of social behaviour are followed.

HABITAT Open moor and heath (both highland and lowland) as well as the richer lowland pastures.

TRACK The track will vary in size with the breed and individual. It is fairly long in proportion to its width (e.g. 6 cms. by 4.5 cms.), is rounded at both ends and has only a small gap between the toes, which are only slightly concave on the inner walls towards the front. One toe is usually larger than the other. The dew claws do not show as they are set high up on the limb.

151

TRAIL The stride will again be dependent on the breed and the animal concerned. At a walking gait the tracks do not register, and will show individually with the toes pointing outwards, and splaying a little, either side of the median line. When galloping the feet show in the characteristic groups of four and point outwards very obviously.

SIGNS The animal feeds on grass, heather and almost any type of ground vegetation. In especially difficult conditions (e.g. the hills of north-west Scotland) bushes will also be nibbled. The droppings are composite and are made up of faceted sections, which fit together in such a way as to leave their one rounded face turned outwards. These are dropped at random. Regular paths are followed, and there are usually well-defined tracks which can often be mistaken for footpaths in hill country. These tracks usually follow contours.

DWELLING PLACE In the more closely controlled habitats shelter may be provided by man, but in the case of the hill sheep and the almost wild island sheep no shelter is constructed, and the animals will group against walls or under vegetation for protection.

Bos taurus

Cattle
Family: Bovidae

The male is termed Bull, the female, Cow, and the young, Calf.

OCCURRENCE There are many breeds of cattle in the British Isles today and, whether for meat or milk, they form standard elements of the rural economy. Cattle are found in almost every stretch of open countryside and are excluded only by the unfavourable conditions found over 600 metres in Ireland, Scotland, Wales, parts of northern England and the moors of the south-west.

HABITS Highly modified by being under the control of man. The animal is gregarious, and spends much of the day grazing. If on free range shelters by walls, under trees or hedges at night. Regular movements, paths and activities are enforced by man.

HABITAT Controlled by man. Fields and open heath and moorland, largely the former in the summer. Permanent shelter is usually provided by the farmer.

TRACK Large. The toes are heavy, rounded and very broad in proportion to their length. Size of track, 10 cms. long, 9.5 cms. wide (very variable). The toes are often of uneven size, with only a small gap between them; their inner walls are distinctly concave and tend to converge towards the back. Dew claws will never be present in the track of a normal cow, and the outline will often be blurred as the animal tends to drag its feet.

TRAIL There will be a great variation in the stride depending on the size and breed of the individual, but as a general rule the feet will be placed well to either side of the median line, and the tracks will not register, although they may just be touching at walking pace.

SIGNS The food consists largely of grass and rough pasture, supplemented with specially produced foods. The droppings are very distinctive and are a positive means of identification. They consist of amorphous, almost liquid, circular masses often 30 to 60 cms. in diameter and are brown in colour. If the animal is on the move a long trail of small 'pats' may be found. When the droppings harden they become darker in colour and remnants of undigested herbage shows through. The

152

horns are permanent, unlike the antlers of the Cervidae, but in the case of many breeds are removed early in life. Flattened areas in the grass indicate resting places.
DWELLING PLACE Usually man-made, but flattened areas of vegetation under trees and hedges show where the animals lie up and shelter when in the open.

Capra hircus

Goat   Family: Bovidae

The male is termed Billy, the female, Nanny, and the young, Kid.

OCCURRENCE No truly wild herds exist in the British Isles, but feral herds are found in the remote parts of the Scottish Highlands, the Hebrides, Lundy, Holy Island, the Cheviots, North, Central and South Wales. Usually they live in high, inaccessible exposed rock zones. The domestic goat is not widely kept in this country and is in many ways the least domesticated artiodactyl. Whenever escapes occur in favourable terrain wild herds are likely to start. In some cases deliberate releases have been engineered so that the goats will graze higher, rougher pasture and restrict sheep to lower and more suitable terrain. The herds of Wales and Wester Ross may be of very ancient introduced stock.

HABITS This is a herding species controlled by one master male or billy. Generally they are gregarious, although, as with many of the artiodactyls, fighting between males takes place at the beginning of the breeding season.

HABITAT In the wild state high, isolated areas of rough pasture are occupied. When in captivity the animals are usually tethered on small plots near to the farm buildings.

TRACK Like other domestic species, the track of the goat is broad in proportion to its length (6 by 5 cms.). The track is curved and rounded at the ends. The cleaves tend to spread and their inside edges are markedly concave. The dew claws do not show.

4 : 39 Fallow deer lying-up place.

4 : 40 Damage to young conifer by Roe deer.

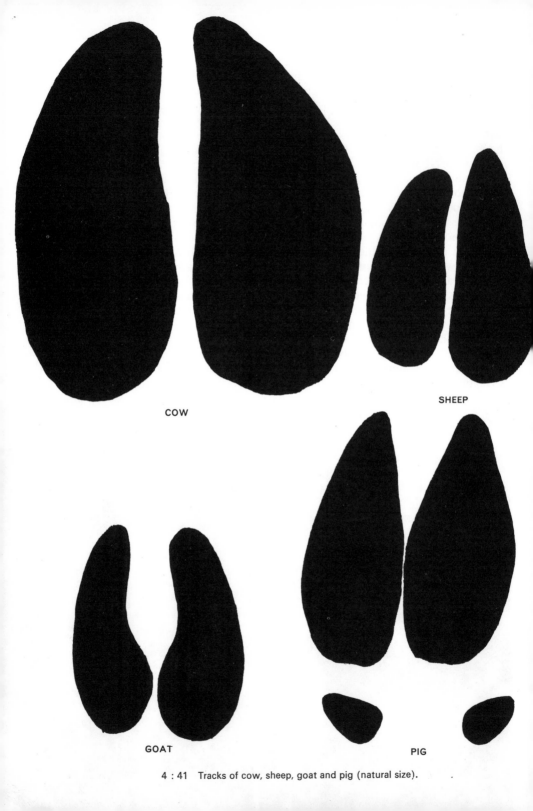

COW

SHEEP

GOAT

PIG

4 : 41   Tracks of cow, sheep, goat and pig (natural size).

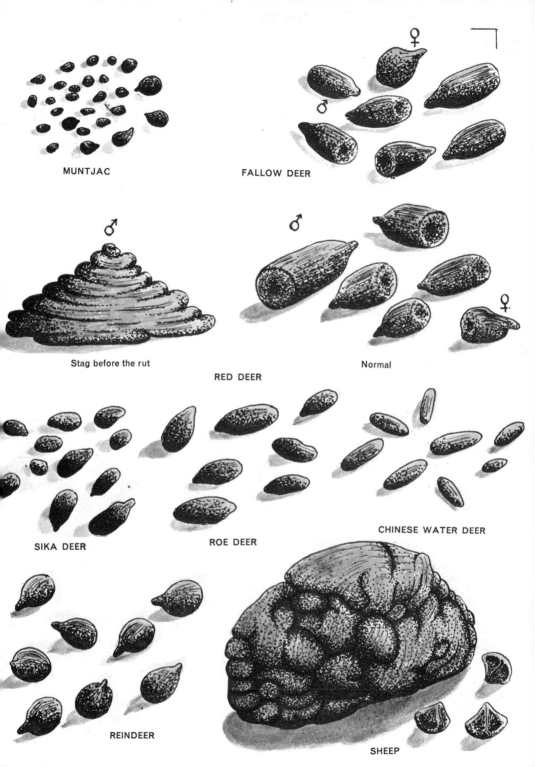

MUNTJAC

FALLOW DEER
♀
♂

RED DEER

♂ Stag before the rut

♀ Normal

SIKA DEER

ROE DEER

CHINESE WATER DEER

REINDEER

SHEEP

4 : 42 Droppings of deer (natural size). The male and female signs apply to the droppings below them.

TRAIL At a walking pace a stride of from 60 to 65 cms. is taken. The feet are placed close to the median line in pairs, so that the tracks are side by side. When the animal runs the stride is increased, and the tracks are almost registered.

SIGNS The droppings are almost cylindrical, about 1 cm. in length and flattened at the ends. These are dropped in groups, and no definite latrine is used.

DWELLING PLACE In captivity this is controlled by man. In the wild mountain or moorland herds, lying-up places will be in isolated hollows.

Sus scrofa

Pig Family: Suidae

The male is termed Boar, the female, Sow, and the young, Piglet.

OCCURRENCE Pigs are widely spread, but are particularly prominent in the poorer forms of agricultural activity where an inexpensive waste product consumer is useful.

HABITS A gregarious animal kept usually in small herds. General routine of life is governed by man, but within the limitations of its captivity the pig moves about freely. The animal enjoys wallowing, and also spends a considerable amount of the day sleeping. In certain areas farmers have common grazing rights (e.g. certain of the enclosures and unfenced lands of the New Forest) and small herds of pigs, fending for themselves, may be seen moving about for a few weeks during the autumn.

HABITAT Largely the farms on which the animals are kept, and here their range is likely to be very limited. Where circumstances permit the animals are allowed to roam free range at certain times of the year.

TRACK The track is distinctive in that the dew claws show in almost every print as they are set very low on the limb. The front two toes are large with only a small space between them at the back, although they taper on the inside, as well as the outside, to form a rounded point at the front. The two back toes are set fairly far back and are slightly to the outside of the others.

TRAIL When walking the feet are placed toe to 'heel' so that they almost register. The front two toes tend to merge into a mass at the back, to splay slightly and to point outwards from the median line. They are slightly straddled across the line. When galloping the tracks are placed in groups of four with a further distinct pairing within each group. The toes splay widely and point outwards and the dew claws are deeply impressed. Length of stride will again vary with the individual and breed involved.

SIGNS Food is almost entirely provided by man. Those animals wandering on common land and feeding on acorns will turn over the leaves where they have been rooting for the nuts. The droppings vary greatly, but are cylindrical and brownish in colour. In close confinement, however, these are usually trampled almost immediately and are rarely seen in a recognisable form.

DWELLING PLACE Almost always a shelter provided by man, but in the open, temporary lying-up places under the shelter of bushes or trees.

ORDER PERISSODACTYLA

There is little need for detailed discussion on this Order as it is only represented by the horse in this country, and all breeds are either domesticated or only semi-wild.

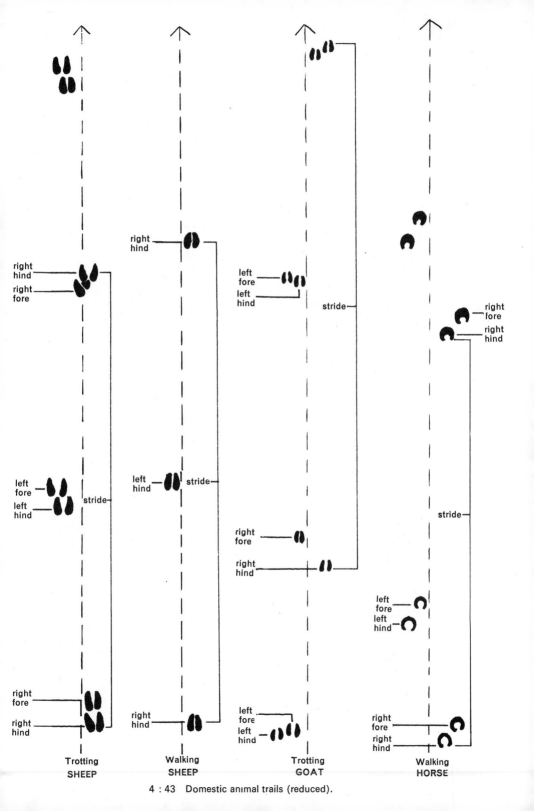

right hind

right fore

left fore

left hind

right fore

right hind

stride

Trotting
SHEEP

right hind

left hind

stride

right hind

Walking
SHEEP

left fore

left hind

stride

right fore

right hind

left fore

left hind

Trotting
GOAT

right fore

right hind

stride

left fore

left hind

right fore

right hind

Walking
HORSE

4 : 43 Domestic animal trails (reduced).

Soft mud

Hard mud

4 : 44 Track of horse (natural size). There are many different breeds and the size of tracks will vary greatly.

It occurs widely, and will be seen almost anywhere except in bleak uplands above 600 metres, although there are exceptions to this (e.g. Dartmoor ponies).

As in the artiodactyls the limbs are modified for running but there has been even greater reduction·and only the third digit remains. The tracks of the horse are extremely distinctive and the only variations will be in size. The small, unshod tracks found in the many wild parts of the country indicate the existence of semi-wild ponies, while those near to man's habitation are shod.

Equas calabus

Horse   Family: Equidae

The male is termed Stallion, the female, Mare, and the young, Foal.

OCCURRENCE There are many breeds of the domesticated horse in this country and, although formerly the most important means of power in agriculture, the horse has now been largely relegated to the uses of recreation and display. The distribution is wide, however, and individuals are to be found in most stretches of cultivated country. Breeds of semi-wild pony occur in the New Forest, on Dartmoor, Exmoor, in the Lake District, the Welsh Uplands, Northumberland and Cumberland fells, Shetlands, the Western Isles and part of Connemara. Even these animals require some attention and need extra food in hard weather. In general the habits and habitat of this species are dependent on man.

TRACK The track is large and almost circular. The size will vary greatly with the age and breed, but the unshod hoof-mark is distinctive. The sides are flat, the front blunt and rounded. There is a deep notch in the back. The track shown is that of a small pony and measures about 12 by 12 cms. Usually the tracks will be those of shod feet, in which case almost all other detail will be obscured.

TRAIL The trail size will vary with the individual, but the shape of the tracks provides a positive means of identification. The feet are placed wide astride the median line and, at a walking pace, will be seen in groups of two. At a galloping gait the tracks will register imperfectly or not at all. This is true of all domestic species of artiodactyl and perissodactyl.

SIGNS Since the food consists largely of grass taken on the open range or hay in stables, the droppings are the only important means of identification other than tracks. The droppings vary in size, but are recognised by their yellow-green colour when fresh, the remnants of unchanged cellulose matter, usually hay or grass stems, forming the texture of the faeces, which have imperfect cohesion.

4 : 45   Red deer hind with new born calf.

4 : 46   Red deer stag, showing the recent loss of left antler.

ORDER MARSUPIALIA (Pouched Mammals)

Macropus rufogriseus   Family: Macropidae

Bennett's or Red-necked Wallaby

OCCURRENCE The time at which this species established itself extends over a period from the 1940's until the present time. They are currently found in the Peak District and Sussex. The origin of this species has arisen from private collections. The Wallaby comes from Eastern Australia.

HABITS They feed on heather and bilberry. Generally the animals remain solitary but they do form groups and these are probably mating groups. Although the severe winter of 1962–63 dealt a heavy blow to the population a few survived and the population has steadily increased though not rapidly.

HABITAT In the Peak District (Moorland) the animals live predominantly in areas of heather, with some bracken, grasses and bilberry.

TRACK A large five-toed fore track, 6–7 cms. long by 6–7 cms. wide. In soft ground conditions it will show as a neat hand-shaped impression with strong claw marks and plantar pads; thumb print tends to be small and may be absent in some tracks. The hind track is very striking – a walking or jumping track is normally 10–14 cms. in length and two-toed, one toe being very large and one much smaller; occasionally the third vestigial toe will show. If the animal has been resting the full length of the track, i.e. 20–25 cms. may show to the heel; claw marks show strongly.

TRAIL Very distinctive. The normal walking trail shows a strong tail drag which is not present in a jumping trail; the tail drag tends to disappear near the tracks which are situated each side of the tail drag.

The hind tracks lie to the side or ahead of the fore-tracks but in groups of four. The distances between the groups of tracks is about 30–40 cms.

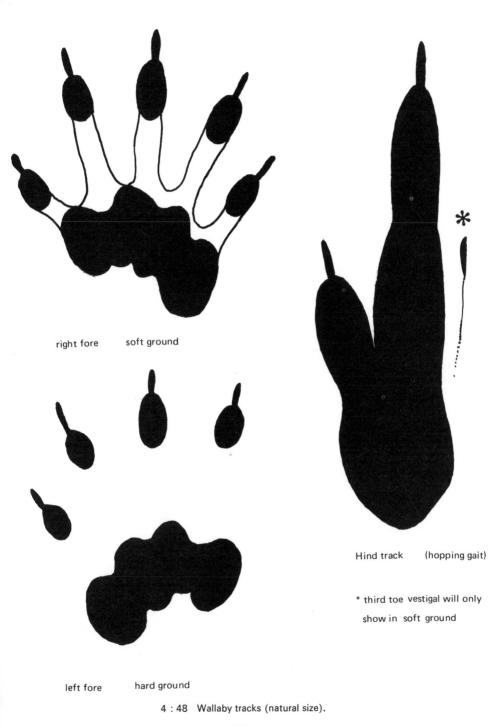

right fore   soft ground

Hind track   (hopping gait)

* third toe vestigal will only
  show in soft ground

left fore   hard ground

4 : 48   Wallaby tracks (natural size).

161

4 : 47 Wallabies in natural conditions.

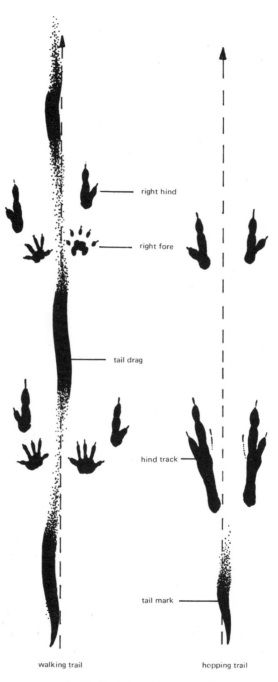

right hind

right fore

tail drag

hind track

tail mark

walking trail   hopping trail

4 : 49   Trail of wallaby (reduced).

162

5 Mammal Identification from Teeth, Skulls and other Bones

Tracks and other direct signs such as droppings provide an important means of identifying mammal species in the field, but other, indirect evidence, especially the feeding remains of carnivorous animals, contributes valuable information. A 'kill' may be found in open country, or outside a carnivore's home and, although this will not always consist of mammal remains, good evidence is sometimes obtained by analysing them. Further, in the droppings of some carnivores and in owl pellets, the indigestible parts of the animals' meals give important clues. The information gained from these various signs is extremely important and no book on mammal field work would be complete without dealing with them in some detail. It must be emphasised, however, that the remains of mammals found under these circumstances will be far from complete and indeed they may only be fragmentary, a small piece of jaw or skull only being found. In order to facilitate the use of the smallest section of an animal which can reasonably be used to identify it, a systematic classification of the species, and all the skeletal features which provide a positive means of identification have been included here. This information consists of a series of drawings of the various bone structures and comprehensive explanatory notes which enable the remains discovered in the field to be identified with considerable accuracy. Before moving on to this, however, it is necessary to mention briefly the conditions under which the material dealt with in this chapter is likely to be found.

In barns, church towers, ruined buildings, roofs of inhabited buildings, and under trees, pellets of fur, feathers, bone and insect remnants will sometimes be found.* These are the undigested remains of a meal, which an owl or bird of prey has regurgitated while resting. Often these will contain the remains of small birds and insects only, but some will consist of fur and pieces of mammal bone. Unless part of the skull or jaws is contained within the pellet it will be difficult to identify the species; however, in some species the scapula and pelvis are distinctive, and these are described along with the various features of the skull and jaws of the species concerned. Most commonly, mice, voles and shrews will be found, but many other species of small mammals are taken, and the frequency with which a particular species is discovered in the pellets of a given roost often reflects its density in the area far more accurately than simple observations of direct signs can (except for bats which are not commonly taken). Only on rare occasions will a complete skull be found, more usually parts of an upper or lower mandible will be intact. To facilitate identification Figs. 5 : 5, 5 : 6, 5 : 15, 5 : 19–20, 5 : 24, 5 : 34–40, 5 : 51–58, 5 : 62–63, 5 : 67–73 show the complete skulls of mammal types likely to be taken by owls. Obviously more detailed information is needed to identify a small piece of jaw and for this reason other figures show the teeth of the left upper and right lower jaws, while yet others show the cavities occupied by the teeth of these same jaws. Teeth cusp patterns provide a reliable means of identifying insectivore, rodent and small carnivore species, and the drawings of teeth given here are suffici-

* See tables of owl pellet analyses, pp. 201–6.

163

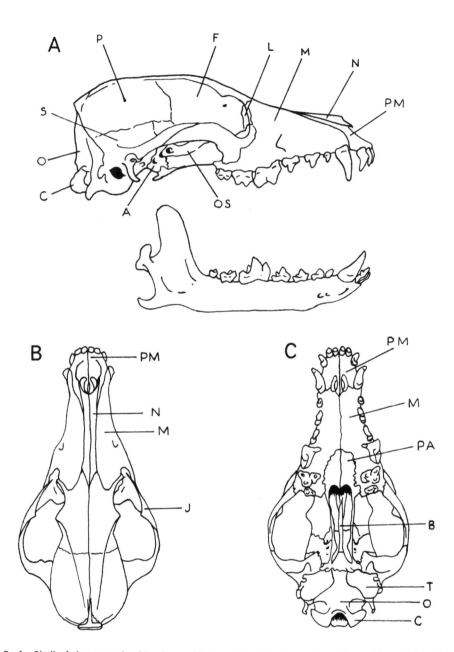

5 : 1   Skull of dog, seen in side view, with lower jaw (*a*), from above (*b*), and from below (*c*).
A, alisphenoid. B, basiphenoid. C, condyle. F, frontal. J, jugal. L, lachrymal. M, maxilla. N, nasal.
O, occipital. OS, orbitosphenoid. P, parietal. PA, palatine. PM, premaxilla. S, squamosal. T, tympanic.
From *British Mammals*, Collins.

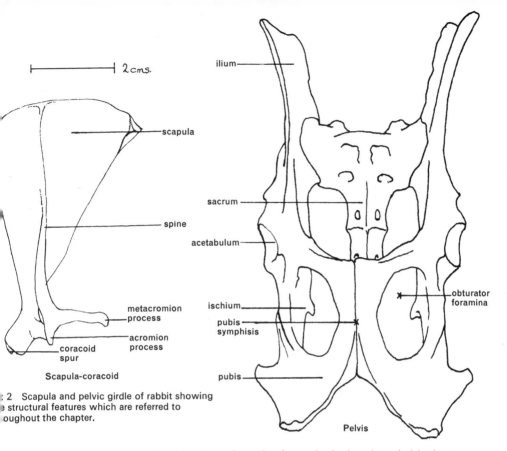

2 cms.

scapula

spine

metacromion process

acromion process

coracoid spur

Scapula-coracoid

ilium

sacrum

acetabulum

ischium

pubis symphisis

pubis

obturator foramina

Pelvis

2   Scapula and pelvic girdle of rabbit showing
e structural features which are referred to
oughout the chapter.

ently detailed to enable identification of species from the isolated teeth (the largest
units of the skull commonly to be found whole) removed from the pellets. The
illustrations cover all species likely to be found and, although small mammals are
most commonly taken, the remains of rats and animals the size of young rabbits
are sometimes found in pellets. The scapulae of various species which have distinctive characteristics are shown in Figs. 5 : 13, 5 : 59, 5 : 74. No specific reference
has been made to the great variety of size and contents of pellets (factors controlled
by the species of owl and the nature of the meal). The photograph gives some
indication of the general characteristics.

The droppings of some of the carnivores (viz. Wild cat, otter, badger and fox)
may contain the remains of other mammals. These will consist largely of shattered
bones and fur (as well as much non-mammalian material), but occasionally enough
of a skull will be found to make identification possible. Remains of all the species
illustrated in this chapter may occur in this form, but generally speaking the larger
species (e.g. rabbit, hare, hedgehog, squirrel) are the most likely, since they have
strong enough skeletons to emerge from the carnivore digestive tract with almost
any part of them recognisable. The teeth themselves and the pattern of cavities they
occupy in the jaws give a reliable means of identification.

Outside the dens of some carnivores (e.g. fox, weasel, stoat) the remains of kills

165

will be found. Often these will be mammalian and by examining skull remains it will be possible to identify species. The type of prey likely to be taken by a parti- cular species will depend on the size of the predator and the relative distribution and density of both prey and predator. By looking at the prey–predator relationship key it will be possible to ascertain the likelihood of the remains of a given species being found outside the den of another and by checking in the occurrence section of the species concerned where this is likely to happen.

In addition to remains found in owl pellets, skull and other skeletal remains are often found in the field. These include the larger carnivores and herbivores which are not normally taken as prey. Seals and Whales are sometimes washed up on the shore. In order that these may be identified keys and sets of illustrations of the skulls, scapulae and pelvic girdles are presented here. Complete records and collec- tions of stranded whales are kept in the British Museum (Natural History).

The descriptions given here refer to bones from the adult animals. It is possible to identify juveniles of species, but clearly one must be aware of the changes which occur with ageing. Plate 5 : 4 demonstrates this with reference to an age series of badger skulls. In *a* the suture lines on the skull are still evident and there is no sign of a sagittal crest. In *c*, an older animal, most of the sutures on the cranium are closed and a sagittal crest has started to form. The process continues through to *f*, an old mature individual, where all the sutures have disappeared and the sagittal crest is very strongly developed. It is worth noting that from *d* onwards the jaws are still attached to the skull due to the characteristic 'locking' which typifies maturity in this species.

The following text should be used in close conjunction with the figures in the chapter and takes the form of a systematic study of the various forms of bone ma- terial likely to be encountered. The material is arranged by Orders, and consists of a brief outline of the general features characteristic of the Orders, then brief notes on the various aspects of each family, the jaw, skull, teeth, root patterns,* scapula and pelvis (Os innominatum). See Glossary.

ORDER MARSUPIALIA

There are several skull characters distinguishing the *marsupials* from the placentals, although here we are only concerned with the wallaby. Below are listed the *major* skull differences between the two groups and a more detailed description of the Wallaby skull.

Marsupial (Wallaby)	*Placental*
(*a*) Four incisors in upper jaw	(*a*) Three incisors in upper jaw
(*b*) Palatal vacuities in palate	(*b*) Palatal vacuities *absent*; except in the Hedgehog *erinaceus*
(*c*) Angle of lower jaw inflected	(*c*) Angle of lower jaw *not* inflected
(*d*) 2 ducts in lachrymal bone	(*d*) 1 duct present in lachrymal bone.

Family: Macropidae

Genus *Macropus*

Macropus rufogriseus

SKULL: Approximately 120–40 mm. in condylobasal length; zygomatic width 65 mm. In lateral view a robust skull tapering anteriorly. The zygomatic arch is well developed and at the anterior end there is a strongly developed flange formed from a posterior protruberance of the maxilla. There is no postorbital process. The ex-occipital is well developed and peg-like in shape. Viewed ventrally there are two deep cavities placed posterior to the palate and in line with the tooth row. The palatal vacuities are sometimes fenestrated. There is a large gap (diastema) between the incisors and premolars.

TEETH: The four upper incisors overlap from the anterior to the posterior. The premolars and molars are multicusped and not unlike the dentition of an artiodactyl; wear takes place anteriorly and progresses posteriorly with age. In the lower jaw there are two well-developed, tusk-like incisors.

ORDER INSECTIVORA

The teeth of this Order are the least specialised of any, but the dentition is far from simple. The cheek-teeth (premolars and molars) generally have modified cusps. Usually there are three or more with pointed cusps. There is great variation in the premolars, canines and incisors; often the variations from the basic pattern are wide. There are never less than two pairs of incisors in the mandible and no special carnasial teeth exist. The upper and lower incisors are conical and pointed while the canines are usually weak.

There is much variation in the skull features; the cranial cavity is small and never greatly elevated. The facial bones are considerably elongated, the nasals and pre-maxilla being well developed. The zygomatic arch is usually slender or incomplete.

Family: Erinaceidae

There is only one British representative of this family, a member of the genus *Erinaceus* (dental formula $\frac{3.1.3.3.}{2.1.2.3.}$ = 36) (Fig. 5 : 6c, 5 : 9c and d).

Erinaceus europaeus

SKULL: It is over 50 mm. in length. The palatal bones have two large unossified

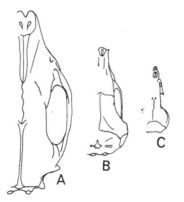

5 : 3   Right half of the skull of (*A*) hedgehog, (*B*) mole, (*C*) shrew, seen from above. The zygomatic arch is stout in the hedgehog, slender in the mole and absent in the shrew. All drawn to the same scale. From *British Mammals*, Collins.

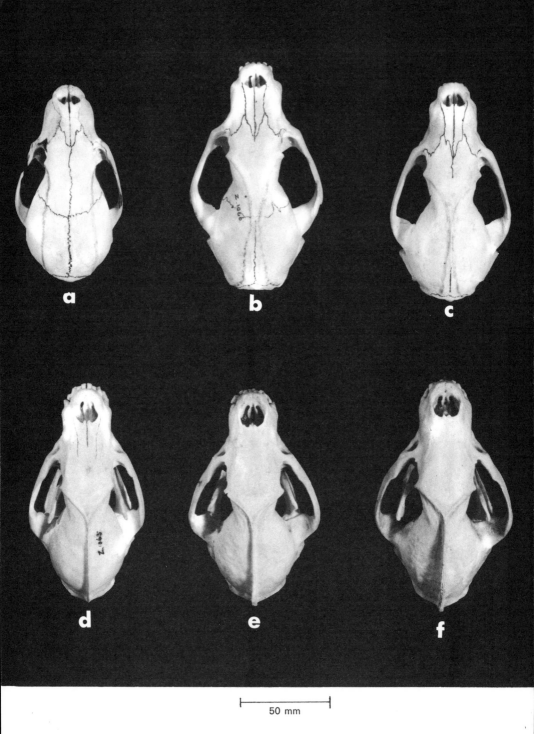

a

b

c

d

e

f

50 mm

5 : 4   Aged series of badger skulls.

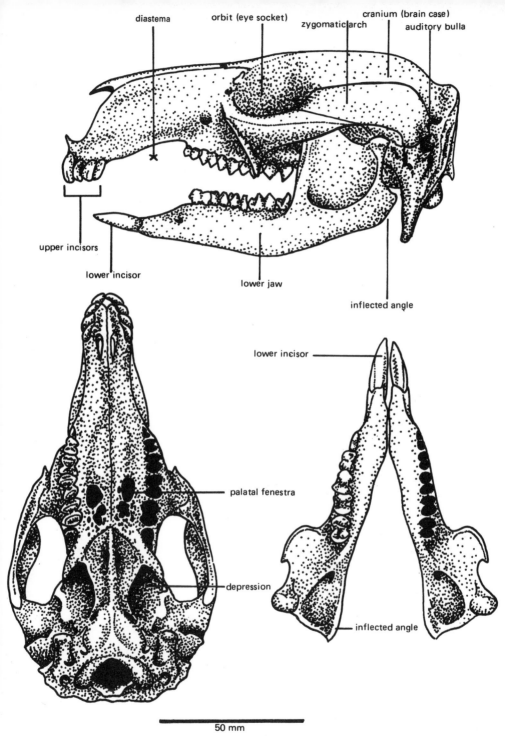

diastema

orbit (eye socket)

zygomatic arch

cranium (brain case)

auditory bulla

upper incisors

lower incisor

lower jaw

inflected angle

lower incisor

palatal fenestra

depression

inflected angle

50 mm

5 : 5 Wallaby skull.

spaces in front of the transverse ridge immediately behind the posterior molars. The sagital crest is well developed. The tympanic bulla is very slightly developed forming a small ring and the zygomatic arch is very slender.

TEETH: The first incisor in each jaw is comparatively large and projects forwards, but not as much as in the shrew. There are five upper and four lower unicuspids, of which the first three upper and two lower are incisors, the fourth upper tooth is a canine, and the fifth a premolar. In both jaws the unicuspids are succeeded by four molar-like teeth of which the first is a premolar and the other three are molars.

ROOT PATTERN: The lower jaw displays a linear root pattern structure. In the upper jaw the third incisor and the canine may be double rooted.

SCAPULA: (Fig. 5 : 72). The total length is about 4.5 cms. The bone is long and narrow and has a large glenoid cavity with a small stumpy coracoid spur. The spine is very long and high, the end bifurcating, forming well-developed acromion and metacromion processes.

Family: Talpidae

The Mole (*Talpa europaea*) is the only British representative of this family. The dental formula is $\dfrac{3.1.4.3.}{3.1.4.3.} = 44$

SKULL: (Fig. 5 : 6b). The total length of the skull is about 40 mm. It is elongated and possesses auditory bullae and slender zygomatic arches, but no post-orbital processes.

TEETH: The upper canine is always double rooted, and the lower canines are not differentiated from the incisors, the first lower premolar taking its place (Fig. 5 : 7b).

ROOT PATTERN: The large double-rooted upper canine is the distinctive feature of the root pattern in the upper jaw (Figs. 5 : 5, 5 : 9a and b.)

SCAPULA: This has a total length of 2.5 cms., and is long and very narrow. The spine and acromion are not very prominent. (See also Fig. 5 : 12.)

PELVIS: The length is about 2.8 cms. It is completely fused to the sacrum, but there is no pubic symphysis. The acetabulum is large (Figs. 5 : 75, d, e, f).

Family: Soricidae

There are three British genera of this family. *Sorex* (dental formula $\dfrac{3.1.3.3.}{1.1.1.3.} = 32$) represented by two species, the Common and Pygmy Shrew; *Neomys* (dental formula $\dfrac{3.1.2.3.}{1.1.1.3.} = 30$) with one species, the Water Shrew; and *Crocidura* (dental formula $\dfrac{3.1.2.3.}{1.1.1.3.} = 30$) again represented by one species, the White-toothed Shrew.

SKULL: Is very small, long and tapers markedly towards the snout (Fig. 5 : 6a). The zygomatic arch is absent, as are the post-orbital processes and the tympanic bullae. The tympanium is ring-like. An important feature is the double joint on the lower jaw (Fig. 5 : 7a). The total length of the skull in *Sorex araneus* is 19–20 mm., and in *S. minutus* 15–16 mm., and of *Neomys fodiens* over 20 mm. The total length of *Crocidura saveolens* is under 18.5 mm. (Figs. 5 : 8a, 5 : 8b, 5 : 10, 5 : 11.)

170

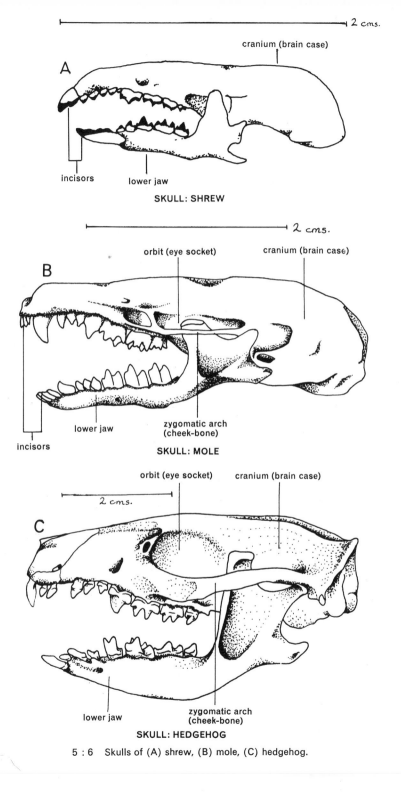

2 cms.

A

cranium (brain case)

incisors

lower jaw

SKULL: SHREW

2 cms.

B

orbit (eye socket)

cranium (brain case)

lower jaw

zygomatic arch
(cheek-bone)

incisors

SKULL: MOLE

orbit (eye socket)

cranium (brain case)

2 cms.

C

lower jaw

zygomatic arch
(cheek-bone)

SKULL: HEDGEHOG

5 : 6   Skulls of (A) shrew, (B) mole, (C) hedgehog.

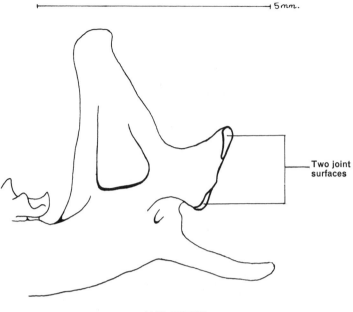

JAW: SHREW

5 : 7a   Drawing of shrew jaw to show double joint surfaces.

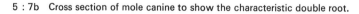
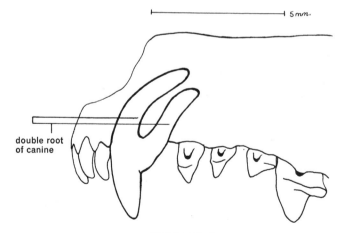

SNOUT: MOLE

5 : 7b   Cross section of mole canine to show the characteristic double root.

5 upper unicuspids

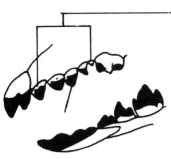

PYGMY SHREW

COMMON SHREW

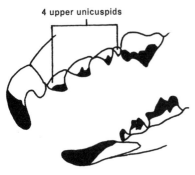

4 upper unicuspids

WATER SHREW

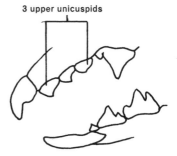

3 upper unicuspids

SCILLY SHREW

5 : 8a   Teeth of shrews.

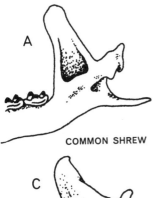

A

COMMON SHREW

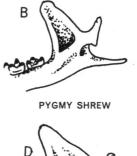

B

PYGMY SHREW

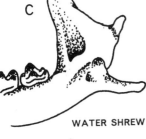

C

WATER SHREW

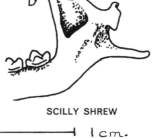

D

SCILLY SHREW

1 cm.

5 : 8b   Jaw characteristics of shrew species.

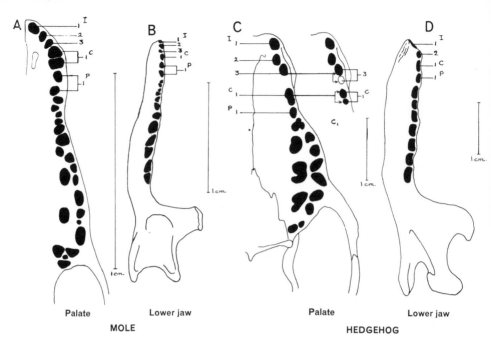

5 : 9 Root patterns on the palates and lower jaws of mole and hedgehog.

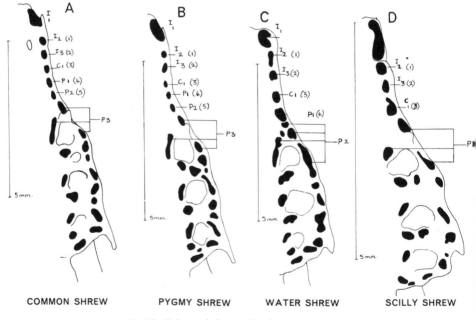

5 : 10 Palates of shrews showing root patterns.

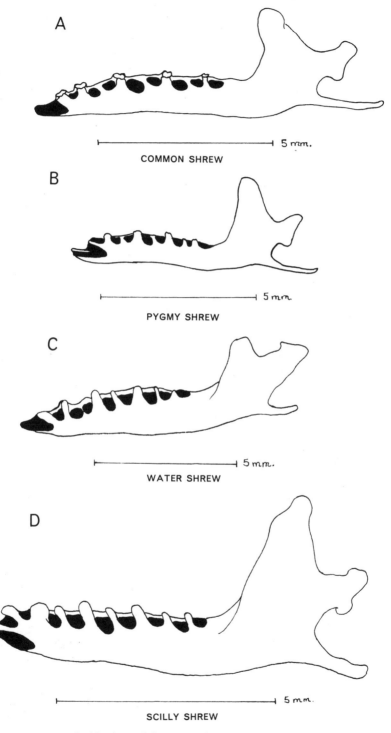

A

5 mm.

COMMON SHREW

B

5 mm.

PYGMY SHREW

C

5 mm.

WATER SHREW

D

5 mm.

SCILLY SHREW

5 : 11   Jaws of shrews showing root patterns.

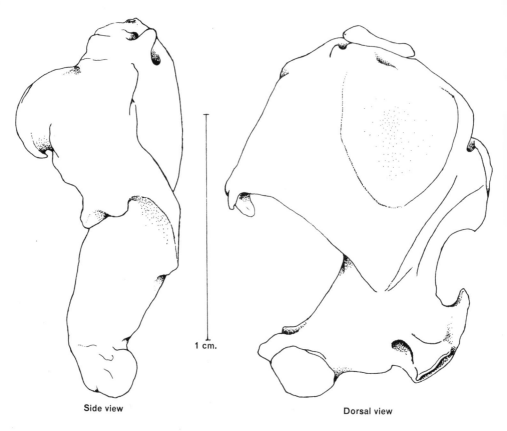

1 cm.

Side view

Dorsal view

5 : 12 Mole humerus.

SCAPULAE: May be dealt with collectively for the group. Total length is under 9 mm. It is long and narrow with a well-developed spine which bifurcates at the end into the acromion and metacromion processes which are also well developed.

ORDER CHIROPTERA

There are two types of skull within this Order, but they have certain general characteristics in common. The upper incisors are widely separated on either side of a deep, round concavity or borne on a slender bone projecting from the base of such a cavity. The total length of the skull is under 25 mm., the width more than half of the total length. The cheek-bone is a slender bar, and the ring of bone encircling the ear passage is not fused with the rest of the skull, but is loosely attached. The most characteristic feature of bat skulls is the reduction in the size of the premaxillae, the two small bones at the front of the upper jaw, which carry the incisor teeth. The lower jaws are very slender. The skull is that of a *Rhinolophid* bat if there are two bulbous projections on the top of the skull behind the nasal cavity (Figs. 5 : 15a, 5 : 16). These projections are absent from a *Vespertilionid* skull.

176

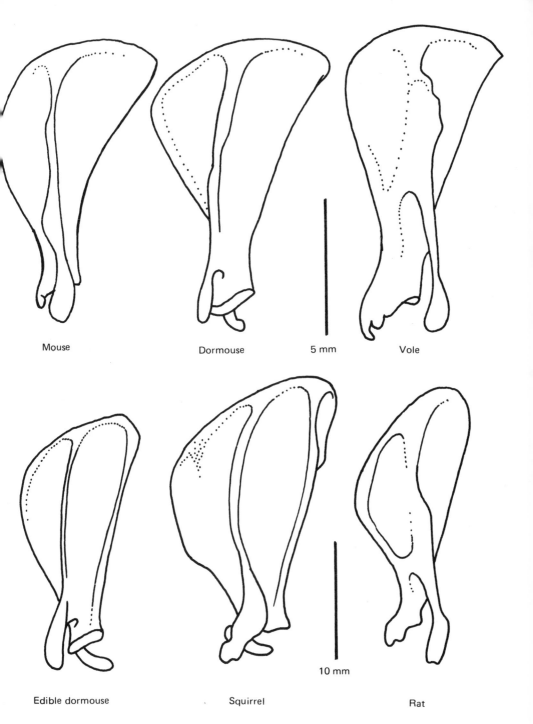

Mouse   Dormouse   5 mm   Vole

Edible dormouse   Squirrel   10 mm   Rat

5 : 13   Scapulae of rodents.

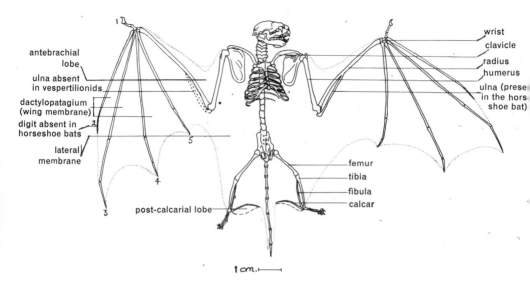

5 : 14 Bat skeleton with the wing membrane shown. The post-calcarial lobe is shown as a broken line because it is absent from some species. 1–5 digits.

TEETH: The total number of teeth is never more than thirty-eight (the dental formula in the case of this skull being $\frac{2.1.3.3.}{3.1.3.3.} = 38$). The incisors are small and in the upper jaws are reduced in number, never more than two on each side. The canines are large and the premolars are pointed, similar in shape to, but much smaller than the canines. The last premolar resembles a molar. The molars bear three main pointed cusps and several smaller ones.

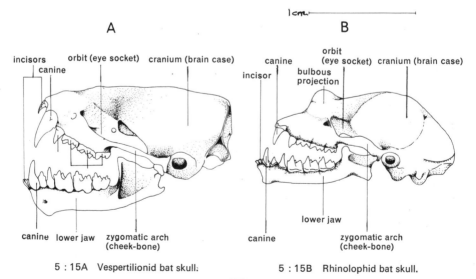

A

B

5 : 15A Vespertilionid bat skull.

5 : 15B Rhinolophid bat skull.

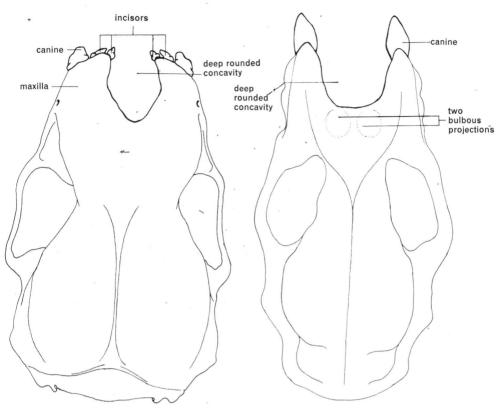

incisors

canine

maxilla

deep rounded
concavity

canine

deep
rounded
concavity

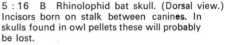

two
bulbous
projections

5 : 16   A   Vespertilionid bat skull. (Dorsal view.)

5 : 16   B   Rhinolophid bat skull. (Dorsal view.)
Incisors born on stalk between canines. In
skulls found in owl pellets these will probably
be lost.

Family: Vespertilionidae

Genus *Nyctalus*

(The dental formula for this genus is $\dfrac{2.1.2.3.}{3.1.2.3.} = 34$). Represented by two species
(Fig. 5 : 23a).

SKULL: This is massive and flat, the brain case is angular and the nasal region somewhat inflated. The premaxillary gap is large and somewhat pointed above and
deeply rounded below. The zygomatic arch is moderately flattened and the cranial
crests are not prominent. The auditory bullae are moderately large.

Nyctalus noctula

SKULL: The total length is over 18 mm. This is typical of the genus and is characterised by a strong lambdoid, but, as a rule, a weak sagittal crest. There is considerable variation in the size and proportions with individuals (Fig. 5 : 19e).

TEETH: The inner upper incisor is bicuspid in immature animals, but the outer cusp
is lost in the adult. The upper, outer incisor is much shorter than the inner, and its

179

crown is hollowed out to receive the tip of the lower canine. The lower incisors are crowded and overlap, so that their large crowns are oblique and parallel to the jaw (Fig. 5 : 21e).

Nyctalus leisleri

SKULL: The total length is from 15–17 mm. The bone structure is weaker than *Nyctalus noctula*, and the crests, especially the sagittal, are totally absent or feebly developed (Fig. 5 : 19f).

TEETH: The teeth are similar, but smaller than those of *Nyctalus noctula*. The outer upper incisor is comparatively small, while the anterior upper premolar is relatively larger. The lower incisors are smaller and less crowded and do not usually overlap (Fig. 5 : 21f).

Genus *Pipistrellus*

Dental formula $\frac{2.1.2.3.}{3.1.2.3.} = 34$). (Fig. 5 : 23b.) There are two representatives of this genus in Great Britain.

Pipistrellus nathusii

SKULL: Larger than *P. pipistrellus*, the condylobasal length being 14.0 mm. The bullae are not as large relatively as in *P. pipistrellus*.

(Dental formula $\frac{2.1.2.3.}{3.1.2.3.} = 34$). (Fig. 5: 23b.)

TEETH: The teeth are long and slender. The upper canine is almost half as long again as in *P. pipistrellus* measured from the cingulum. The first upper premolar is clearly visible from the outside. The first incisor is strongly bifurcated and longer than the inner.

Pipistrellus pipistrellus

SKULL: The total length of the skull is under 13.5 mm. It is weak and rounded with a saddle-shaped facial region. The premaxillary gap is moderately conspicuous while the zygomatic arch is weak, and the cranial crest is usually absent. The auditory bullae are more prominent than they are in *Myotis*, but are less so than in the *Barbastella* (Fig. 5 : 20a).

TEETH: The inner upper incisor is both more bicuspid and longer than the outer. The outer upper premolar is moderately large. The lower incisors tend not to overlap (Fig. 5 : 22a).

Genus *Eptesicus*

(Dental formula $\frac{2.1.1.3.}{2.1.3.3.} = 32$). (Fig. 5 : 23c.) There is only one representative of this genus in this country.

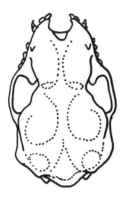
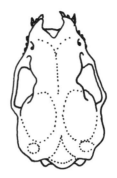

Pipistrellus nathusii

Nathusius pipistrelle

Pipistrellus pipistrellus

Common pipistrelle

5 : 17   Skull and teeth of Pipistrelle bats.

Eptesicus serotinus

SKULL: The total length of the skull is under 17 mm., but it is more heavily built, is flatter, stronger and larger than that of *P. pipistrellus*. Compared with *Nyctalus* it is longer and less massive with a more rounded brain-case. The zygomatic arch is expanded and the cranial crest is posteriorly prominent. The auditory bullae are small (Fig. 5 : 20b).

TEETH: The inner upper incisor is long, strongly bifid and is twice as long as the outer incisor. The anterior lower premolar attains about half the length and breadth of the posterior (see Fig. 5 : 22b).

Genus *Myotis*

(Dental formula $\frac{2.1.3.3.}{3.1.3.3.}$ = 38). (Fig. 5 : 23d.) This is a larger genus represented by five species.

181

SKULL: The skull varies in strength according to the size of the species. Usually it has a rounded brain-case elevated above the facial region, which is narrow, depressed and markedly saddle-shaped. The premaxilla is developed to an intermediate degree between that of *Nyctalus* and *Vespertilio*. The zygomatic arch is flattened and the auditory bullae are moderately developed.

TEETH: The upper incisors are almost equal in size, with generally divergent points – the outer slightly outwards, the inner inwards. The two anterior upper premolars are small, especially the anterior which is so often minute and crowded out of the tooth row internally. The lower outer incisors are much larger than the inner, and the lower premolars are the same, except that the central one is not as minute as the corresponding tooth in the upper jaw.

Myotis daubentoni

SKULL: The total length is from 14–15 mm. The profile of the cranium is almost horizontal, that of the face is slightly concave (Fig. 5 : 19b).

TEETH: The upper incisors are equal in size, short and broad. The first two premolars in the upper and lower jaws are smaller than the rest of the teeth, and the lower incisors are broad and flattened (Fig. 5 : 21b).

Myotis nattereri

SKULL: Total length is 15–16 mm. The skull is saddle-shaped or like a shallow S, the brain-case is prominently raised above the face line and is rounded (Fig. 99, C).

TEETH: The upper premolars are very small while the lower incisors are wide and overlapping (Fig. 5 : 21c).

Myotis mystacinus

SKULL: The total length is under 14 mm. The profile is similar to that of *M. nattereri*, but the frontal region is depressed, and the narrow muzzle is horizontal. The bullae are small (Fig. 5 : 19a).

TEETH: The first two premolars in each jaw are small, the first two lower incisors are broad, but the third is narrower (Fig. 5 : 21a).

Myotis bechsteini

SKULL: The total length is from 16–19 mm. The skull is larger than that of *M. nattereri*, but is relatively narrower. It (Fig. 5 : 19d) carries more prominent cranial ridges, and has much larger bullae.

TEETH: The first upper premolar is larger than the second (Fig. 5 : 21d).

Myotis myotis

SKULL: Total length over 21 mm.

Genus *Plecotus*

(Dental formula $\frac{2.1.2.3.}{3.1.3.3.} = 36$). (Fig. 5 : 23e.) There are two British representatives.

Plecotus auritus

SKULL: The total length is under 17 mm. The skull is weak, the profile descends gradually from the inflated brain-case to the depressed, broad, but not saddle-shaped facial region. The zygomatic arch is flattened and the cranial crests are very slightly developed. The auditory bullae are very large, equalling or exceeding those of *N. noctula*, *V. serotinus* or *M. myotis* in size (Fig. 5 : 20d).

TEETH: The upper incisors point inwards; the inner being bifid, with the inner cusps exceeding the outer; the outer is smaller and unicuspid. The anterior upper premolar, although very small is distinctly visible externally, while the upper premolar is large. The three lower premolars graduate in from the posterior which is largest to the central, which is the smallest (Fig. 5 : 22d).

Genus *Barbastella*

(Dental formula $\frac{2.1.2.3.}{3.1.2.3.}$ = 34). (Fig. 5 : 23f.) There is only one representative in Britain.

Barbastella barbastellus

SKULL: Total length is from 13.5–15 mm. It is weak with prominent rounded brain-case, has a broad, somewhat concave facial region and flattened zygomatic arches. The cranial crests are weaker or absent while the auditory bullae are moderately developed (Fig. 5 : 20c).

TEETH: The upper incisors are oblique, the outer pair being small while the inner pair is large and bifid. The upper canine has small anterior and posterior cusps at its base. The anterior upper premolar is minute and lies in the inner angle between the canine and posterior premolar which makes it invisible externally. The anterior lower premolar is about half the length and breadth of the posterior (Fig. 5 : 22c).

Genus *Vespertilio*

(Dental formula $\frac{2.1.1.3.}{3.1.2.3.}$ = 32). (Fig. 5 : 23c) Only one British representative of this genus.

Vespertilio murinus

SKULL: The total length is over 18 mm., and the general shape is similar to *Eptesicus serotinus*.

TEETH: The anterior premolar is absent from the upper jaw and is diminutive in the lower one.

Family: Rhinolophidae

This family is represented by one genus in the British Isles, *Rhinolophus* (dental formula $\frac{1.1.2.3.}{2.1.3.3.}$ = 32). In this genus the lower incisors which are tricuspid, plus

183

the upper incisors, although tiny, are always present in the premaxilla. The anterior upper premolar is minute and is often crowded out of the tooth line externally by the large canine and posterior premolars. The central lower premolar is frequently in a similar position between the neighbouring teeth. The molars are well developed and their cusps are 'W' shaped (Fig. 5 : 15b).

Rhinolophus ferrumequinum

SKULL: The total length is over 18 mm. The palatal bridge is long – a third or more of the length of the maxillary tooth-row, but is never as short as a quarter. The auditory bullae are small, and the basi-occipital is not particularly narrowed between them (Fig. 5 : 20e).

TEETH: The anterior upper and central lower premolars are either minute or absent and if present, are squeezed out of the tooth-row externally. The upper canine and posterior premolars overlap, the latter being external. The central and posterior lower premolars make contact with each other (Fig. 5 : 22e).

Rhinolophus hipposideros

SKULL: The total length is under 18 mm. The auditory bullae are so large that the basi-occipital is very much narrowed between them, so that it becomes only a bridge of bone. Sometimes the bullae are almost touching (Fig. 5 : 20f).

TEETH: The anterior upper premolar, although small, is in the tooth row. The upper canine and the posterior premolars are well separated. In the lower jaw the anterior and posterior premolars are usually in contact, but this varies (Fig. 5 : 22e).

SCAPULA: The spine is not very well developed, but does give rise to a strongly developed acromion process. The coracoid spur is always long and strong (Fig. 5 : 13c).

PELVIS: Is strongly fused to the several sacral vertebrae; there is no pelvic symphysis. In the Rhinolophid bats however, there is a complete fusion between the two pubic bones. In the Vespertilionid bats the two pubic bones are not fused, but are joined by a band of cartilage. (Fig. 5 : 59a) Vespertilionid, (Fig. 5 : 59a–c) Rhinolophid.

5 : 18   Photograph of a bat in walking position.

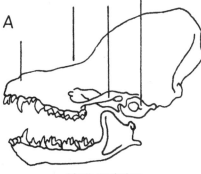

A

Myotis mystacinus

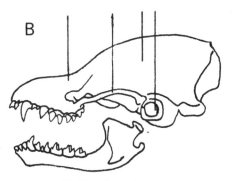

B

Myotis daubentoni

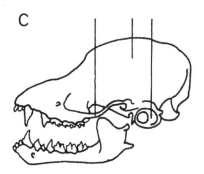

C

Myotis nattereri

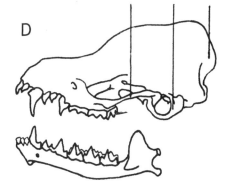

D

Myotis bechsteini

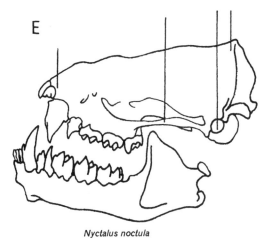

E

Nyctalus noctula

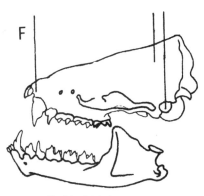

F

Nyctalus leisleri

5 : 19 Drawings of bat skulls, diagrammatic and enlarged to show distinguishing characteristics. Lines indicate features of identification for comparison (see text).

185

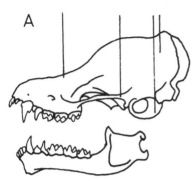

A

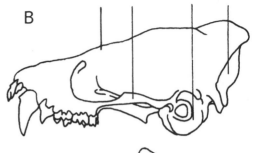

B

Pipistrellus pipistrellus

Eptesicus serotinus

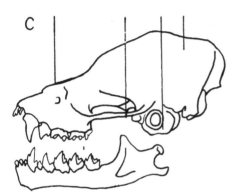

C

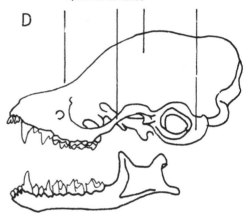

D

Barbastella barbastellus

Plecotus auritus

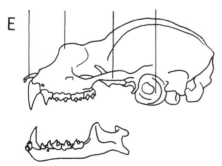

E

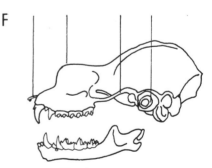

F

Rhinolophus ferrumequinum

Rhinolophus hipposideros

5 : 20 Drawings of bat skulls, diagrammatic and enlarged to show distinguishing characteristics. Lines indicate features of identification for comparison (see text).

186

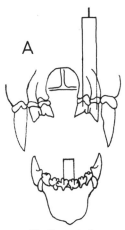

A

Myotis mystacinus

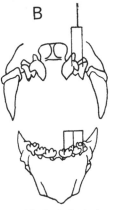

B

Myotis daubentoni

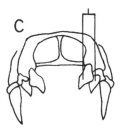

C

Myotis nattereri

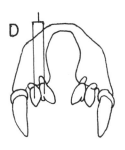

D

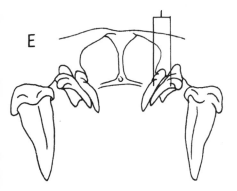

E

Myotis bechsteini

Nyctalus noctula

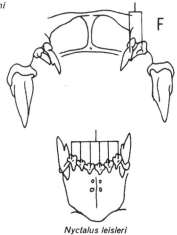

F

Nyctalus leisleri

5 : 21   Front view of bat skulls to show dentition characteristics. Lines indicate features of identification
for comparison (see text).

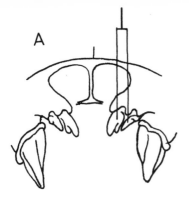

Pipistrellus pipistrellus

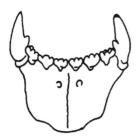

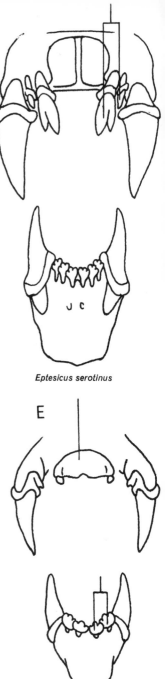

Eptesicus serotinus

Barbastella barbastellus

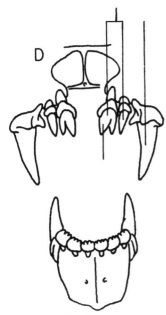

Plecotus auritus

Rhinolophus spp.

5 : 22   Front view of bat skulls to show dentition characteristics. Lines indicate features of identification for comparison (see text).

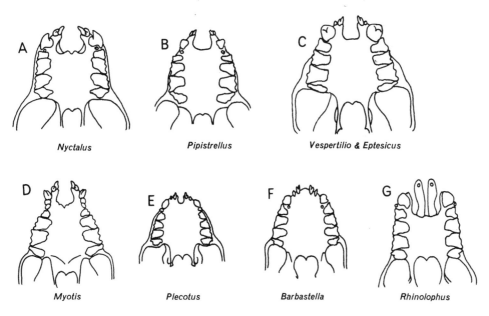

A	B	C
Nyctalus	Pipistrellus	Vespertilio & Eptesicus

D	E	F	G
Myotis	Plecotus	Barbastella	Rhinolophus

5 : 23 Drawings of palates of bat genera showing distinguishing features of dentition.

ORDER LAGOMORPHA

SKULL: The skull is long but there is a small brain-case, the nasal bones are also very long. There are sutures between the basi-occipital and the basi-sphenoid, while the basi-sphenoid and pre-sphenoid remain open throughout life. Much of the maxilla forming the side of the face in front of the orbit is fenestrated. The optic foramina are united to form a single hole, while the coronoid process is slightly differentiated from the ascending portion of the mandible. There is a large gap (diastema) between the incisors and premolars.

The canines are absent, but there are two upper incisors on each side, the second being smaller and lying behind the first. There are six grinding teeth with transverse ridges. The incisors are covered by enamel. In Rodents, however, this is only present on the front.

Family: Leporidae

There are two British genera in this family.

Genus *Oryctolagus*

Oryctolagus cuniculus

SKULL: Not more than 85 mm. in length. The sutures of the interparietal and supra-occipital are not fused. The palate is longer than the width of the posterior nares. (Fig. 5 : 26b)
TEETH: There are four incisors in the upper jaw and six grinding cheek-teeth separated by a diastema. There are only two incisors in the lower jaw.

189

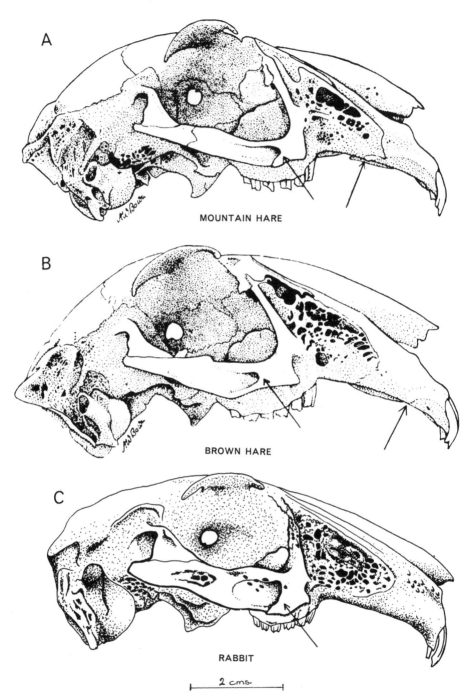

A

MOUNTAIN HARE

B

BROWN HARE

C

RABBIT

|— 2 cms. —|

5 : 24 Skulls of A, Mountain hare. B, Common hare. C, Rabbit. A and B by kind permission of the Trustees of the British Museum (Natural History).

Genus *Lepus*

There are two species representing the genus in this country. The skull differs from that of *O. cuniculus*. The posterior nasal opening is wider than the narrowest part of the palatal ridge; the interparietal is fused with the supra-occipital. (Fig. 5 : 26a.)

Lepus capensis (= *L. europeus*)

SKULL: The root of the upper incisor does not reach the suture between the maxilla and premaxilla. At the anterior end of the cheek bone the distance from the end of the groove to the front edge is greater than the depth between these points (Fig. 5 : 24b).

Lepus timidus

SKULL: The root of the upper incisor extends behind the suture of the maxilla and premaxilla. At the anterior end of the cheek bone the distance from the end of the groove to the front edge is less than the depth between these points (Fig. 5 : 24b).

SCAPULA: This may be dealt with collectively for the members of this Order. It is triangular in shape and has a well-developed spine which bifurcates, giving rise to an acromion and metacromion process of which the latter is well developed. The coracoid spur is short.

PELVIS: In (*O. cuniculus*), the ilium is over half the length of the bone (pelvis) and is considerably flattened towards the anterior end. The ischium and pubis are separated by a wide obturator foramen. On the inner surface of the ilium there is a large scar left by the symphysis.

ORDER RODENTIA

This is one of the largest Orders of British mammals, and is represented by several families. There are several features which are common to the groups in this Order.

5 : 25   Snail shells which have been broken open by voles (note that they are broken round the spiral).

SKULL: The zygomatic arch is large and complete, while the nasal cavities are long. The post-orbital processes are absent, and in many rodents there is an infra-orbital foramen. The palate is narrow, and there is a very long diastema. The canines are completely absent.

TEETH: The incisors are reduced to $\frac{1}{1}$, and are large with open roots so that they never stop growing. The ends of the incisors wear to a chisel shape. The teeth sometimes have cusps on a series of ridges. The majority of the molars have closed roots, but some are open-rooted giving rise to continuous growth. In all rodents the premolars are never more than $\frac{2}{1}$ and are in many cases absent.

Family: Sciuridae

Genus *Sciurus*

SKULL: The skull is broad, smooth and rounded, and has short broad nasals, widest and well arched at the front. These protrude beyond the incisors. The post-orbital bar is absent and the tympanic bullae are small. The lower jaw is heavily built (Fig. 5 : 33).

TEETH: The cheek-teeth are arranged $\frac{5}{4}$, the upper cheek-tooth being very small (Fig. 5 : 44e).

Sciurus vulgaris

SKULL: The total length is under 54 mm., and is smaller than that of *S. carolinensis*. The greatest length of the nasals is under 16 mm.

Sciurus carolinensis.

SKULL: The total length is up to 65 mm., and the greatest length of the nasals is over 17 mm.

ROOT PATTERNS: The first upper cheek-tooth has one root only; the first lower cheek-tooth has three roots (Figs. 5 : 47b; 5 : 50b).

Both the pelvis and scapula of both species may be dealt with collectively.

SCAPULA: The spine rises to an acromion process. The spine does not bifurcate and there is a false spine on the ventral edge. The coracoid spur is moderately developed.

PELVIS: The ilium is long, slender and slightly curved. The symphysis is well developed. The obturator foramen and acetabular foramina are shown in Fig. 5 : 76.

Family: Muridae (= Cricetidae)

Genus *Clethrionomys*

This is represented by only one species in the British Isles.

Clethrionomys glareolus

SKULL: The total length is under 32 mm., and the outlines are full and rounded. The interorbital region is broad, and the auditory bullae are large and inflated. The zygomatic arch is usually slender (Fig. 5 : 37).

TEETH: The incisors are weak and slender, and the cheek-teeth are small, narrow and, in the young, rootless. The surfaces consist of a pattern of alternating triangles rounded at the edges. (Fig. 5 : 41b.)

Genus *Microtus*

Represented by two species in this country.

SKULL: This is ridged and angular, and the interorbital region is narrow. The temporal ridges are well developed, and the bony palate terminates posteriorly in a median ridge sloping dorsally between the two lateral pits. It becomes narrower and sharper with age.

TEETH: The cheek-teeth are rootless. The surfaces are characterised by a pattern of very sharp alternating triangles (Fig. 5 : 41c).

Microtus agrestis

TEETH: The second upper cheek-tooth has *three* inwardly projecting loops (Fig. 5 : 41c).

Microtus arvalis

TEETH: The second upper cheek-tooth has *two* inwardly projecting loops (Fig. 5 : 41c).

Genus *Arvicola*

Arvicola terrestris

SKULL: The total length is over 32 mm. It has large prominent ridges. The auditory bullae are relatively small and the basioccipital is wide.

TEETH: The upper incisors are large and deep yellow in colour on the anterior surface; they do not project conspicuously. (Fig. 5 : 41b).

ROOT PATTERNS: *C. glareolus* The upper and lower jaws have six root cavities (Figs. 5 : 41a; 5 : 46a, c, d; 5 : 49a, c, d).

Microtus and *Arvicola*. There are no true roots to the teeth at all, but the cavities they occupy in the jaws can be clearly seen.

SCAPULA: This is triangular in shape and has a spine which is long and slender, but does not bifurcate. The coracoid spur is short and sturdy (Fig. 5 : 13e).

PELVIS: The ilium is very long and slender; the symphysis is small. The obturator foramen is of medium size (Fig. 5 : 76e).

Family: Muridae

There are six British representatives of this family.

Genus *Apodemus*

There are two species in this genus but as yet it is difficult to identify the differences with any certainty between *A. sylvaticus* and *A. flauicollis*. For this reason, only the former is described.

Apodemus sylvaticus

SKULL: A total length of 26.5 mm. The bones are lightly built. The brain-case is very smooth and of oval form. The interorbital is short but very wide. The zygomatic arches are very slender, as are the nasal bones, these are as long as the maxilla. The diastema is nearly twice as long as the tooth row. The brain-case is rounded at the sides (Fig. 5 : 38).

TEETH: There are three cheek-teeth in each jaw, the anterior cheek-tooth being the largest. The first and second upper cheek-teeth have three cusps on their inner sides (Fig. 5 : 42b). The anterior lower cheek-tooth has three cusps at its extreme anterior end.

ROOT PATTERNS: Upper jaw – the first cheek-tooth has four roots, giving a total of eleven in the jaw. Lower jaw – total of six roots (Figs. 5 : 45b; 5 : 48b).

Genus *Mus*

Only one representative in Britain.

Mus musculus

SKULL: The brain-case is depressed and oval, with poorly developed temporal crests. The zygomatic arch is relatively strong. The nasals do not advance beyond the incisors as they do in *A. sylvaticus*. The lower jaw is relatively shorter and deeper than in *Apodemus*.

TEETH: The upper incisor is strongly curved and notched on the inner edge. The first and second upper cheek-tooth have only two cusps on the inner side while *Apodemus* has three. The first lower cheek-tooth has only one cusp at its extreme anterior end (Figs. 5 : 42c, d).

ROOT PATTERNS: Three cavities for the first upper molar, five cavities altogether in the lower jaw (Figs. 5 : 45c; 5 : 48c).

Genus *Micromys*

One British representative.

Micromys minutus

SKULL: Under 20 mm. Small size is one characteristic, and the great development of the cerebral and corresponding shortening of the facial regions is another. The nasals fuse at an early age, and the diastema is short.

TEETH ROOT PATTERNS: Upper jaw – five roots in first upper molar, with total of twelve in whole. Lower jaw – total of seven roots; second smaller than rest (Figs. 5 : 45d; 5 : 48d).

Genus *Rattus*

Two British representatives.

SKULL: The skull is strongly built with well marked supra-orbital ridges, which generally extend to the outer corners of the interparietal (Figs. 5 : 35; 5 : 36).

TEETH: The incisors are much deeper than they are broad and their working surfaces are normally notched. There are three upper and lower cheek-teeth. The first and second upper cheek-teeth have two cusps on their inner surface (Fig. 5 : 44a, b).

194

Rattus rattus

SKULL: The lateral ridges are distinctly curved (Fig. 5 : 26bB).

Rattus norvegicus

SKULL: The lateral ridges on the brain-case are almost parallel (Fig. 5 : 26bA).

Family: Gliridae (= Muscardinidae)

There are two genera representing this family in the British Isles, the Common and Edible dormice.

Genus *Muscardinus*

Muscardinus avellanarius

SKULL: This is similar to that of the Muridae, except that the angular portions of the mandibles are bent outwards, and the brain-case is less oval in shape than, for example, that of *A. sylvaticus*. There is a considerable constriction between the brain-case and the nasals. The tympanic bullae are proportionally very large.

TEETH: Dental formula $\frac{1.0.1.3.}{1.0.1.3.} = 20$. The premolars are small and single rooted. The anterior molar is the largest tooth. There are transverse ridges on the teeth (Figs. 5 : 43a, b; 5 : 45a, b; 5 : 48a).

Genus *Glis*

Glis glis

SKULL: There are no ridges on the cranium. The post-orbital bar is almost absent. The nasals widen anteriorly, and the whole structure is broad in relation to its length. The bullae are very large and the zygomatic arch is strong, while the infra-orbital foramen is very small (Fig. 5 : 34).

TEETH: There are four upper and four lower cheek-teeth all with lateral ridges. The first upper and lower cheek-teeth are small (Figs. 5 : 43c, d; 5 : 47c; 5 : 50c).

Family: Capromyidae

Only one introduced species represents the family in this country.

Genus *Myocastor*

Myocastor coypus

SKULL: This is very strongly built. The infra-orbital foramen is small as are the bullae, and the post-orbitals are almost absent. There is a prominent occipital crest. The nasal bones are not as long as the maxilla. The skull is flat. The occipitals are greatly elongated. The lower jaw is angular and is flattened at the posterior end (Fig. 5 : 39).

TEETH: There are four cheek-teeth in the upper and lower jaws, and a total of four well-developed incisors. The incisors are dark yellow on the front edges; there are

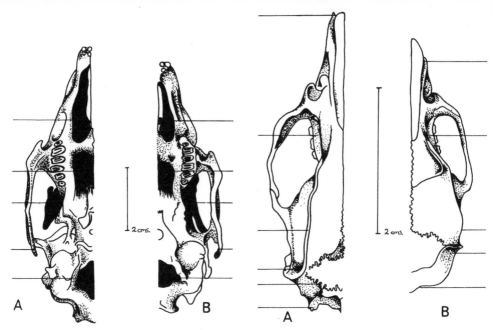

5 : 26a Underside of A, Hare skull, B, Rabbit skull. (Ventral view.)

5 : 26b Skulls of A, Brown rat, B, Black rat. (Dorsal view.)

Lines indicate features of identification for comparison.

notches on the backs of the upper incisors. The cheek-teeth in the upper jaw point outwards and downwards. The lower cheek-teeth point inwards and upwards. The lines of teeth converge anteriorly. The teeth are ridged (Fig. 5 : 42c).

From Brown, J. C. and Twigg, G. I. (1969)

The morphology and its variation of the bony pelvis in British species of Muridae and Cricetidae have been studied. The investigation began with the application of a mensural method for demonstrating sexual dimorphism and it is shown that for all species except those of *Rattus* the male os coxa can be distinguished from the female over a wide range of ages. During the study it became obvious that there are ranges of morphological variation in os coxae both inter- and intra-specific. There are constant inter-specific differences which allow identification of os.coxae of these rodents at least to genus and in

5 : 27 Photograph of a weasel eating a mouse.

many cases to species. Detailed descriptions of the morphology of the os coxa of each species are given together with an identification key. Intra-specific variation is mainly sex-dependent and comprises sexual dimorphism, male pubertal changes and female parturition changes. The changes in the male are from epicene, through pubertal, to post-pubertal phase, with the first of these resembling the agonadal, female form, and the last with a posterior border thickend and tuberculate in relation to the hypertrophied penis and its associated glands and musculature. These phases are not equally obvious in all species, but the pelvis in all except *Rattus* and *Mus* shows some evidence of the sexual development of the animal. In females the form of the pelvis may be modified during successive pregnancies to allow a wider pelvic outlet for parturition. Resorption and remoulding of the female pelvis allows the recognition of ono-parous, uniparous and multi-parous animals in all Cricetid species, in *Micromys* and, more doubtfully, in *Mus*, but not in *Apodemus* and *Rattus*. Non-sex-dependent intra-specific variation, comprising differences in rugosity related to muscularity, is also described.

The observations are discussed in relation to earlier experimental work, to the need for basic research on small mammal reproduction and population structure, and to the use of the pelvis in the analysis of osteological assemblages such as occur in owl pellets.

Interspecific variation and the identification of os coxae

When the several morphological characters described in the preceding section are tabulated comparatively (Table II) certain of them emerge as constant distinctions between Muridae and Cricetidae. In order of importance and clarity these are:

(1) Pubis: Broad and stra-like in murids; narrow, waisted and rounded in cricetids.
(2) Pubic symphysis: Long curved and inconspicuous in murids; short, straight and obvious because of the hooked symphyseal region resulting from the waisted pubis in cricetids.
(3) Obturator foramen: in murids, essentially trapezoid ranging to sub-ovoid, its dorso-ventral axis short so that the foramen hardly extends dorsal to the ventral rim of the acetabulum and falls far short of the iliac axis; in cricetids, essentially semi-circular with a high dorsoventral axis which almost reaches or extends beyond the iliac axis.
(4) Consequent on the difference in size of the obturator foramen, there is a large body of the ischium in murids and a restricted body in cricetids.
(5) Acetabulum: with the os coxa laid in the study position the acetabulum opens towards the ischeal tuberosity in murids and directly towards the observer in cricetids.
(6) Pectineal fossa: shallow in murids and deep in cricetids due to the essential difference in pubis shape.
(7) Gemellus fossa: a straight dorsal margin in all murids except *Rattus* and curved and projecting in all cricetids.
(8) Ischial angle: a right-angle or a modified right-angle in murids; curved in cricetids.

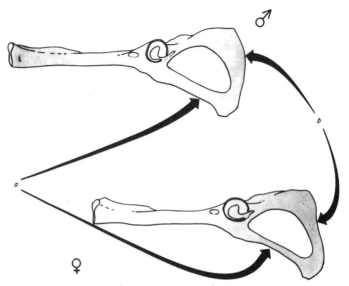

5 : 28   The essential sexual differences in the os coxae of murid
and cricetid rodents *(a)* Pubis is longer and thinner in females
(b) Posterior margin is convex in the male and concave in the
female. The diagram illustrates a microtine male and female.

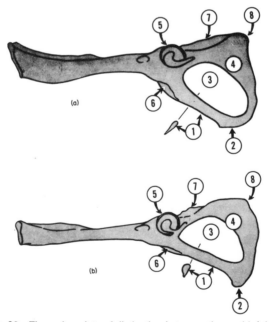

5 : 29   The main points of distinction between the murid *(a)* and
the cricetid *(b)* os coxae. The numbers are those referred to on
page 197.

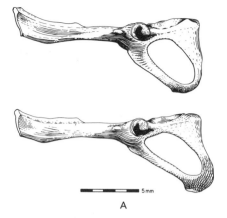

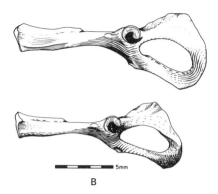

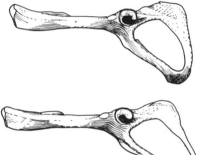

scale 5mm

A

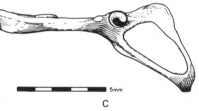

scale 5mm

B

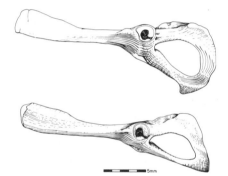

scale 5mm

C

scale 5mm

D

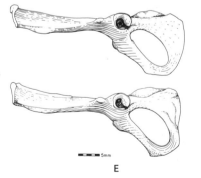

scale 5mm

E

scale 5mm

F

5 : 30
A   *Apodemus sylvaticus*
B   *Mus musculus*

C   *Micromys minutus*
D   *Microtus arvalis
    orcadensis*

E   *Rattus norvegicus*
F   *Arvicola terrestris
    amphibicus.*

199

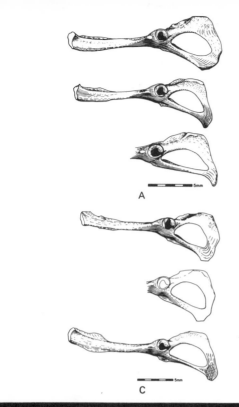

A

B

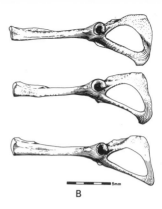

C

5 : 31   A *Microtus agrestis*
B *Clethrionomys glareolus glareolus*
C *Clethrionomys glareolus skomerensis.*

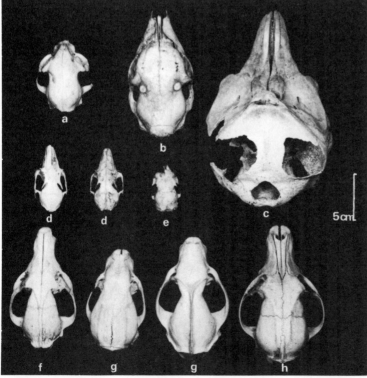

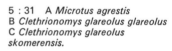

5 : 32   (Below) Collection of skulls kindly lent by Miss Clare Lloyd.
a. Cat. *b.* Roe deer. *c.* Porpoise. *d.* Rabbit. *e.* Squirrel. *f.* Fox. *g.* Badger. *h.* Dog.

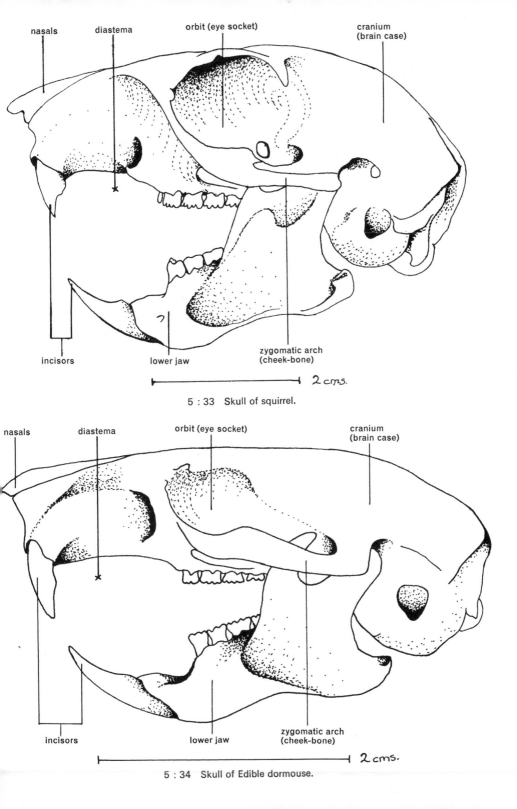

nasals

diastema

orbit (eye socket)

cranium (brain case)

incisors

lower jaw

zygomatic arch (cheek-bone)

2 cms.

5 : 33   Skull of squirrel.

nasals

diastema

orbit (eye socket)

cranium (brain case)

incisors

lower jaw

zygomatic arch (cheek-bone)

2 cms.

5 : 34   Skull of Edible dormouse.

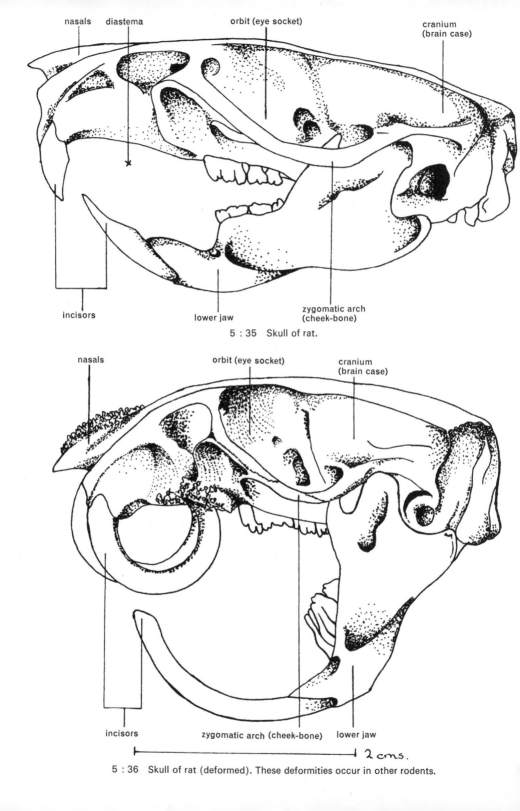

nasals   diastema   orbit (eye socket)   cranium (brain case)

incisors   lower jaw   zygomatic arch (cheek-bone)

5 : 35   Skull of rat.

nasals   orbit (eye socket)   cranium (brain case)

incisors   zygomatic arch (cheek-bone)   lower jaw

2 cms.

5 : 36   Skull of rat (deformed). These deformities occur in other rodents.

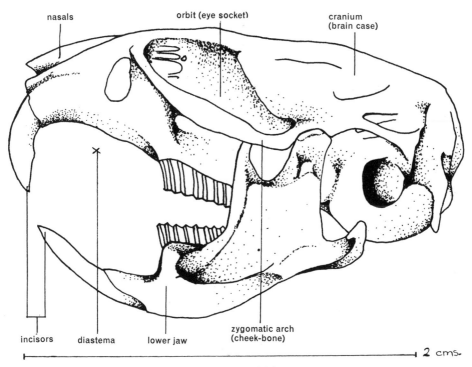

nasals

orbit (eye socket)

cranium
(brain case)

incisors   diastema   lower jaw   zygomatic arch
(cheek-bone)

2 cms.

5 : 37   Skull of vole.

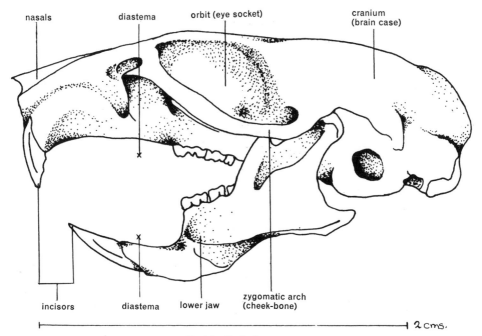

nasals   diastema   orbit (eye socket)   cranium
(brain case)

incisors   diastema   lower jaw   zygomatic arch
(cheek-bone)

2 cms.

5 : 38   Skull of mouse.

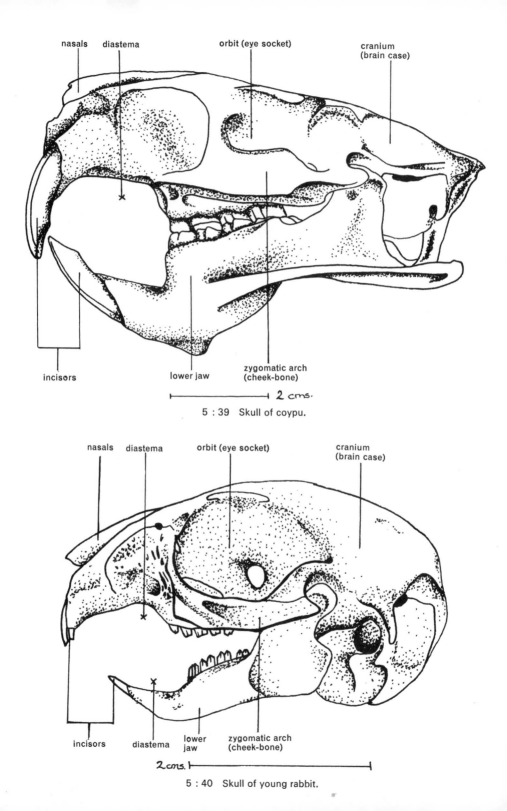

nasals   diastema   orbit (eye socket)   cranium (brain case)

incisors   lower jaw   zygomatic arch (cheek-bone)

2 cms.

5 : 39   Skull of coypu.

nasals   diastema   orbit (eye socket)   cranium (brain case)

incisors   diastema   lower jaw   zygomatic arch (cheek-bone)

2 cms.

5 : 40   Skull of young rabbit.

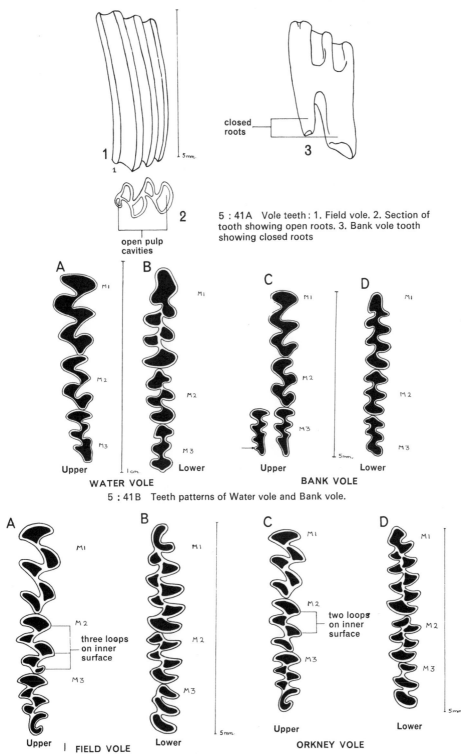

5 : 41A Vole teeth : 1. Field vole. 2. Section of tooth showing open roots. 3. Bank vole tooth showing closed roots

closed roots

open pulp cavities

WATER VOLE

Upper

Lower

BANK VOLE

Upper

Lower

5 : 41B Teeth patterns of Water vole and Bank vole.

three loops on inner surface

two loops on inner surface

FIELD VOLE

Upper

Lower

ORKNEY VOLE

Upper

Lower

5 : 41C Teeth patterns of Field vole and Orkney vole.

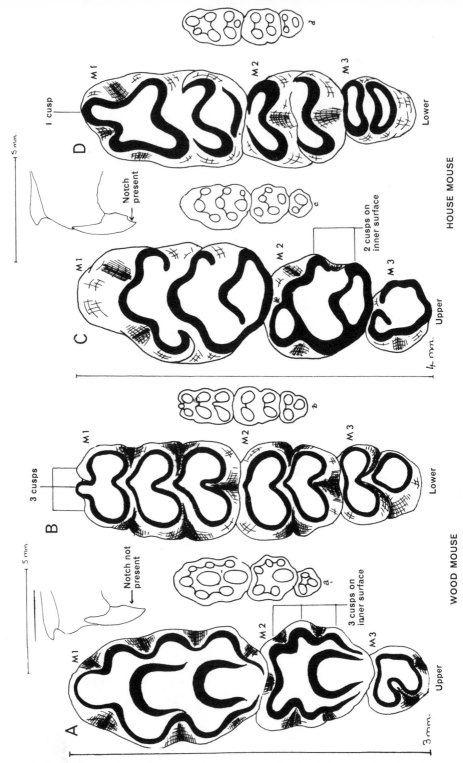

5 : 42 Teeth patterns of Wood mouse and House mouse showing lack of notch on Wood mouse incisors, and showing presence on House mouse incisors.

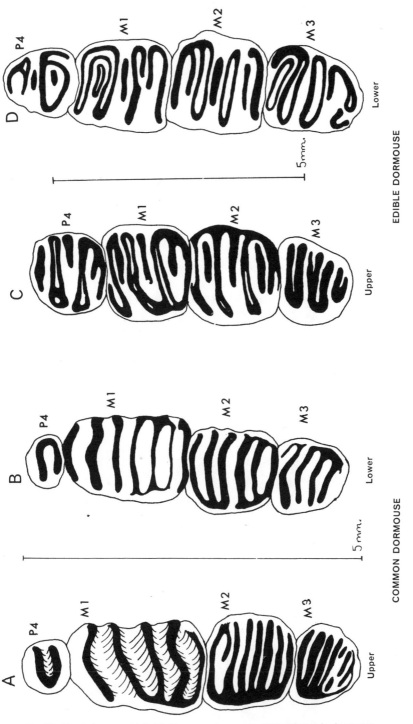

EDIBLE DORMOUSE

COMMON DORMOUSE

5 : 43   Teeth patterns (A & B) Common dormouse. (C & D) Edible dormouse.

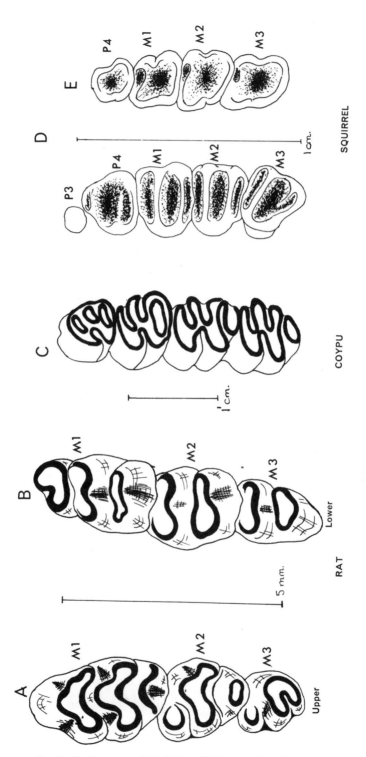

5 : 44 Teeth patterns (A & B) Rat. (C) Coypu. (D & E) Squirrel.

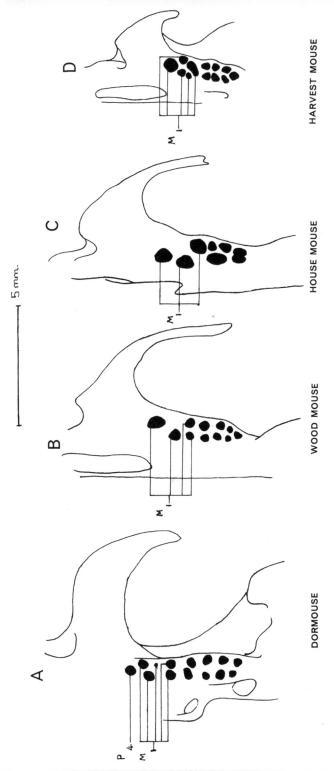

5 : 45 Mice palates showing root patterns.

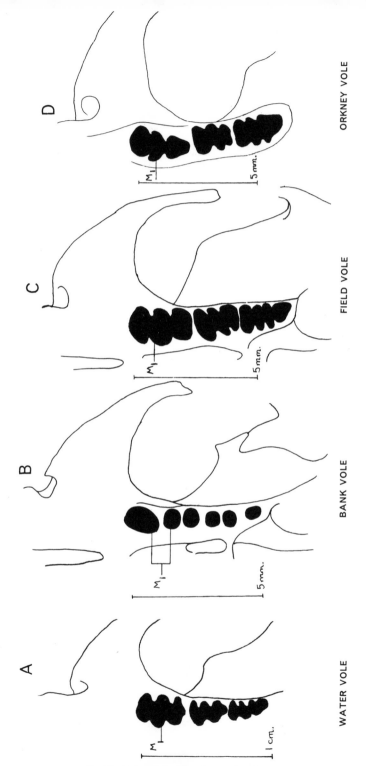

5 : 46 Vole palates showing root patterns.

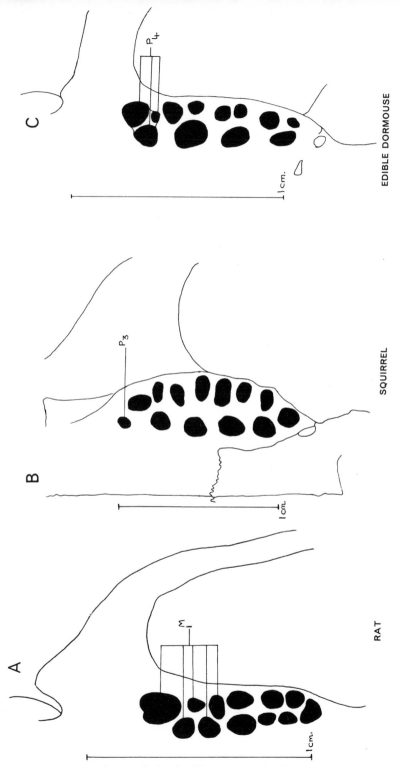

5 : 47   Palates of rat, squirrel and edible dormouse showing root patterns.

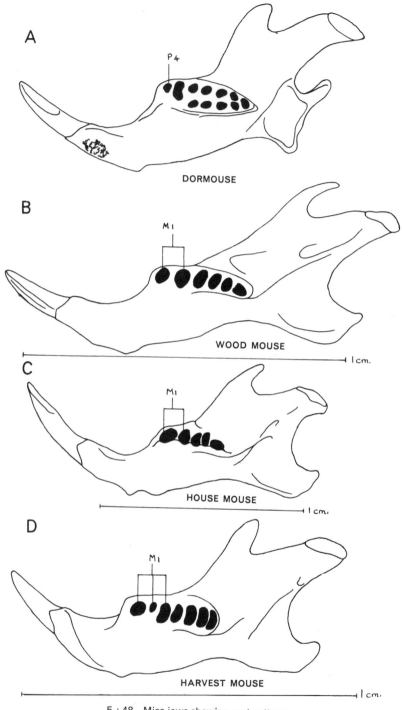

A — P4 — DORMOUSE

B — M1 — WOOD MOUSE — 1 cm.

C — M1 — HOUSE MOUSE — 1 cm.

D — M1 — HARVEST MOUSE — 1 cm.

5 : 48   Mice jaws showing root patterns.

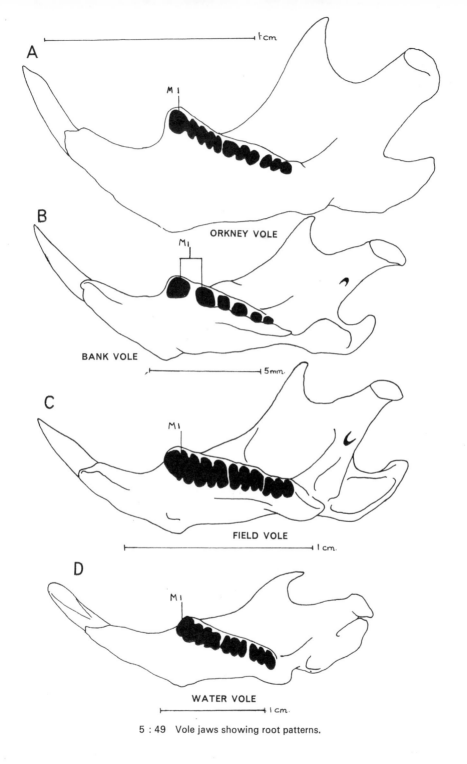

A

1cm

M1

ORKNEY VOLE

B

M1

BANK VOLE

5mm.

C

M1

FIELD VOLE

1 cm.

D

M1

WATER VOLE

1 cm.

5 : 49   Vole jaws showing root patterns.

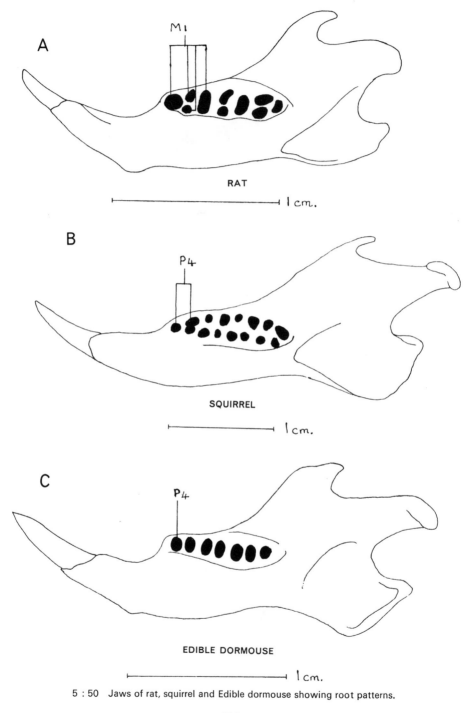

A

M1

RAT

⊢————————————⊣ 1 cm.

B

P4

SQUIRREL

⊢————————————⊣ 1 cm.

C

P4

EDIBLE DORMOUSE

⊢————————————⊣ 1 cm.

5 : 50   Jaws of rat, squirrel and Edible dormouse showing root patterns.

214

ORDER CARNIVORA

SKULL: A large brain-case on which there is a sagittal crest in the centre and transverse ridges running to the occipital. There is a strong zygomatic arch. The orbit and
temporal fossa communicate freely since the post-orbital bar is incomplete. There
is a deep glenoid fossa and a well-developed post-glenoid cavity. The condyle on
the lower jaw is transversely elongated.

TEETH: The canines are well developed and the carnassial is commonly present as a
large tri-lobed tooth (Fig. 5 : 57).

Family: Canidae

The skull is long and tapered, the upper jaw is much greater than half the length of
the skull, as is the lower jaw. The brain case (cranium) is less than half the length of
the skull.

Genus *Vulpes*

Vulpes vulpes

SKULL: the dental formula of the one British representative of this genus is:

$$\frac{3.1.3.3.}{3.1.4.3.} = 42$$

The condylobasal length varies between 115–59 mm. The rostrum is long and
slender. The palate is also long, but only reaches as far as the last upper molar. The
sagittal crest (when developed) is placed posteriorly on the cranium. The infra-
orbital foramen is very small and is well anterior to the orbit. The lower jaw is long
and slender and the angle is not very prominent.

TEETH: The canines, compared with those of the domestic dog, are very long.
Viewed apically a line between the tips of the lower canines passes through the
nareal cavity. Viewed laterally the tips of the upper canines clearly protrude below
the lower jaw.

Family: Mustelidae

The skull is long and the upper jaw is less than half the total length of the skull.
The lower jaw is just over half the total length. The brain-case is long and narrow.

Genus *Mustela*

Mustela putorius

SKULL: Condylobasal length varies between 57.5 and 71 mm. Viewed dorsally the
post-orbital portion of the cranium tapers gradually to its junction with the cranium
proper. The breadth of the junction (post-orbital constriction) is about 25% of the
condylobasal length (Corbet, 1966). The mastoid width is over 50% of the condylobasal length. In ventral view the roof of the meatus can be clearly seen.

Mustela vison

SKULL: The condylobasal length varies from 56–74 mm. The post-orbital constriction, viewed dorsally, is very much less than 20% of the condylobasal length. The

mastoid width is about 50% of the condylobasal length. The posterior incissure of the palate tends to be laterally constricted and elliptical in outline. In ventral view the lower margin of the auditory meatus is expanded and obscures the roof of the meatus.

Mustela nivalis

SKULL: Long, slender and flat on top. The upper jaw is less than half the total length of the skull, and the sagittal crest is not well developed, but the transverse ridge is. The zygomatic arch is very slender, and the brain-case is very long. The total length is under 42 mm. (Fig. 5 : 53).

TEETH: The incisors are small, the canines are large. There are four upper and four lower cheek-teeth with only one premolar in each jaw.

ROOT PATTERNS: The third upper molar has three roots (Fig. 5 : 53). The second lower molar has two roots (Fig. 5 : 53).

SCAPULA: This is short and triangular in shape with a poorly-developed spine, which bifurcates strongly at the end to give a strong acromion process, but a weak metacromium process (Fig. 5 : 59A).

PELVIS: The ilium is long yet thick. The pubis is thin, the ischium is heavier Fig. 5 : 60A).

Mustela erminea

SKULL: Similar to, but larger than, that of the weasel. The zygomatic arch is relatively thinner and the post-orbital process is poorly developed as in the weasel (Fig. 5 : 53). The total length is over 42 mm.

TEETH: See weasel.

ROOT PATTERNS: The third upper molar has four roots, the second lower molar having the same number as well (Fig. 5 : 53).

Genus *Meles*

The one representative of this genus in the British Isles has a dental formula of:

$$\frac{3.1.3.1.}{3.1.4.2.} = 36$$

This is because the first upper premolar is often shed after erupting.

Meles meles

SKULL: The condylobasal length varies between 110–43 mm. The sagittal crest is well-developed (especially in old mature animals) and often protrudes posteriorly beyond the occipital crest. The mastoid process is large, extending downwards and forwards. The palate is extremely long, extending well beyond the last upper molar – up to 3–4 times longer than the width between the carnasials. The infra-orbital is much larger than the canine alveolus. The inter-orbital and anterior cranial regions are relatively broad and measure about one-third of the zygomatic width.

TEETH: The upper molar is much larger than the neighbouring carnassial and is at least as long as it is broad. In the lower carnassial the sectorial section is much restricted whilst the talus is very large and tuberculate.

216

Genus *Lutra*

Represented by one species with a dental formula $\dfrac{3.1.4.1.}{3.1.3.2.} = 42$

Lutra lutra

SKULL: The condylobasal length is 104–24 mm. The post-orbital constriction is the most noticeable feature in *Lutra* since it is very narrow. The skull is broad and much compressed dorso-ventrally, the zygomatic width is greater than the mastoid width, and the bullae are flattened. The palate is almost four times as long as the width between the cheek teeth. The infra-orbital foramen is relatively larger than in *Meles*. The rostrum is also very much shortened.

TEETH: The upper molar is about the same size as the carnassial and broader than it is long. The lower carnassial is of more normal form than is *Meles* but bears a large flattened talus.

Genus *Martes*

Martes martes

There is only one British representative of this genus dental formula $\dfrac{3.1.4.1.}{3.1.4.2.} = 38$.

SKULL: The brain-case is slightly rounded and the sagittal crest is poorly developed, or almost absent. The zygomatic arch is strong, but the post-orbital process is weak. The lower jaw is over one half of the total length of the skull (Fig. 5 : 57).

TEETH: The canines are large, but the carnassials are not. The last molar in both upper and lower jaws is greatly flattened. There are six upper and five lower cheek-teeth (Fig. 5 : 57).

SCAPULA: This is slightly triangular in shape with a poorly-developed spine, bifurcating to a strong acromium process and a weak metacromium process. The glenoid cavity is well developed (Fig. 5 : 59A).

PELVIS: The ilium is long but very stout, and the pubis and ischium are also well developed. The ilium is greater than half the total length of the structure, which is altogether very strong (Fig. 5 : 60A).

Family: Felidae

The skull is short and broad being almost equal in dimensions. The brain case is equal to half the condylobasal length.

Genus *Felis*

Dental formula: $\dfrac{3.1.3.1.}{3.1.2.1.} = 30$

SKULL: There are two species of the genus in the British Isles, the Domestic cat and the Scottish Wild cat. It is not possible to distinguish them from their skulls. The following description is of a known specimen of a Scottish Wild cat. *Felis*

217

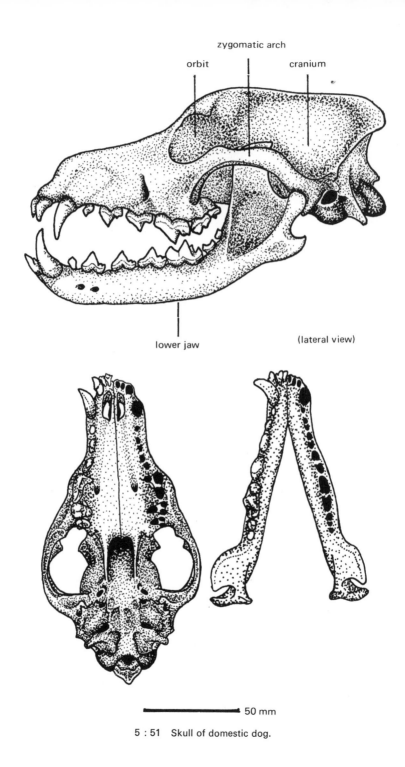

orbit

zygomatic arch

cranium

lower jaw

(lateral view)

50 mm

5 : 51   Skull of domestic dog.

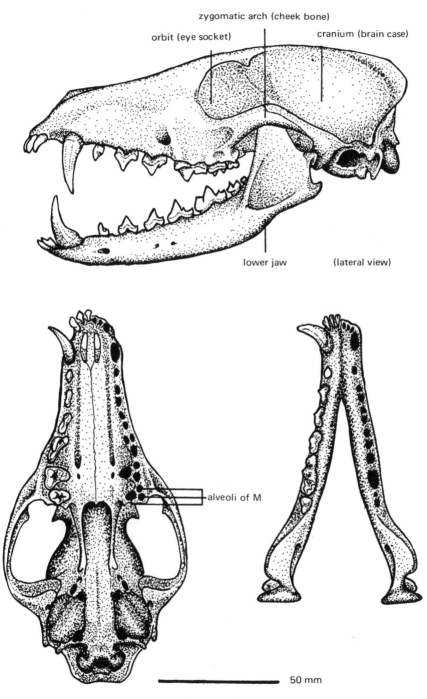

zygomatic arch (cheek bone)

orbit (eye socket)

cranium (brain case)

lower jaw   (lateral view)

alveoli of M

50 mm

5 : 52   Skull of fox.

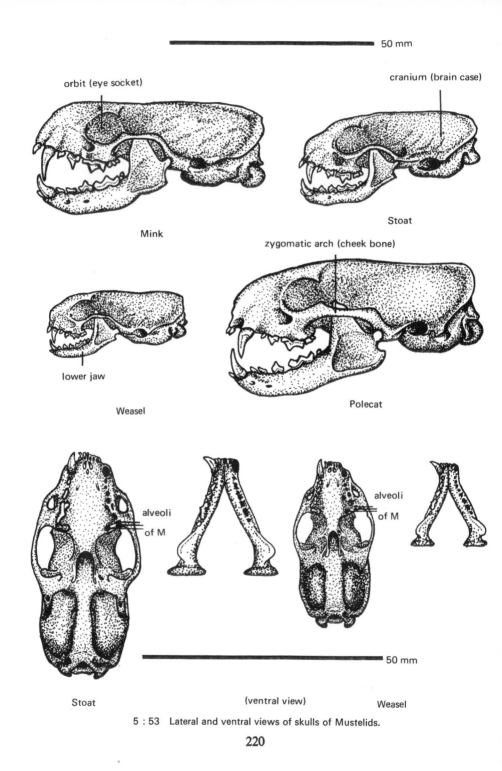

50 mm

orbit (eye socket)

cranium (brain case)

Stoat

Mink

zygomatic arch (cheek bone)

lower jaw

Weasel

Polecat

alveoli
of M

alveoli
of M

Stoat

(ventral view)

Weasel

50 mm

5 : 53   Lateral and ventral views of skulls of Mustelids.

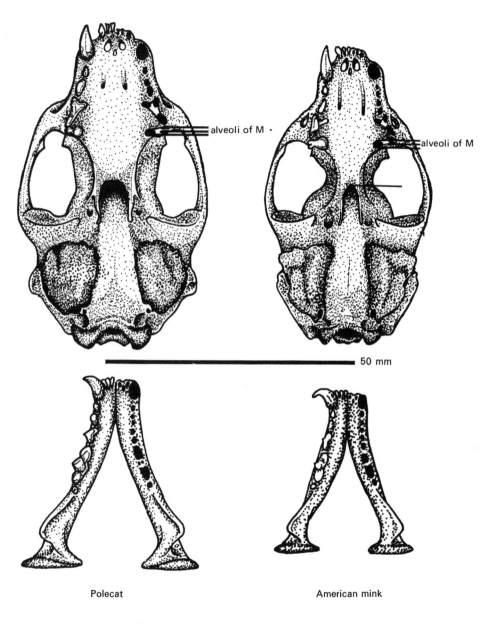

alveoli of M ·

alveoli of M

50 mm

Polecat

American mink

5 : 54   Ventral view of skulls of polecat and American mink.

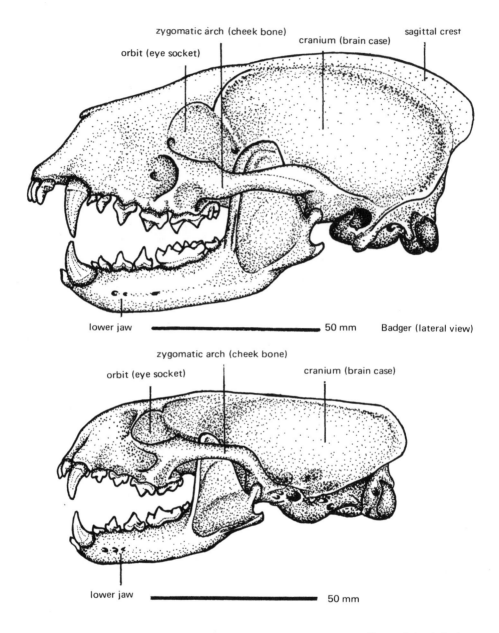

5 : 55 Skulls of badger and otter.

222

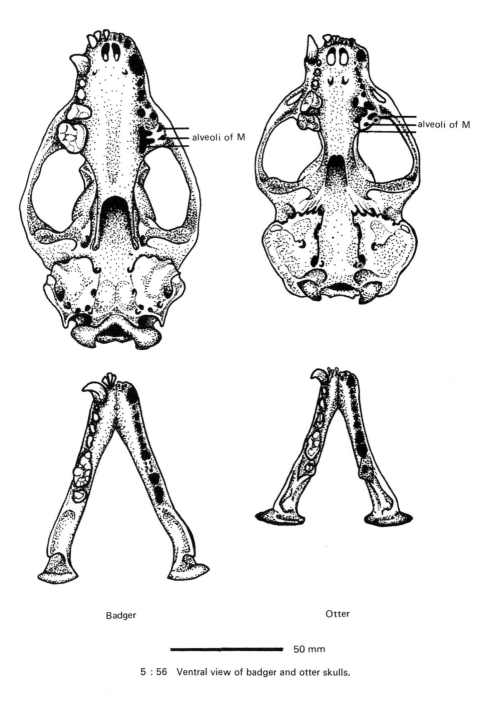

alveoli of M

alveoli of M

Badger   Otter

50 mm

5 : 56   Ventral view of badger and otter skulls.

223

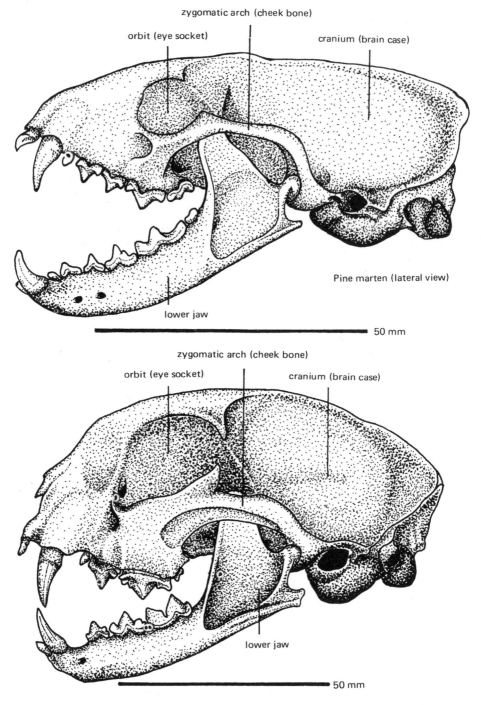

orbit (eye socket)

zygomatic arch (cheek bone)

cranium (brain case)

Pine marten (lateral view)

lower jaw

50 mm

zygomatic arch (cheek bone)

orbit (eye socket)

cranium (brain case)

lower jaw

50 mm

Scottish Wild Cat   (lateral view)

5 : 57   Skulls of pine marten and Scottish wild cat.

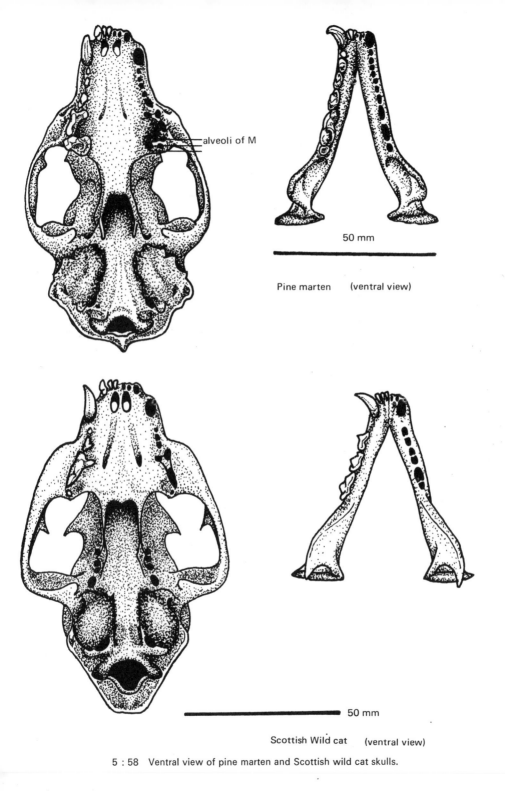

alveoli of M

50 mm

Pine marten   (ventral view)

50 mm

Scottish Wild cat   (ventral view)

5 : 58   Ventral view of pine marten and Scottish wild cat skulls.

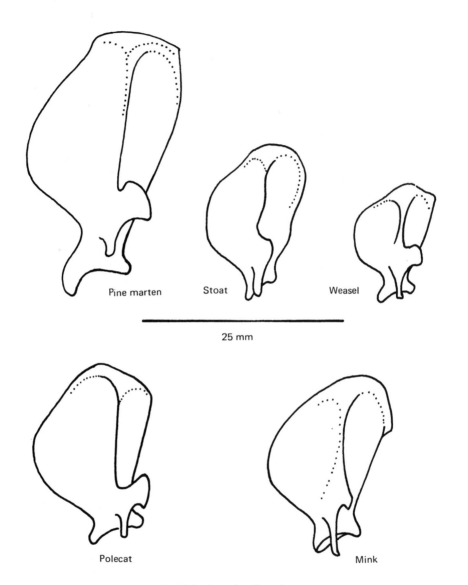

Pine marten

Stoat

Weasel

25 mm

Polecat

Mink

5 : 59A   Scapulae of carnivora.

226

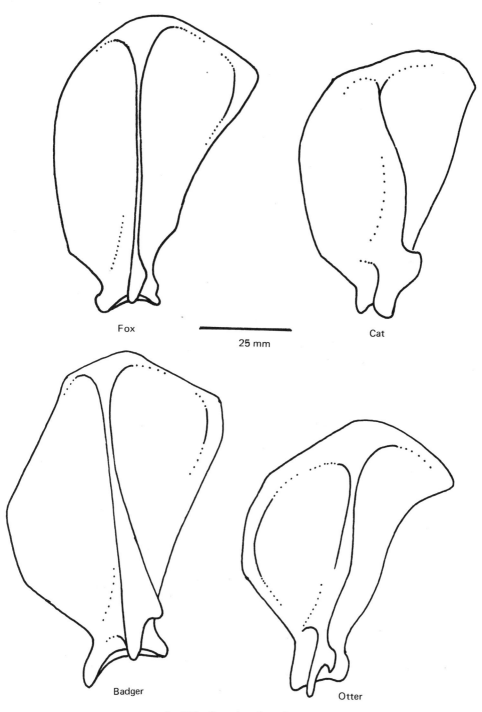

Fox

Cat

25 mm

Badger

Otter

5 : 59B   Scapulae of carnivora.

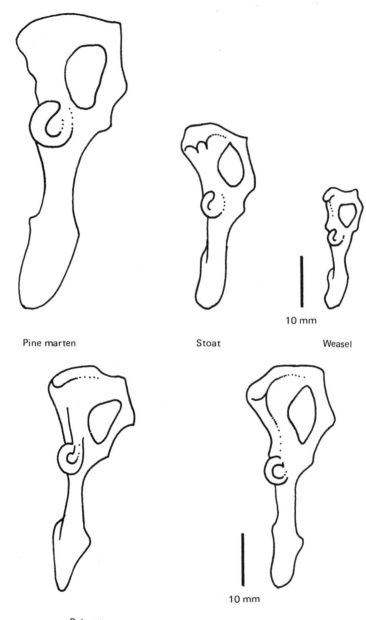

Pine marten   Stoat   Weasel

10 mm

Polecat   Mink

10 mm

5 : 60A Pelvic girdle of carnivora.

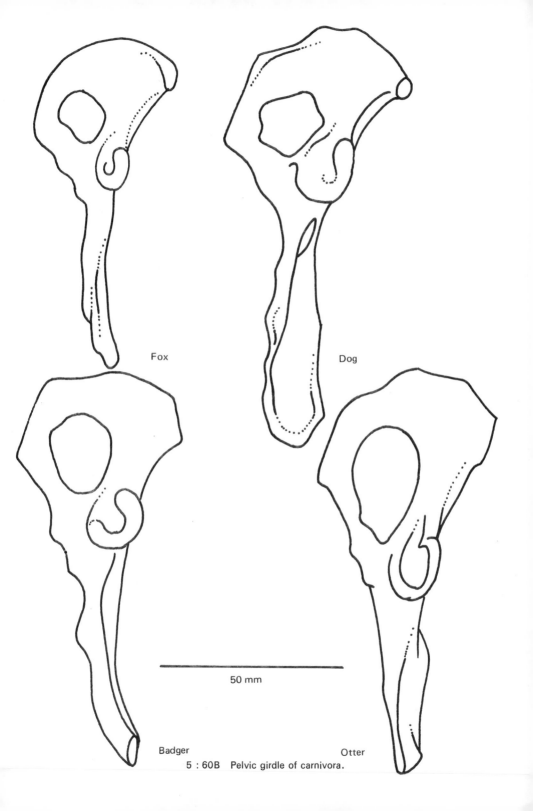

Fox

Dog

Badger

Otter

50 mm

5 : 60B Pelvic girdle of carnivora.

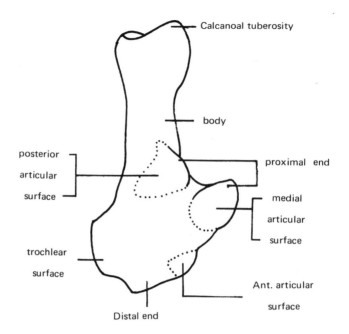

Calcanoal tuberosity

body

posterior
articular
surface

proximal end

medial
articular
surface

trochlear
surface

Ant. articular
surface

Distal end

Dorsal view of a generalized calcaneum

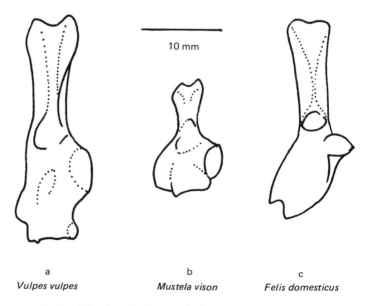

10 mm

a
Vulpes vulpes

b
Mustela vison

c
Felis domesticus

5 : 61   Calcanium. The bone at the base of the foot (heel).
Commonly found in owl pellets and will probably provide good
identification of species. A very hard bone and not easily broken,
like skulls.

230

sylvestris. The condylobasal length varies between 80.5–125 mm. In general form the skull is broad, the zygomatic width is approximately 75% of the condylobasal length and the extreme width of the palate about equal to or slightly less than its length. The post-orbital process sometimes forms a post-orbital bar. The bullae are large and bulbous, the brain viewed dorsally appears hemispherical and its post-orbital constriction is marked.

TEETH: This species shows the most extreme degree of tooth reduction found in the carnivora. The incisors are relatively small and arranged in a straight line. The first upper premolar and first and second lower premolars have been lost. The remaining premolars (apart from the second upper) are well-developed, the upper carnasials having three highly sectorial buccal cusps. The tooth row is less than half the condylobasal length.

ORDER: PINNIPEDIA

Family: Phocidae

The brain case is less than half the length of the condylobasal length, as is the tooth row. The bullae are very large and inflated, the rostrum is short and the inter-orbital constriction is extremely narrow. The sagittal crest is absent.

Genus: *Phoca*

There is one common member of this genus in British waters.

Phoca vitulina

SKULL: Compared with *Halichoerus* the inter-orbital region is not as wide and the nasals are longer. The orbit is large. The jugal is far longer than its depth at the narrowest point.

TEETH: The tooth row is straight and the palate wedge-shaped and relatively flat. The teeth are tri-cuspid.

Genus: *Halichoerus*

Again, there is only one common representative in British waters.

Halichoerus grypus

SKULL: The most noticeable aspect of this skull is the extreme depth of the rostrum, the short nasals and the parallel line of the premaxilla and maxilla. The depth of the rostrum is equal to its length. The nasal aperture is extremely large. The inter-orbital region is robust (but not as is *Phoca*) and cylindrical in cross-section. The lateral wall of the maxilla anterior to the base of the zygomatic arch is large and inflated.

TEETH: The tooth row is straight and the palate tapers very greatly anteriorly and bears a deep concavity anteriorly. The teeth are not as in *Phoca*, but are peg-like in appearance. The canine is powerful and single rooted.

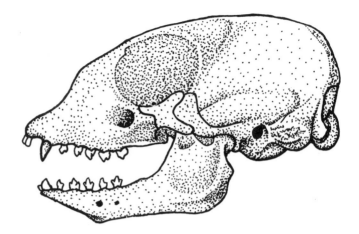

Bearded seal *Erignathus barbatus*

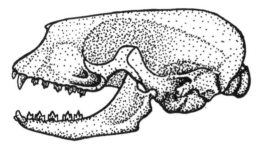

Ringed seal *Phoca hispida*

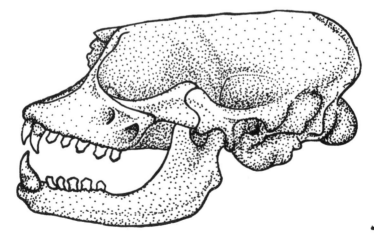

Hooded seal *Cystophora cristata*

50 mm

5 : 62 Lateral view of seal skulls.

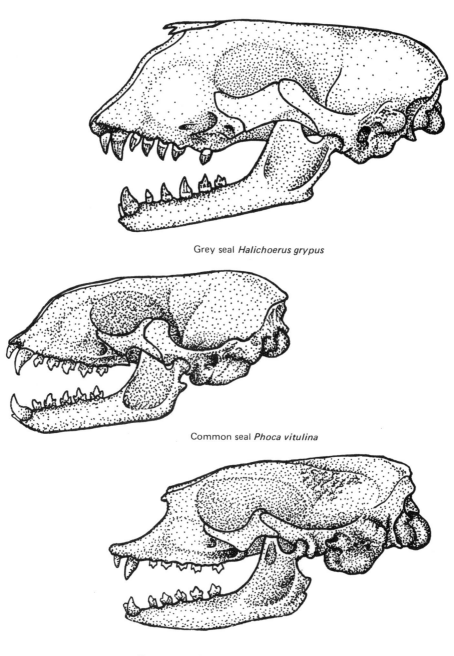

Grey seal *Halichoerus grypus*

Common seal *Phoca vitulina*

Greenland or Harp seal *Pagophilus groenlandicus*

5 : 63   Lateral view of seal skulls.

233

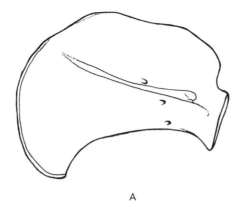

A

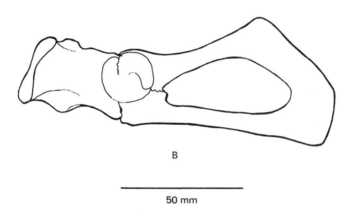

B

50 mm

5 : 64   Seal A. shoulder; B. hip girdle.

ORDER: ARTIODACTYLA (Deer)

SKULL: Characterised in the case of the male animals by deciduous bony antlers (with the exception of the Reindeer in which both male and female possess antlers, and the Chinese Water deer where neither sex has antlers). The post-orbital process is complete, the orbit prominent and nearly circular. The palatines and pterygoids are moderately large. The squamosal is small. There is a large paraoccipital process.
TEETH: The premolars and molars are usually dissimilar, the premolars being one-lobed, the molars being two-lobed. In the case of the Red and Sika deer the differences in structure are less well marked. The canines are absent, excepting in the Red, Sika and Chinese Water deer (in the last case they amount almost to tusks). There are six cheek-teeth in both upper and lower jaws.

Genus *Dama*

Dama dama

SKULL: The total length is up to 25 cms. The canines are completely absent. The zygomatic arch is fairly thick and straight (Fig. 5 : 71).

TEETH: There are six upper cheek-teeth, three molars and three premolars. The first upper premolar has three roots which are arranged as the points of a triangle. The roots are large, irregular and very close together.

Genus *Cervus*

Cervus elaphus

SKULL: The total length is up to 40 cms. There is a small canine in the upper jaw. The zygomatic arch is broad, thickening in the anterior region (Fig. 5 : 71).

TEETH: There are six cheek-teeth in the upper jaw and one small canine. The premolars are smaller than the molars, but are not as simple as they are in other species, as they show a marked tendency towards two lobes. The first upper premolar has three roots, two very large ones to the outside and one very small one to the inside.

Cervus nippon

SKULL: The skull is generally similar to that of *Cervus elaphus*, except that it is never greater than 30 cms. in length. There is again a small canine in the upper jaw (Fig. 5 : 71).

TEETH: There are six cheek-teeth and one small canine in the upper jaw. The premolars are slightly more complicated in surface structure than in other species. The first upper premolar has three widely spaced roots which form the corners of a triangle.

Genus *Hydropotes*

Hydropotes inermis

SKULL: The total length is not greater than 20 cms. The zygomatic arch is heavy, broadening and curving in the anterior section. The large canine in the upper jaw and the lack of antlers are distinctive features (Fig. 5 : 70).

TEETH: There are six cheek-teeth in the upper jaw and a very large canine. The premolars are simpler and smaller than the molars. The first upper premolar has three roots of irregular shape, which are widely spaced in an irregular fashion.

Genus *Capreolus*

Capreolus capreolus

SKULL: The total length is from 15 to 20 cms. The zygomatic arch is considerably extended in the anterior region. No canines are present (Fig. 5 : 70).

TEETH: There are six upper cheek-teeth, three molars and three premolars. The latter are simpler than the former, but they are not very much smaller. The first upper premolar has two parallel roots (at right angles to the surface of the jaw), the posterior is almost divided into two, the anterior has approximately straight sides.

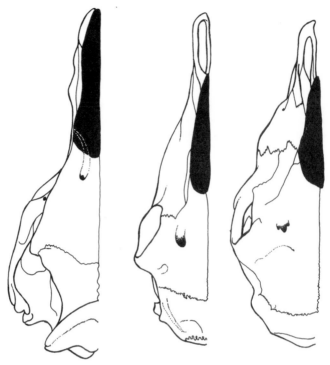

5 : 65   Dorsal views of pig, goat and sheep skull.

Genus *Muntiacus*

Muntiacus (muntjac and reevesi)

SKULL: The total length is under 15 cms. The skull is broad in relation to its length. Canines are totally absent, and there is a very long pedicle. The zygomatic arch is broad (Fig. 5 : 70).

TEETH: There are six cheek-teeth in the upper jaw, the molars being distinct from the premolars both in size and greater complexity of shape. The first upper premolar has three roots, two circular posterior ones and a single, elongated anterior one, which tends to show two distinct bulges at the ends.

5 : 66   Red deer stag with the antlers losing their velvet.

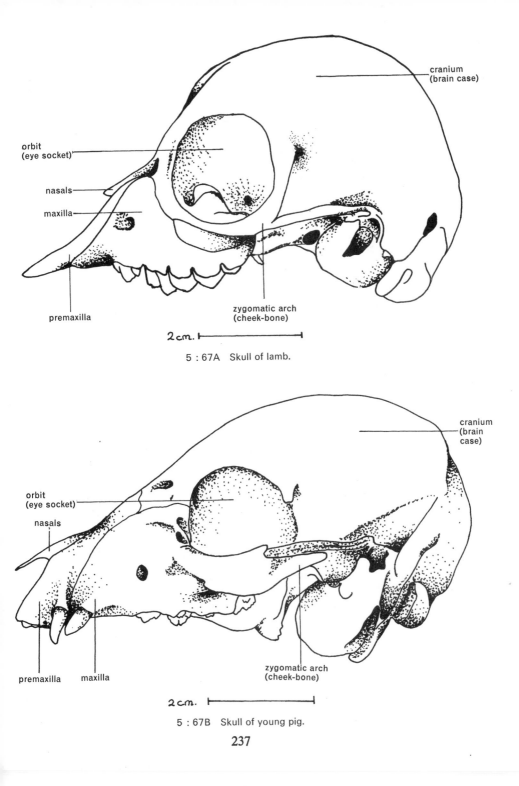

cranium
(brain case)

orbit
(eye socket)

nasals

maxilla

premaxilla

zygomatic arch
(cheek-bone)

2cm.

5 : 67A   Skull of lamb.

cranium
(brain
case)

orbit
(eye socket)

nasals

premaxilla

maxilla

zygomatic arch
(cheek-bone)

2cm.

5 : 67B   Skull of young pig.

237

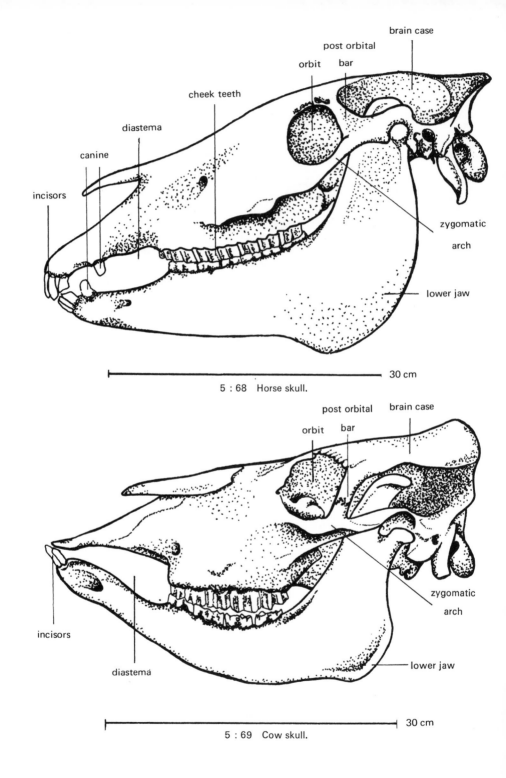

brain case

post orbital
orbit bar

cheek teeth

diastema

canine

incisors

zygomatic
arch

lower jaw

30 cm

5 : 68   Horse skull.

post orbital
orbit bar   brain case

zygomatic
arch

lower jaw

incisors

diastema

30 cm

5 : 69   Cow skull.

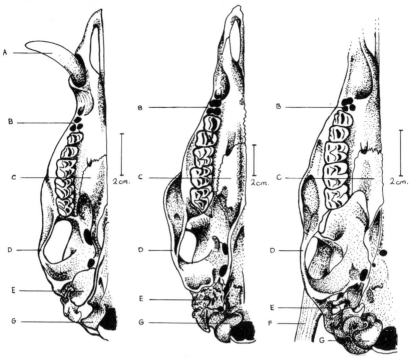

CHINESE WATER DEER **ROE DEER** **MUNTJAC**

5 : 70 Ventral surface of Chinese Water deer, Roe deer, muntjac. A canine ; B tooth removed to show root patterns ; C palatine ; D zygomatic arch (cheek bone) ; E bulla ; F pedicle ; G condyle.

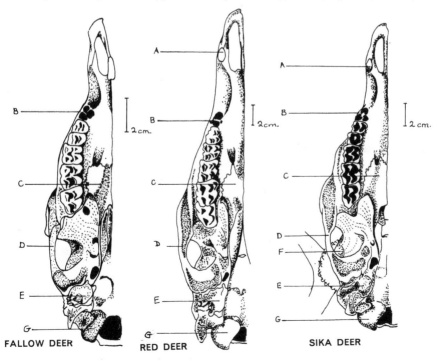

FALLOW DEER **RED DEER** **SIKA DEER**

5 : 71 Ventral surface of skulls of Fallow deer, Red deer, Sika deer (*Key as above*).

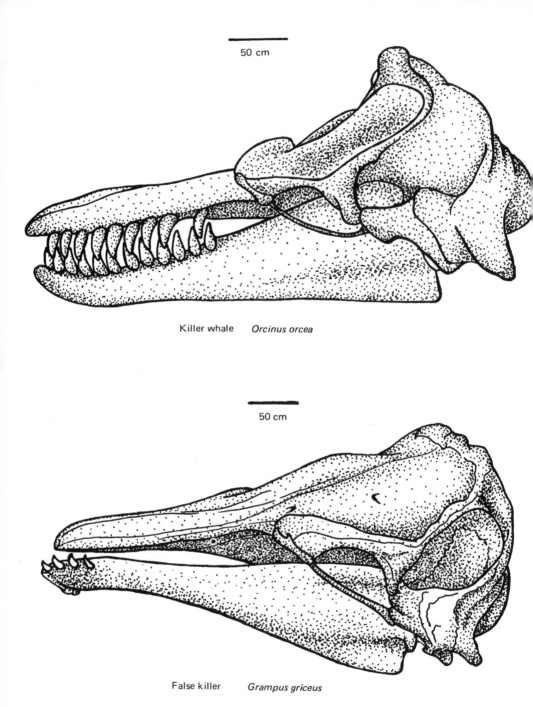

50 cm

Killer whale   *Orcinus orcea*

50 cm

False killer   *Grampus griceus*

5 : 72   Cetacea (whale) skulls.

240

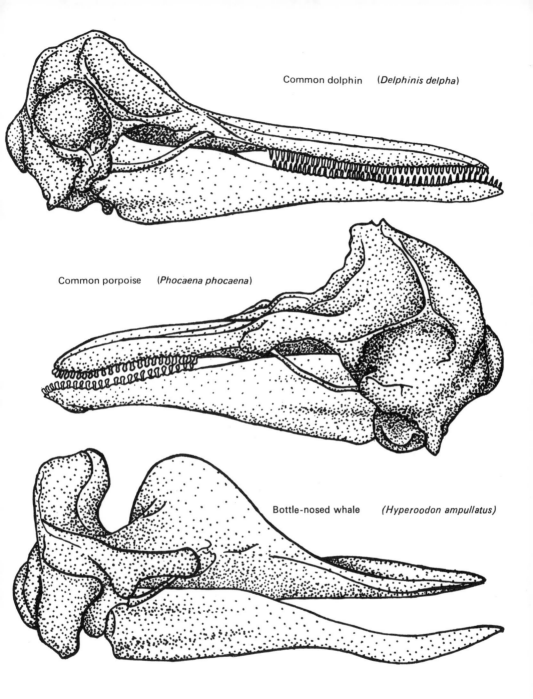

Common dolphin   (*Delphinis delpha*)

Common porpoise   (*Phocaena phocaena*)

Bottle-nosed whale   (*Hyperoodon ampullatus*)

5 : 73   Cetacea (dolphin and porpoise) skulls.

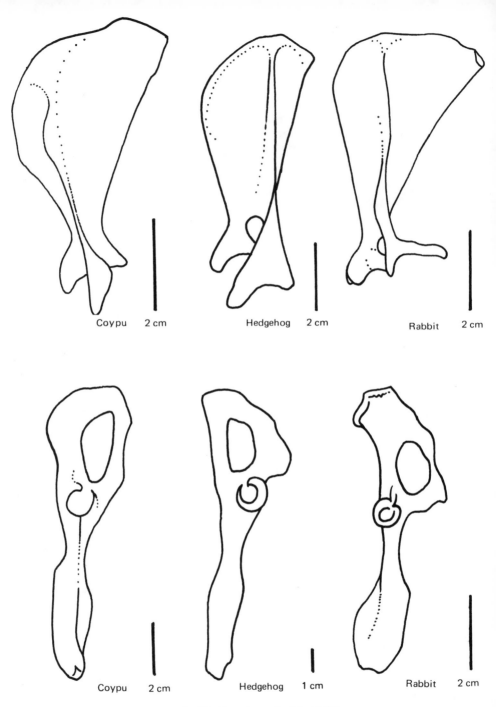

Coypu   2 cm   Hedgehog   2 cm   Rabbit   2 cm

Coypu   2 cm   Hedgehog   1 cm   Rabbit   2 cm

5 : 74   Scapulae and pelvic girdles.

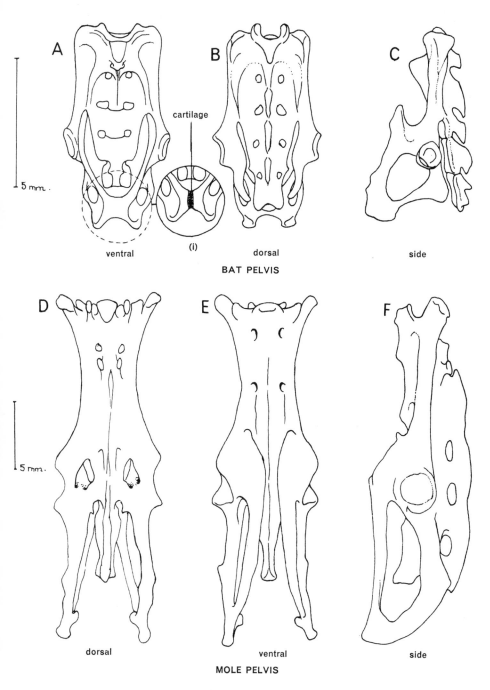

A

cartilage

(i)

ventral

B

dorsal

C

side

BAT PELVIS

D

dorsal

E

ventral

F

side

MOLE PELVIS

5 mm.

5 mm.

5 : 75   Pelvis of Rhinolophid Bat (A, B, C) Vespertilionid Bat (i) and Mole (D, E, F).

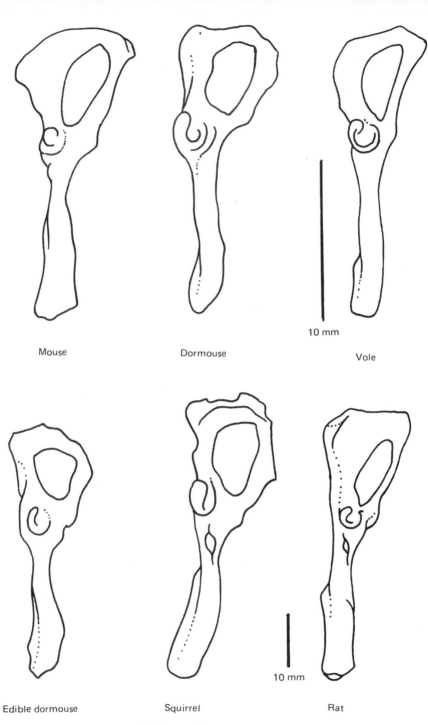

Mouse

Dormouse

Vole

10 mm

Edible dormouse

Squirrel

Rat

10 mm

5 : 76   Pelvic girdles of rodents.

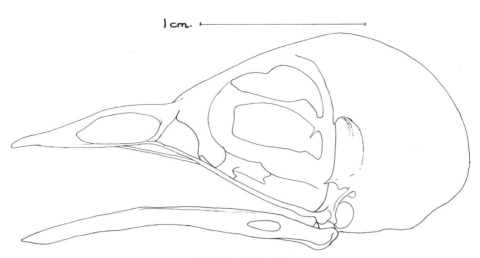

1 cm.

5 : 77a   Bird scull.

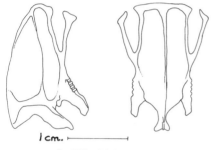

1 cm.

5 : 77b   Bird sternum.

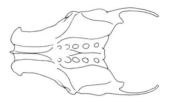

5 : 77c   Bird Pelvis.

Key to skulls and lower jaws of small animals found in owl pellets (Reference to figures advised)

1. Teeth present 2
   Teeth *not* present 3
2. Teeth all same shape 4
   Teeth different 5
3. Beak present ... ... Bird
   Beak *not* present ... ... Toad
4. Teeth conical (peg-like) in shape ... ... Lizard
   Teeth pointing backwards and sharp ... ... Snake
   Teeth very small and in upper jaw only ... ... Frog
5. Incisors *not* separated by gap from cheek-teeth 6
   Incisors separated by wide gap (diastema) from cheek-teeth 20
6. Upper incisors or canines separated by deep rounded concavity (horse-shoe bats have incisors borne on stalk, in such a cavity, but will probably be absent; canines will, however, be separated by deep rounded concavity) 7
   Upper incisors and canines are *not* separated by deep rounded concavity 14
7. Bats: Two bulbous projections on top of skull behind nasal cavity... ... 8
   Bulbous projections absent 9
8. Length 18 mm. ... ... *Rhinolophus ferrumequinum*
   Length under 18 mm. ... ... *Rhinolophus hipposideros*
9. Upper and lower cheek-teeth $\frac{6}{6}$ 10
   Upper and lower cheek-teeth $\frac{5}{5}$ 11
   Upper and lower cheek-teeth $\frac{4}{5}$ 12
   Upper and lower cheek-teeth $\frac{5}{6}$ 13
10. Genus *Myotis*
    Total length of skull 21 mm. ... ... *M. myotis*
    Total length of skull 16–19 mm. upper premolar very small *M. bechsteini*
    Total length of skull 15–16 mm. ... ... *M. nattereri*
    Total length of skull 14–15 mm. upper incisors very small *M. daubentoni*
    Total length of skull under 14 mm. skull saddle-shaped *M. mystacinus*
11. Genus *Nyctalus*
    Total length of skull 18 mm. ... ... *N. noctula*
    Total length of skull 15–17 mm. ... ... *N. leisleri*
    Genus *Barbastella*
    Total length of skull 13.5–15 mm. ... ... *B. barbastellus*
    Genus *Pipistrella*
    Total length of skull under 13.5 mm. ... ... *P. pipistrellus*
12. Genus *Eptesicus*
    Total length of skull over 18 mm. ... ... *E. serotinus*
    Genus *Vespertilio*
    Total length of skull under 17 mm. ... ... *V. murinus*

246

13. Genus *Plecotus*
    Total length of skull under 17 mm. Length of maxillary toothrow (upper canine to last molar) under 5.6 mm. ... ... *P. auritus*
    Total length of skull over 17 mm. Length of maxillary toothrow over 5.6 mm. (after G. B. Corbet) ... ... *P. austriacus*
14. Zygomatic arch (cheek-bone) absent. Shrews 15
    Zygomatic arch present 18
15. Teeth entirely white, three upper unicuspids. *Crocidura sauveolens*
    Teeth with red pigment on tips – four or five unicuspids 16
16. Four upper unicuspids – lower incisor with one lobe on cutting edge. *Neomys fodiens*

    Five upper unicuspids on each side – lower incisor with three lobes on cutting edge ... ... *Sorex* sp. 17
17. Third upper unicuspid smaller than second – skull 19–20 mm. *Sorex araneus*
    Third upper unicuspid as large as second – skull 15–16 mm. *Sorex minutus*
18. Sagittal crest absent – skull widest at brain-case (length under 40 mm.); upper canine double rooted ... ... *Talpa europaea*
    Sagittal crest present – skull widest at zygomatic arch 19
19. Total length of skull over 42 mm.; four roots at position of last molar in upper jaw. Lower jaw over 22 mm.; four roots at position of second molar. *Mustela erminea*

    Total length of skull under 42 mm.; three roots at position of last molar in upper jaw. Lower jaw under 22 mm.; four roots at position of second molar. *Mustela nivalis*

20. One pair of incisors in upper jaw ... ... Rodents 21
    Two pairs of incisors in upper jaw (only very young animals) *Oryctolagus cuniculus*

21. Rodents. Surface of cheek-teeth with *transverse* ridges cheek-teeth $\frac{4}{4}$ Dormice 22
    *Surface of cheek-teeth with *rounded* cusps – Rats and mice ... 23
    Surface of cheek-teeth with pattern of alternating triangles – Voles 27
    *Surface of cheek-teeth with cusps cheek-teeth $\frac{5}{4}$ – Squirrels ... 30

22. Total length of skull under 25 mm.; first cheek-tooth in upper and lower jaw very small and with one root. Second upper cheek-tooth has five roots, four teeth together under 5 mm. ... ... *Muscardinus avellanarius*
    Total length of skull over 25 mm. First upper and lower cheek-tooth small but not as small proportionally as in the Common Dormouse. Three roots on first upper cheek-tooth. Length of four cheek-teeth over 5 mm. *Glis glis*
23. Total length of skull over 30 mm.; five roots on first upper cheek-tooth, four roots on first lower cheek-tooth. First and second upper cheek-tooth with two turbercles on their inner sides 24
    Total length under 30 mm. 25

* In old animals cusps will be worn down, and teeth will appear flat.

24. Rats. Lateral ridges almost parallel ... ... *Rattus norvegicus*
    Lateral ridges curved ... ... *Rattus rattus*
25. Mice. Upper incisors notched, first and second upper cheek-teeth with two cusps on inner side. Five roots on lower jaw. First upper cheek-tooth with three roots ... ... *Mus musculus*
    Upper incisors not notched, first and second upper cheek-teeth with three cusps on inner surface 26
26. Total length over 20 mm. Four roots on first upper cheek-tooth. Six roots on lower jaw ... ... *Apodemus spp.
    Total length of skull under 20 mm. Five roots on first upper cheek-tooth, seven roots on lower jaw ... ... *Micromys minutus*
27. Total length of skull over 32 mm. ... ... *Arvicola terrestris*
    Total length of skull under 32 mm. 28
28. Angles of cheek-teeth rounded and with roots (roots absent in very young animals) (Fig. 5:37A. 3) ... ... *Clethrionomys glareolus*
    Angles of cheek-teeth sharp and without roots ... *Microtus spp.* 29
29. Second upper cheek-tooth with three inwardly projecting loops.
    Microtus agrestis
    Second upper cheek-tooth with two inwardly projecting loops.
    Microtus arvalis
30. Total length of skull under 54 mm. Greatest length of nasal bones under 16 mm. ... ... *Sciurus vulgaris*
    Total length of skull up to 65 mm. Greatest length of nasal bones over 17 mm. ... ... *Sciurus carolinensis*

* Species identification not possible at present.

Identification of the Appendicular Skeleton (Limb Bones) in the Carnivora

This section will consider the identification of the appendicular skeleton only in so far as it considers the following 'long bones', i.e. Humerus, Radius, Ulna, Femur, Tibia and Fibula. Arrows in diagram are features of identification.

Key to Appendicular Skeleton (Limb Bones) of the Order Carnivora
(*Reference to the illustrations is advised*)

Bone Types

1. Canal (hole) present at distal end of bone ... ... Humerus
   Canal (hole) *not* present at distal end of bone 2
2. Large round knob (head) on end of projection at proximal end of bone
   Femur
   Large round knob absent from proximal end of bone 3
3. Bone has a deep rounded concavity to one edge and near proximal end of bone ... ... Ulna
   Bone does *not* have a deep rounded concavity at proximal end 4
4. Bone at proximal end has a distinctly triangular cross-section (*x- -y*).
   Tibia
   Bone *not* triangular at proximal end and approximately elliptical in cross-section 5

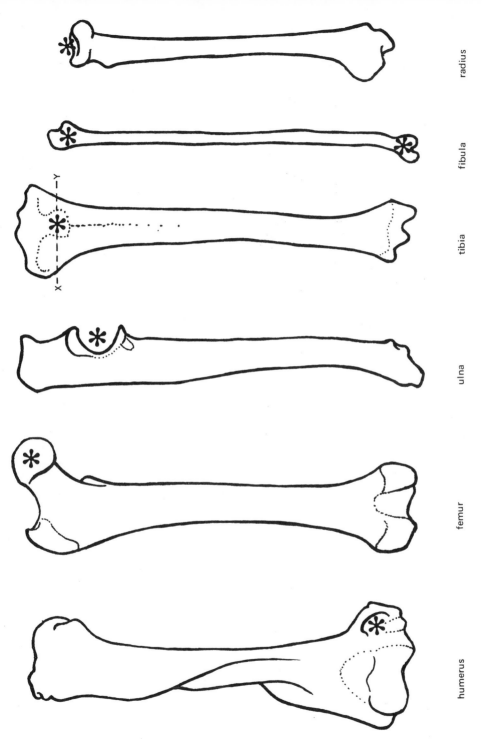

radius

fibula

tibia

ulna

femur

humerus

5 : 78   Limb bone types.

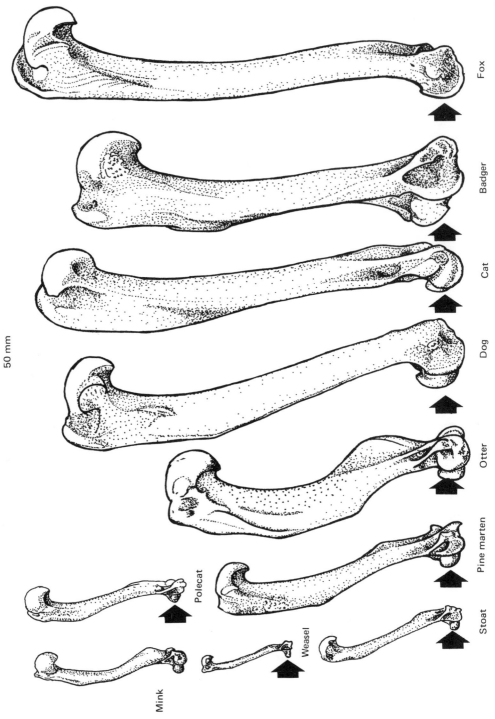

Fox

Badger

Cat

Dog

Otter

Pine marten

Polecat

Stoat

Mink

Weasel

50 mm

5 : 79A   Humeri of the carnivora.

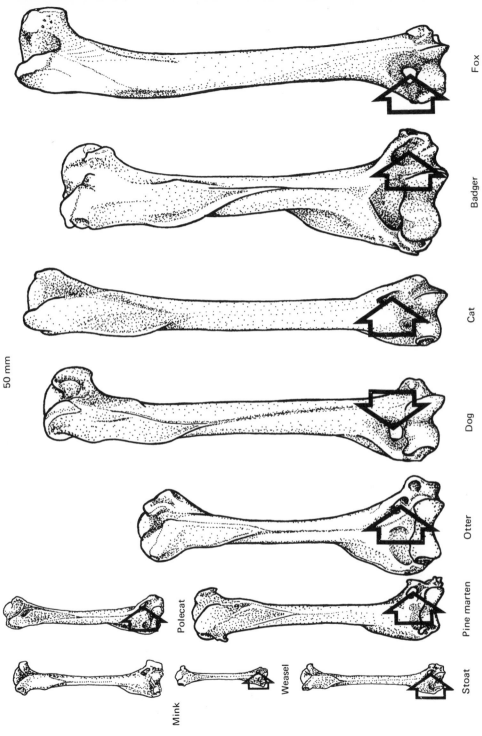

Fox

Badger

Cat

Dog

Otter

50 mm

Pine marten

Polecat

Stoat

Mink

Weasel

5 : 79B   Humeri of the carnivora.

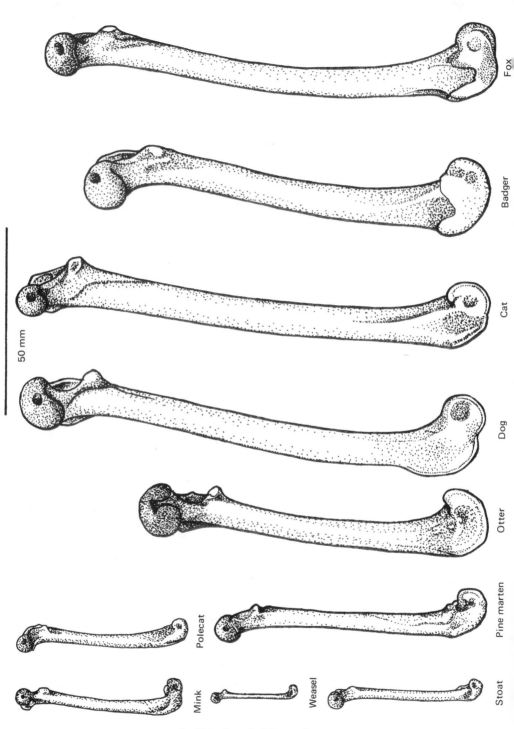

Fox

Badger

50 mm

Cat

Dog

Otter

Pine marten

Polecat

Mink

Weasel

Stoat

5 : 80A   Femuri of the carnivora.

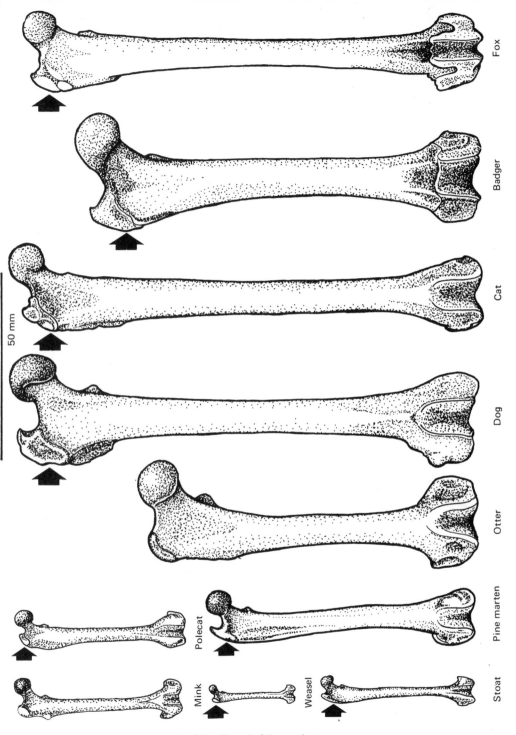

Fox

Badger

Cat

50 mm

Dog

Otter

Pine marten

Polecat

Stoat

Mink

Weasel

5 : 80B   Femuri of the carnivora.

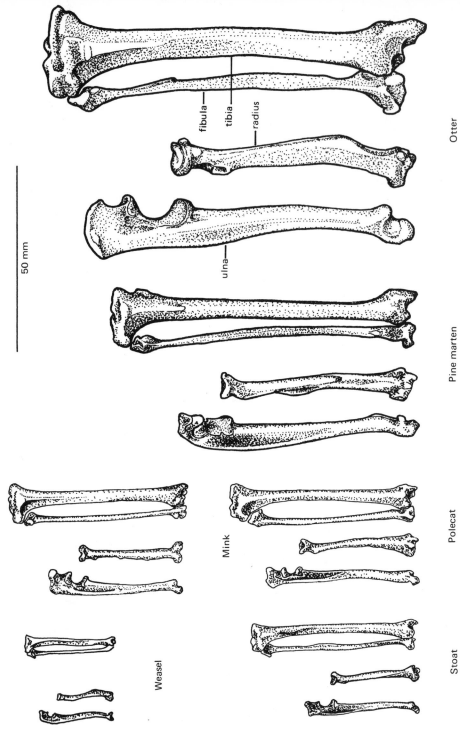

fibula
tibia
radius

50 mm

Otter

ulna

Pine marten

Mink

Polecat

Weasel

Stoat

5 : 81   Tibia and fibula of the Mustelidae.

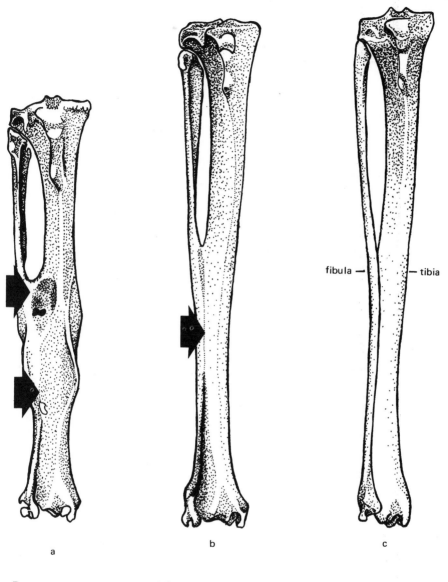

fibula — —— tibia

a

b

c

Fox   natural size

5 : 82   Tibia and fibula of fox showing progressive ossification
(a) Injury causing complete ossification as shown between arrows,
(b) partial ossification, (c) normal condition.

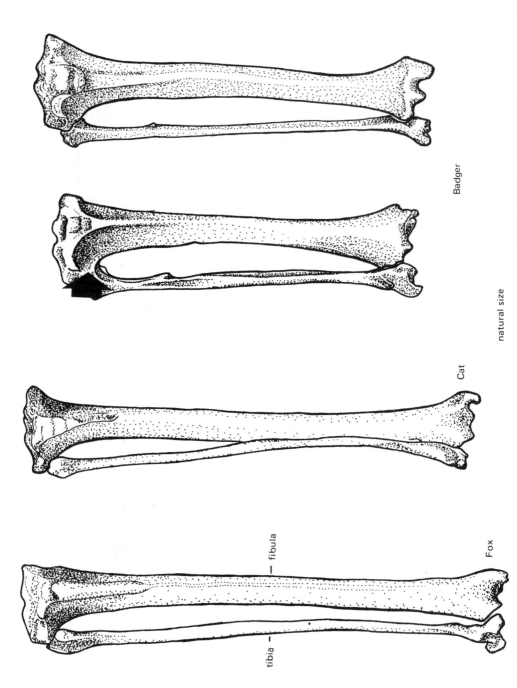

Badger

natural size

Cat

Fox

fibula

tibia

5 : 83A   Tibia and fibula of fox, cat and badger.

256

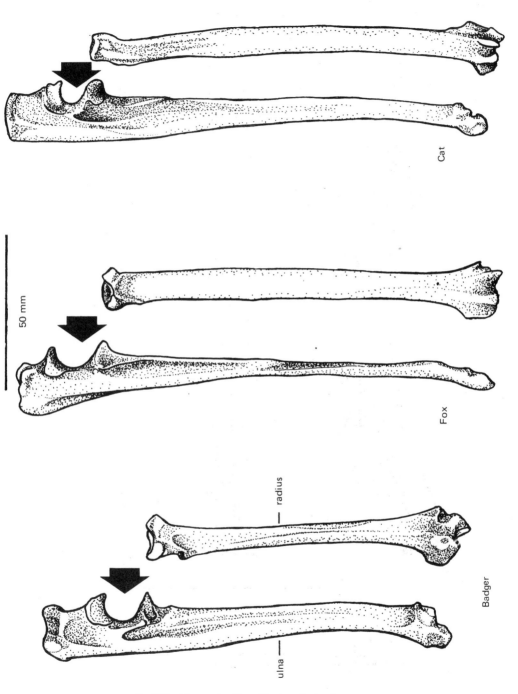

50 mm

Cat

Fox

radius

ulna

Badger

5 : 83B Ulna and radius of badger, fox and cat.

257

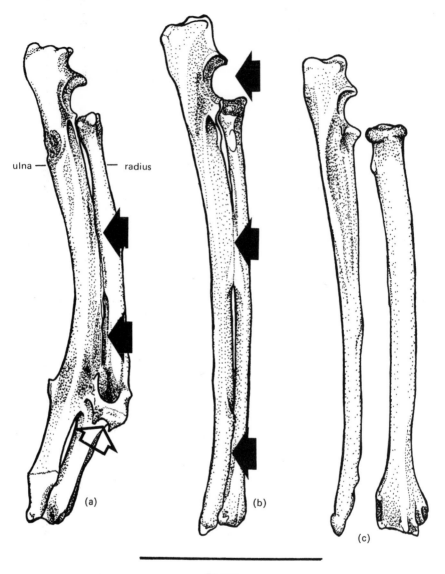

ulna — radius

(a)

(b)

(c)

50 mm

Fox

5 : 84 Ulna and radius of fox (*a*) Injury has caused partial
ossification. Open arrow shows where bone enclosed blood vessel.
(*b*) Partial ossification. (*c*) Normal condition.

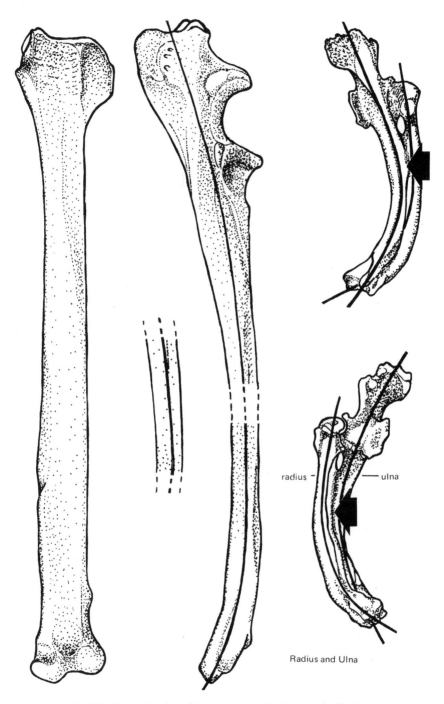

radius   ulna

Radius and Ulna

5 : 85 Ulna and radius of Great Dane and Pekingese. Ossification in Pekingese is normal.

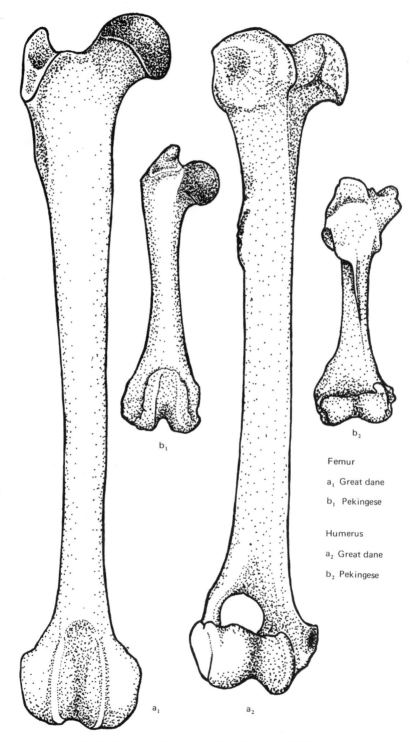

Femur

a₁ Great dane

b₁ Pekingese

Humerus

a₂ Great dane

b₂ Pekingese

5 : 86   Femur and humerus of Great Dane and Pekingese.

5. Bone *very* long and *slender* and having a small knob at both proximal and distal end ... ... Fibula

Bone with a concave depression at extreme proximal end ... Radius

Key to Skulls and Lower Jaws of the Order Carnivora

1. Upper cheek teeth six, lower cheek teeth seven ... ... Canidae 2

Upper cheek teeth fewer than six, lower cheek teeth three to six

Felidae and Mustelidae 3

2. Upper surfaces of post-orbital processes *convex* shape of skull variable (e.g. Alsatian or Bulldog) ... ... *Canis familiaris*

Upper surfaces of post-orbital processes distinctly *concave Vulpes vulpes*

3. Width of brain case (mastoid width) under 75% of zygomatic width. Upper cheek teeth three ... ... Felidae

Felis sylvestris and *domesticus*

Width of brain case over 75% of zygomatic width. Upper cheek teeth three–five lower cheek teeth four–six... ... ... Mustelidae 4

4. Length of skull *over* 100 mm., mandible *over* 65 mm. 5

Length of skull *under* 100 mm., mandible *under* 65 mm. 6

5. Upper molar (last upper cheek tooth) much *larger* than preceding tooth; not elongate. First lower molar crowned (four lower premolars)

Meles meles

Upper molar *equal* to or *smaller* than preceding tooth; transversely elongate. First lower molar carnassial, inter-orbital constriction *extremely* narrow, one-sixth of zygomatic width ... ... *Lutra lutra*

6. Premolars 4/4; greatest width across upper premolars 70% of upper tooth row ... ... *Martes martes*

Premolars 3/3; greatest width across upper premolars equal to upper tooth row ... ... *Mustela* spp. 7

7. Total length of skull *under* 55 mm., sides of muzzle *not* parallel sided, mandible under 32 mm. 8

Total length of skull *over* 55 mm., sides of muzzle are parallel sided, mandible *over* 32 mm. 9

8. Total length of skull *over* 42 mm., lower jaw over 22 mm. *Mustela erminea*

Total length of skull *under* 42 mm., lower jaw under 22 mm.

Mustela nivalis

9. Mastoid width 50% of skull length or *less*. Post-orbital constriction *under* 15 mm. ... ... *Mustela vison*

Mastoid width *over* 50% of skull length. Post-orbital constriction *over* 15 mm. ... ... *Mustela putorius*

Key to Skulls and Lower Jaws of the Order Pinnipedia found in British Waters

1. Alisphenoid canal *present*. Osseus bulla relatively thick-walled and flattened. Canine in upper jaw enormous, becoming powerful tusks. Odobaenidae ... ... *Odobenus rosmarus*

Alisphenoid canal *absent*. Osseus bulla relatively thin-walled and inflated. Canine in upper jaw does not become tusk-like, but remains small

Phocidae 2

261

2. Premaxilla does clearly *not* reach the nasals. Only one incisor in each side of lower jaw ... ... *Cystophora cristata*
   Premaxilla clearly reaches the nasals. Two incisions in each side of lower jaw 3
3. Profile of nasals, frontals and parietals form a straight line
   Halichoerus grypus
   Profile of nasals, frontals and parietals is convex 4
4. Jugal bone short and deep, depth of jugal *not* less than half its length
   Erignathus barbatus
   Jugal bone long and narrow, so that depth of jugal is *less* than half its length 5
5. Bony nasal septum reaches, or almost, the rear edge of the bony palate
   Rear edge of bony palate forms a more or less straight line *or* shallow double arch ... ... *Pagophilus groenlandica*
   Bony septum fails to reach rear of bony palate. Rear edge of palate forms a high arch, usually pointed at the top 6
6. Nasal bones are short and broad, teeth large, infra-orbital foramen small, its diameter 2/3–1/3 that of the alveolus of the upper canine
   Phoca vitulina
   Nasal bones are longer and narrower, teeth small, infra-orbital foramen well developed, approximately the same size as the alveolus of the upper canine ... ... *Phoca hispida*

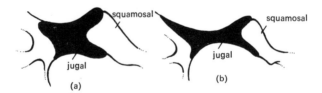

Shape of jugal in (a) *Erignathus* and (b) *Phoca*

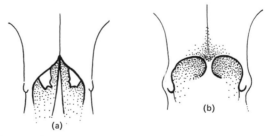

Shape and form of posterior palate in (a) *Phoca* and (b) *Pagophilus*

Key to Skulls and Lower Jaws of Orders Lagomorpha and Rodentia

1. *Two* pairs of incisors in upper jaw ... ... Lagomorpha 2
   One pair of incisors in upper jaw ... ... Rodentia 4

2. Distinct suture between the supra-occipital and the inter-parietal. Posterior nasal opening narrower than or just as wide as the narrowest part of the palatal bridge (length under 86 mm. in wild specimens)

Oryctolagus cuniculus

Supra-occipital fused with parietal. Posterior nasal opening wider than the narrowest part of the palatal bridge ...   .   *Lepus*   3

3. Pulp cavity of first upper incisors reaching the maxillae; fossae of zygomatic arch more anterior   ...   . *Lepus timidus*

Pulp cavities of first upper incisors *not* reaching the maxillae; zygomatic fossa more posterior ...   .*Lepus capensis*

4. Cheek teeth 5/4 first upper cheek tooth very small

Total length of skull 45–65 mm.   ...   .   Squiridae   5

Cheek teeth 3/3 with *rounded cusps* ...   .   Muridae   6

Cheek teeth 3/3 with pattern of *alternating triangles*   ...   Cricetidae   10

Cheek teeth 4/4 with *transverse ridges*   ...   .   Gliridae   13

Cheek teeth 4/4 *without* transverse ridges. Skull very angular and over 50 mm. long; tooth rows diverge behind   ...   ...   Capromyidae

Myocastor coypus

5. Total length of skull *under* 54 mm. Greatest length of nasal bones under 16 mm. ...   .   *Sciurus vulgaris*

Total length of skull *up to* 65 mm. Greatest length of nasal over 17 mm.

Sciurus carolinensis

6. Total length of skull *over* 30 mm. five roots on first upper cheek tooth, four on first lower cheek tooth.

First and second upper cheek tooth with two tubercules on inner sides

Rats   7

Total length of skull *under* 30 mm. ...   .   Mice   8

7. Lateral ridges almost parallel   ...   .   *Rattus norvegicus*

Lateral ridges curved ...   .   *Rattus rattus*

8. Upper incisors notched, first and second upper cheek tooth with two cusps on inner side. Five roots on lower jaw, first upper cheek tooth with three roots   ...   .   · *Mus musculus*

Upper incisors not notched, first and second upper cheek tooth with three cusps on inner side   9

9. Total length of skull *over* 20 mm. Four roots on first upper cheek tooth, six roots on lower jaw ...   .   *Apodemus* spp.

Total length of skull *under* 20 mm. Five roots on first upper cheek tooth. Seven roots on lower jaw   ...   .   *Micromys minutus*

10. Total length of skull *over* 30 mm.   ...   .   *Arvicola terrestris*

Total length of skull *under* 30 mm.   11

11. Angles of cheek teeth rounded and with roots (absent in young animals)

Clethrionomys glareolus

Angles of cheek teeth sharp and without roots   ...   *Microtus* spp.   12

12. Second upper cheek tooth with three inwardly projecting loops

Microtus agrestis

Second upper cheek tooth with two inwardly projecting loops

Microtus arvalis

263

13. Total length of skull *under* 25 mm. First upper and lower tooth very small and only one root. Second upper cheek tooth has five roots. Four teeth together under 5 mm. ... ... *Muscardinus avellanarius*
Total length of skull *over* 25 mm. First upper and lower cheek tooth small but not as small proportionally as in *M. avellanarius*. Three roots on first upper cheek tooth. Four teeth together over 5 mm. ... *Glis glis*

Key to the identification of the os coxae (Pelvic girdle) of British Muridae and Cricetidae

From Brown, J. C. and Twigg, G. I., 'Studies on the pelvis in British Muridae and Cricetidae (Rodentia)', J. Zool., Lond. (1969), **158**, *81–132*

1. Pubis broad and strap-like, pubic symphysis long and curved; obturator foramen flattened, its ischial border little curved and not extending much above the lower rim of the acetabulum ... ... Muridae 2
Pubis narrow, waisted and rounded in cross-section; symphysis short and hooked; obturator foramen high, its ischial border strongly curved with the apex reaching the level of the iliac axis ... ... Cricetidae 5
2. The two ischial rami making a near right-angle; ilioischial axis a straight line 3
The ischial angle an imperfect right-angle; ischial axis at an angle to iliac axis 4
3. Size large, over 35 mm. overall length; gemellus border curved and projecting ... ... *Rattus*
Size medium, about 16–20 mm. overall; gemellus border straight
Apodemus
4. Size medium, about 16–20 mm. long; extremely broad pubis ... *Mus*
Size small, about 10–12 mm. overall; obturator foramen subtriangular in shape ... ... *Micromys*
5. Obturator foramen semicircular, its pubic border more or less straight... 6
Obturator foramen oval or irregular in shape, its pubic border sinuous... 7
6. Pectineal fossa small, usually lacking ilio-pectineal eminence; obturator flange on pubis lacking; obturator foramen a perfect semicircle; overall size 16–18 mm. ... ... *Clethrionomys glareolus*
Pectineal fossa large with marked eminence; obturator flange may be present but obturator border of pubis almost straight; overall size about 20 mm. ... ... *Clethrionomys glareolus skomerensis*
7. Size large, up to 43 mm. overall; obturator flange present; obturator foramen asymmetrically oval, large, shallow pectineal fossa with well-developed ilio-pectineal eminence... ... ... *Arvicola terrestris*
Size medium; obturator flange hypertrophied with marked obturator notch; pectineal fossa small; obturator foramen irregular (fig-shaped)... 8
8. Size less than 20 mm. ... ... *Microtus agrestis*
Size 20–25 mm., very robust ... ... *Microtus orcadensis*

Key to Scapulae found in Bird Pellets

1. Spine almost absent acromion and metacromion absent.

Posterior end only twice as wide as an anterior end
Length 2.5 cms. ... ... *Talpa europaea*
Spine present 2
2. Acromion and Metacromion process always *present*
Acromion process always present, metacromion process always *absent* ... 6
3. Acromion and Metacromion very prominent and *almost* equal in width.
Length under 10 mm. ... ... Shrews
Acromion and Metacromion *not* equal in width 4
4. Acromion more prominent than Metacromion and triangular in shape.
Length of scapular 45 mm. Coracoid spur medium in length
Erinaceus europaeus
Metacromion more prominent than acromion process. Width of scapulae
almost equal to length... 5
5. Scapula *under* 20 mm. ... ... *Mustela nivalis*
Scapula *over* 20 mm. ... ... *Mustela erminea*
6. Coracoid spur *very* prominent 7
Coracoid spur *not* very prominent 10
7. Dorsal and ventral edges parallel. Length 9–16 mm. ... Chiroptera
Dorsal and ventral edges not parallel 8
8. False spine on ventral edge. Length 30 mm. ... ... *Sciurus* sp.
No false spine present. Post-scapula and pre-scapula fossa triangular in
outline. Length 10–20 mm. ... ... Dormice 9
9. Scapula 20 mm. or *over* ... ... *Glis glis*
Scapula 10 mm. **or** *less* ... ... *Muscardinus avellanarius*
10. Length 20 mm. or *over* coracoid spur not developed... ... *Rattus* spp.
Length *under* 10 mm. coracoid spur small but well-developed 11
11. Dorsal and ventral edges parallel but curved along their length; being convex dorsally and concave ventrally.
Length 10 mm. or under ... *Mus. Micromys* and *Apodemus* spp.
Dorsal and ventral edges radiating out from just above glenoid cavity and
so forming the apex of an inverted triangle. 12
12. Length *over* 15 mm. ... ... *Arvicola terrestris*
Length *under* 12 mm. ... ... *Microtus* and *Clethrionomys* spp.

Identification of the Cetacea (B.M.N.H.)

1. Whalebone present on palate. Teeth absent. Lower jaw very wide, its
halves arched outwards ... ... Whalebone Whales 2
Whalebone absent. Teeth present, though sometimes concealed beneath
the gum. Lower jaw narrow, at least in front ... Toothed Whales 7

WHALEBONE WHALES
2. Lower surface of throat not grooved. No back fin. Mouth and upper
border of lower lip much arched. Whalebone blades long, up to 6–9 feet
Atlantic Right Whale
Lower surface of throat with numerous parallel grooves 3

3. Flippers extremely long, nearly one-third the length of the animal, some-times white externally, with a scalloped lower margin ... Humpback

Flippers much less than one-third the total length, not scalloped below

Rorquals 4

4. Whalebone, yellowish white or slate-coloured, or both 5

Whalebone black or nearly black 6

5. Size, up to 70 feet. Whalebone, yellow and slate-coloured, except at the front of the right side, where it is white; its hairy fringes, white or yellowish

Tail-flukes white below ... ... Common Fin Whale

Size, up to 30 feet. Whalebone and its hairy fringes, all white or yellowish.

A white region on outer side of flipper ... ... Lesser Rorqual

6. Size, up to 85 feet. Whalebone very black, with coarse black hairs

Blue Whale

Size, up to 50 feet. Whalebone mostly dark, with very fine, white, curling, silky hairs. Tail-flukes not white below ... ... Sei Whale

TOOTHED WHALES

7. Size, that of a large whale. Head square in side view. Lower jaw very nar-row, with many large teeth, several inches long. Upper jaw toothless or with a few irregular teeth, smaller than in lower jaw Sperm Whale 8

Not exceeding about 30 feet in length, and often much smaller

8. Back fin absent 9

Back fin present 10

9. Head short, with prominent 'forehead'. Colour greyish, with black spots or mottlings. Either without visible teeth (females), or with a tusk-like tooth, several feet long, spirally twisted, projecting forwards from the front of the upper jaw (males), exceptionally with two spiral tusks Narwhal

Colour, white all over (greyish-brown in young individuals), 8–10 pairs of teeth in each jaw ... ... White Whale

10. Teeth confined to the lower jaw, or apparently absent 11

Teeth in both jaws 15

11. Back fin large, near middle of body. Teeth 2–7 pairs, at front end of lower jaw ... ... Risso's Dolphin

Back fin considerably behind middle of body. Front end of jaws narrow. Two grooves on throat Whales of the 'Bottle-nosed' type 12

12. Size large, up to 25–30 feet. Distance from tip of snout to blowhole one-fifth to one-seventh the total length. 'Forehead' very prominent. Teeth (one to two pairs) at tip of lower jaw, usually concealed Bottle-nosed Whale

Distance from tip of snout to blowhole less than one-seventh the total length 13

13. Size large, up to 26 feet. Distance from tip of snout to blowhole one-tenth to one-eighth the total length. 'Forehead' not specially prominent. Teeth one pair at tip of lower jaw, massive in males (diameter 1 inch), concealed in females ... ... Culver's Whale

Size smaller, not exceeding 20 feet. Beak long 14

14. Length about 15 feet. Colour mostly black, usually with white marks. One

pair of teeth at middle of length of lower jaw, conspicuous and triangular
in males, concealed in females ...   .   Sowerby's Whale
Size rather larger. Colour not satisfactorily known. One pair of teeth at tip
of lower jaw, conspicuous and flattened sideways in males, concealed in
females ...   .   True's Beaked Whale
15. Size large, 15–30 feet in adults. Teeth 8–13 pairs in each jaw   16
    Seldom exceeding 12 feet, usually less than 9 feet. Teeth not more than $\frac{1}{2}$
    inch in diameter, more than 15 pairs   18
16. 'Forehead' greatly swollen, overhanging the tip of the very short beak.
    Flippers narrow, about one-fifth of the total length. Colour black, with
    only a small amount of white on lower surface. Teeth, 8–12 pairs in each
    jaw, less than $\frac{1}{2}$ inch in diameter   ...   .   Pilot Whale
    'Forehead' not prominent. Teeth, 10–13 pairs in each jaw, at least $\frac{3}{4}$ inch in
    diameter...   17
17. Colour conspicuously black and white (or yellow). Flippers broad, not
    pointed. Teeth about 1 inch in diameter   ...   .   Killer
    Colour black all over. Flippers narrow and pointed. Teeth as in the killer
                                                                    False Killer
18. Size up to $5\frac{1}{2}$ feet. Teeth about 21–24 pairs in each jaw, flattened sideways,
    with spade-shaped crowns. Beak not distinguishable   Common Porpoise
    Size larger, teeth conical, the crowns not flattened sideways. Beak distinct   19
19. Length up to 12 feet. Beak about 3 inches long in middle line. Teeth large,
    20–25 pairs in each jaw; diameter, $\frac{3}{8}$–$\frac{1}{2}$ inch   Bottle-nosed Dolphin
    Teeth not exceeding $\frac{1}{4}$ inch in diameter   20
20. Beak about 2 inches long in middle line. Length, 9–10 feet...   21
    Beak up to 6 inches in middle line. Teeth, 40–50 pairs in each jaw, about
    1/10 inch in diameter. Length up to 7 feet   22
21. Upper lip white. Dark colour of flippers continuous with that of body,
    their lower margin not much curved. Teeth about 25 pairs in each jaw;
    diameter, $\frac{1}{4}$ inch   ...   .   White-beaked Dolphin
    Upper lip black. Flippers, with strongly curved lower margin, arising from
    white part of body, usually connected with dark part by a narrow dark
    streak. A conspicuous white region on each side, behind the back-fin.
    Teeth 30–40 pairs in each jaw; diameter, 3/16 inch   White-sided Dolphin
22. A well-marked, narrow dark band of pigment extending from the eye along
    the flank and curving down to the vent, with a subsidiary branch in the
    region of the flipper insertion...   ...   ...   Euphrosyne Dolphin
    This band wanting, but an arrangement of yellowish, white and dark
    bands on the sides of the body   ...   .   Common Dolphin

In addition to Sowerby's Whale and True's Beaked Whale, the two species of
Mesplodon mentioned in (14), it is probable that a third species (*M. europaeus*),
perhaps reaching 20 feet in length, will be recorded as British. Its external appearance is not well known.

TABLE I

Owl pellet débris collected from floor of disused cottage near Vaynol Park, Caernarvonshire on 5-5-64. Cottage sited on the edge of grazing fields above a pine wood. No other houses in sight, nearest water 100 yds. away at bottom of valley in an overgrown stream.

Species	Crania	Rt. dentary	Lt. dentary	Min. total
Microtus agrestis	130	138	127	138
Clethrionomys glareolus	58	46	50	58
Apodemus sp.	61	70	75	75
Mus musculus	5	7	7	7
Micromys minutus	1	3	3	3
Rattus norvegicus	23	16	22	23
Oryctolagus cuniculus (young)	—	—	1	1
Talpa europaea	2	2	2	2
Sorex araneus	162	126	109	162
Sorex minutus	38	21	16	38
Neomys fodiens	12	10	11	12
Pipistrellus pipistrellus	—	1	—	1
Passer sp? (Bird)	1	—	—	1
Rana temporaria (Frog)	2	—	—	2

Geotrupes (dung beetle),
at least two individuals.

There are every year several hundred thousands of bottles lost from circulation, many of which are discarded in the countryside.

A proportion of these, mainly milk bottles, trap small mammals. These enter through the neck, and cannot get out again. Checking discarded bottles therefore is a good way of collecting mammal records and specimens. So far following spp. found. (Information: Dr. P. A. Morris.)

Common shrew	Harvest mouse	
Pigmy shrew	Yellow-necked mouse	
Water shrew	Bank vole	
Scilly shrew	Short-tailed vole	The Common shrew and Bank vole are most
Brown rat	Stoat	commonly found.
House mouse		
Wood mouse		

They are found in all parts of Britain and its islands, e.g. 1 vole found down a cave, 1 Wood mouse found 3,000 ft. up Snowdon. Usually only 1 or 2 per bottle; max. so far 28 in a quart milk bottle in Essex.

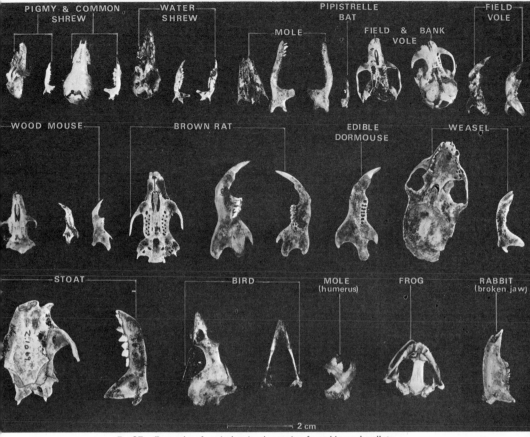

PIGMY & COMMON SHREW — WATER SHREW — MOLE — PIPISTRELLE BAT — FIELD & BANK VOLE — FIELD VOLE

WOOD MOUSE — BROWN RAT — EDIBLE DORMOUSE — WEASEL

STOAT — BIRD — MOLE (humerus) — FROG — RABBIT (broken jaw)

— 2 cm

5 : 87   Example of varied animal remains found in owl pellets.

A

C

G

D

H

B   E   F   J   I

⊢ 10 cms.

5 : 88   Material from one owl pellet.

A Skull jaws and teeth. B Scapulas and pelvis. C Skull bones. D Humeri, ulna and radii.
E Femur and tibia and fibula. F Sacrum. G Vertebrae. H Ribs. I Bones of feet.
J Pelvis, sacrum and longbones of shrew.

TABLE IIa

Analysis of Barn owl (*Tyto alba*) pellets from Claremont, Esher, Surrey. Collected and analysed by D. W. Yalden, P. A. Morris and W. G. Teagle.

Sample 'A' = two batches from Claremont, Esher, Surrey, 1961. Analysed by W. G. Teagle (see London nat. 42).

Sample 'B' = one batch from same roost analysed by P. A. Morris and D. W. Yalden. Collected in 1964, after horses had grazed and trampled the fields making them particularly unsuitable for *Microtus spp*. Note decrease in numbers of this sp. taken and increase in numbers of open-ranging *spp*. (rats and mice). Note also that numbers of Harvest mouse taken has increased, probably because these did not live on the field itself, but in the hedgerows which were not trampled by the horses.

All figures given are 'PREY UNITS', not actual numbers. Percentages calculated on basis of this. (See Southern, Ibis 96.)

Species	'A' Prey Units	% age	'B' Prey Units	% age
Microtus agrestis	41.0	59.83	71.0	32.70
Clethrionomys glareolus	4.5	6.92	41.0	20.08
Apodemus spp.*	12.0	17.88	48.0	23.50
Mus musculus	6.0	8.34	5.0	2.45
Micromys minutus	0.3	0.41	3.3	1.61
Rattus norvegicus	0.00	0.00	20.0	9.98
Sorex araneus	3.0	4.42	13.0	6.36
Sorex minutus	0.9	1.25	3.2	1.57
Neomys fodiens	0.75	1.10	0.75	0.37

* Both the Wood mouse *A. sylvaticus* and the Yellow-necked mouse *A. flavicolus* occur in the neighbourhood, and the skulls cannot always be separated with certainty.

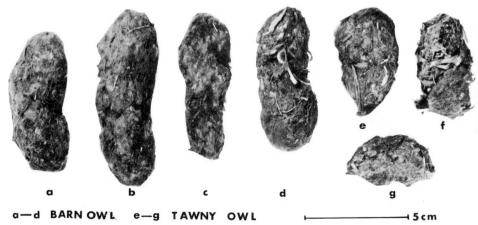

a—d BARN OWL   e—g TAWNY OWL   ⊢————————⊣ 5 cm

5.89 Photograph of complete owl pellets.

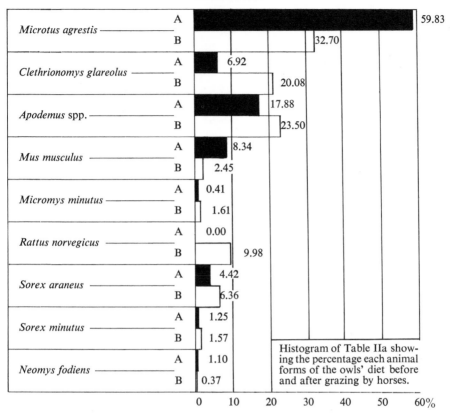

Microtus agrestis	A	59.83
	B	32.70
Clethrionomys glareolus	A	6.92
	B	20.08
Apodemus spp.	A	17.88
	B	23.50
Mus musculus	A	8.34
	B	2.45
Micromys minutus	A	0.41
	B	1.61
Rattus norvegicus	A	0.00
	B	9.98
Sorex araneus	A	4.42
	B	6.36
Sorex minutus	A	1.25
	B	1.57
Neomys fodiens	A	1.10
	B	0.37

0 10 20 30 40 50 60%

Histogram of Table IIa show-ing the percentage each animal forms of the owls' diet before and after grazing by horses.

TABLE III

Analysis of Barn owl (*Tyto alba*) pellets from Tavistock, Devon.
Collected and analysed by Mr. J. R. Cox.
Sample 1
Collected at: Downhouse Farm, Tavistock, Devon.   Date: May 1965.
No. of pellets: 42 from base of ash tree, ⎫
                  and 6 from small stone shed. ⎬ None more than 2 months old.
                                          ⎭
Sample 2
Collected at: Burnshall Farm, Chillaton, Devon.   Date: April 1965.
No. of pellets: About 18.
    The diet of the Barn owl is made up as follows:
1. Primary prey: Short-tailed vole and Common shrew.
2. Secondary prey: (regularly eaten in small numbers):
    Bank vole, Wood mouse, Pygmy shrew.
3. Occasionally eaten in small numbers:
    House mouse, Water shrew, frog, beetles (*Melolontha, Geotrupes, Elateridae*).
    Birds (from warbler size to starling).

4. Rarely eaten:—Harvest mouse, Brown rat, mole, bats, earthworms.

N.B. Another record of Natterer's bat* in Barn owl pellets, found on a farm one mile west of Tavistock. Caught sometime in September or October 1965. Information from Mr. J. R. Cox.

SAMPLE 1

Contents	No.	Prey Units	P.U. %	
Short-tailed vole	82	82.0	56.70	Voles 61.54%
Bank vole	7	7.0	4.84	
Wood mouse	19	19.0	13.40	Mice 13.57%
Harvest mouse	1	0.25	0.17	
Common shrew	53	26.50	18.32	
Water shrew	2	1.50	1.04	Shrews 22.40%
Pygmy shrew	22	4.40	3.04	
*Noctule bat	1	1.0	0.69	
Birds	2	2.0	1.38	
Frog	1	1.0	0.69	

Notes: Bird, one is starling, and one robin-size with slim pointed bill.
For 'Prey units' see H. N. Southern's work on Tawny owls.

SAMPLE 2

Contents	No.	Prey Units	P.U. %	
Short-tailed vole	34	34.0	54.31	Voles 57.50%
Bank vole	2	2.0	3.19	
Wood mouse	4	4.0	6.39	Mice 6.39%
Common shrew	27	13.5	21.59	
Water shrew	2	1.5	2.39	Shrews 26.53%
Pygmy shrew	8	1.6	2.55	
Brown rat	1	5.0	7.98	
*Natterer's bat	1	1.0	1.59	

Notes: Only one fresh pellet – the rest (including the one containing the bat) were up to six months old, but no older. One very large pellet contained remains of 14 mammals: 5 Pygmy shrews, 5 Common shrews, 4 Short-tailed voles.

* Identified at the British Museum (Natural History).

TABLE IV

Analysis of Barn owl (*Tyto alba*) pellets from windmill (G.R. 365176) on the River Ant about one mile from Ludham Bridge, Norfolk Broads. Collected and analysed by M. J. Lawrence.

Number of pellets 41 – most were not fresh.   Date: September 1965.

Species	Skulls	Rt. dentary	Lt. dentary	Min. total
Microtus agrestis	85	85	88	88
Apodémus sp.*	1	1	1	1
Rattus norvegicus	3	3	3	3
Sorex araneus	6	8	5	8
Sorex minutus	1	2	1	2
Rana sp. (frog)	†ilium (pelvis bone) and parasphenoid (skull bone)			

* Species not known.   † See Fig. 5:68, *c.*

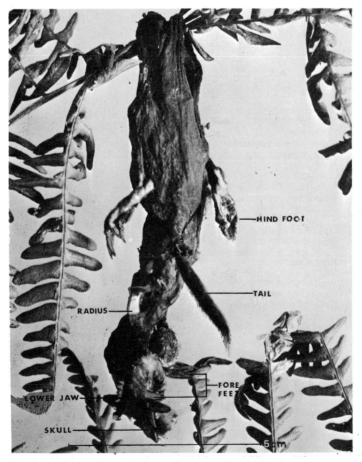

5 : 90 An almost complete mole, partly digested by an owl and regurgitated by the animal from its tree roost. It was found in ferns, in the position shown in the photograph, about four feet from the ground Owl pellets were also found on the ground underneath the ferns.

Date	Material	Authority
Jan. 1	Vegetable remains. Little recognisable.	E. G. N.
,, 6	Rabbit fur from old rabbit. Two or three small bird feathers. Broken fragments of rodent teeth.	,,
,, 8	A great quantity of vegetable material including much grass, leaves, acorns (few).	,,
,, 19	Entirely vegetable remains, much of it grass.	,,
Feb. 9	Vegetable remains. Little recognisable.	,,
,, 20	Vegetable remains. Little recognisable.	,,
March 5	Remains of thorax and back of adult rabbit – ribs and vertebrae only.	,,
,, 10	Beetle elytra and legs. Some vegetable matter.	,,
,, 21	Beetle elytra. Vegetable matter.	,,
,, 26	Large quantity of vegetable matter, mainly grass. One beetle.	,,
April 5	Beetles. Rabbit fur. Vegetable matter. Beetles. Rabbit fur. Broken fragments of rabbit skull.	,,
,, 27	Large number of beetles including *Geotrupes, Melolontha, Carabus.* Young rabbit fur. Leg bones of young rabbit. Small proportion of vegetable matter.	,,
,, ?	Fragments of scaly skin of small bird's foot. Quantity of fragments of small jaw bones with teeth 11 and 16 mm. long. Incisor teeth of young rabbits.	Gwion Davies
May 8	Beetles. Vegetable remains in large amounts.	E. G. N.
,, 16	Little recognisable. Some vegetable matter.	,,
June 10	Much fibrous vegetable matter.	,,
,, 20	Little recognisable.	,,
,, 26	Rabbit fur, beetle elytra.	,,
July 2	Little recognisable. Some plant matter.	,,
,, 25	Rabbit fur, some plant matter.	,,
,, 31	Beetle elytra. Rabbit fur.	,,
Aug. 3	Oats. Few beetle elytra.	,,
,, 5	Oats. Beetle elytra.	,,
,, 6	Corn. Rabbit fur. Beetles.	,,
,, 10	Beetles and corn.	,,
,, 11	Beetles. Corn. Rabbit fur.	,,
,, 13	Beetles. Rabbit fur.	,,
,, 25	Beetles. Much plant material.	,,
,, ?	Great quantity of beetle remains (*Geotrupes*). Three or four larva skins. Few incisors of very young rabbits. A 1-cm. bird quill. Quantity of short rabbit fur. Plant débris including largely husks of wheat and oats.	Gwion Davies
Sept. 1	Plant material. Beetles. Rabbit fur.	,,
,, 2	Corn husks.	,,
,, 10	Blackberries much in evidence. Beetles.	,,
,, 10	Beech. mast. Acorns.	,,
,, 12	Beetles, mainly *Geotrupes*.	,,
,, 15	Beetles. Rabbit fur.	,,
Oct. 3	Beetles in numbers.	,,
,, 12	Vegetable matter mainly. Few beetles.	,,
,, 24	Vegetable remains. Little recognisable.	,,

Date	Material	Authority
Nov. 18	Vegetable remains. Little recognisable.	Gwion Davies
Dec. 10	Vegetable matter.	,,
,, 21	Vegetable matter.	,,
,, 23	Vegetable matter mainly. Woodlice.	,,
,, 30	Vegetable matter.	,,
,, ?	Mainly vegetable remains and rabbit hair. Also acorn shells. Skin of bird's foot with toes 19 and 15 mm. long. Bird's quill 14 mm. × 1 mm. About 8.6 sq. cms. of broken white eggshell, half the thickness of hen's egg. A few splintered bird bones 5 mm. in diameter and a larva skin.	

**Analysis of fifty fox droppings
taken during every month of the
year (1945) on Dartmoor.
Collected and analysed by H. G. Hurrell.**

Per cent by
volume

60......Rabbit (pre-myxomatosis)

16......Beetles

6......Mice

8......Sheep's wool

10......Various: Grass, leaves, earth,
etc. hedgehog fur occasionally.
One domestic hen.

_____

100

_____

The beetle contents varied from only 5 per cent in winter to as much as 95 per cent in September. On one occasion a hedgehog quill had passed right through a fox and become quite soft. The above results do not happen to show the extent to which berries are eaten. Some droppings in summer may contain large quantities of whortleberries.

The following have been recorded from fox faecal pellets (droppings) by H. N. Southern and J. S. Watson.

Rabbit
Apodemus sp.
Microtus agrestis
Small birds
Poultry
Insects
Vegetable remains

For further reading see *Summer food of
the Red Fox* (Vulpes vulpes) *in Great
Britain: a preliminary report* by
H. N. Southern and J. S. Watson.

TABLE SHOWING PREY-PREDATOR RELATIONSHIPS.

PREY	Fox	Pine Marten	Stoat	Weasel	Polecat	Badger	Otter	Wild Cat	Brown Rat	Grey Squirrel	Hedgehog	Dog	Cat	Found in bird pellets
Hedgehog	−			−	−						−			Tawny owl
Mole	−		−	−	−									Tawny owl
Common shrew			?	−				−					−	Barn owl
Pygmy shrew			?	−									−	Short-eared and Long-eared owl
Water shrew			?	−									−	Sparrow hawk
Pine marten	▮													
Stoat	▮					−								Hawks
Weasel	▬	▬	▬		▮	▬							−	Owls
Polecat	?													
Rabbit	−	−	−	−	−	−	−	−	▬		−			Golden eagle
Brown hare	−	?	−	▮			−				−			Buzzards
Mountain hare	−	−	−				−				−			Hawks
Red squirrel	?	−						−		−				Owls
Grey squirrel	▬		−	▬										Hen-harrier
Bank vole			−	−	−	−				−			−	Hawks, Owls
Water vole		−	−		−	−							−	Harriers Buzzards
Field vole	−	−	−	−	−	−		−			−		−	Heron
Orkney vole													−	Short-eared owl
Harvest mouse			−	−						−			−	Tawny owl
Wood mouse	−	−	−	−	−	−		−	−		−		−	Barn owl
Yellow-necked mouse	−		−	−	−	−					−		−	Short-eared and Long-eared owl
House mouse			−	−				−		−			−	Little owl
Black rat	−		−	−	−	−		−				−	−	Kestrel
Brown rat	−	−	−	−	−	−	−					−	−	Sparrow hawk
Edible dormouse			−	−				−						Harriers
Dormouse	−				−									Heron
Coypu (young)	?			−		−	−							Owls, Hawks
Red deer (calves)	▬							−						Golden eagle
Sika? (young)	?													?
Fallow deer (fawn)	−													White-tailed and Golden eagle
Roe deer (young)	−						−							
Chinese Water deer?	?													?
Muntjacs?	?													
Pipistrelle bat														
Noctule bat														Barn owl
Natterer's bat														
Greater horseshoe bat														Tawny owl

▬ = Rare.   ▮ = Very rare.   − = Common.

This table illustrates prey-predator relationships. It represents graphically the likelihood of the remains of a given mammal species being found in close proximity to a particular predator's dwelling place. The smaller mammal remains will be found more commonly in the pellets of birds of prey. While this table is as comprehensive as possible, it does not exhaust all the possible prey-predator relationships.

	Fox	Pine marten	Mink	Stoat	Weasel	Polecat	Badger	Otter	Wild cat
FEEDING TABLE. No. 1 CARNIVORES.									
CARCASES									
(a) Teeth marks with traces of saliva.	■								
(b) Claw lacerations only.									■
(c) Fish with mouthful removed from shoulder, e.g. Salmon or Trout.								■	
(d) Whole or partially eaten voles and field mice outside small hole.					■	■			
(e) Large animal, head torn off, often with brain only eaten, e.g. lamb.								■	
(f) Decapitated remains, e.g. fowl.	■								
(g) Fish remains with tail intact.		?							■
(h) Hedgehog skin turned inside out.	■						■		
(i) Fish remains on river bank.			■			■		■	
(j) Remains (e.g. feet, tail, head and entrails) of small mammals in den.						■			
(k) Large carcase, not necessarily concealed, e.g. Rabbit.							■		
(l) Carcase with bones intact, e.g. Mallard.								■	
(m) Carcase on promontory or tree forks, e.g. Squirrel.		■							
(n) Skulls bitten through at base.					■	■			
GENERAL SIGNS									
(a) Crushed bones, fur and feathers outside large hole.	■								
(b) Deep barking of Sycamore and Beech at ground level.							○		
(c) Shallow pits exposing broken bulbs, fleshy roots, etc.									
(d) Wasp nests dug out.									
(e) Bee-hives torn open.		■							
(f) Crushed remains of marine and freshwater crustaceans and molluscs, often in large quantities.								■	
(g) Stored animal corpses, e.g. small mammals, birds and frogs.						■			

FEEDING TABLE. No. 2
RODENTS.

	Water vole	Voles	Wood mouse	Mice	Dormouse	Squirrel	Thrush	Woodpecker, etc.	Crossbill	Blackbird, etc.	Slugs
CONES											
(a) Scales stripped off.						■					
(b) Isolated piles of scales.						■					
(c) Cones on ground with ends of scales split open.									■		
(d) Cones on ground with scales nibbled irregularly.			■	■							
NUTS											
(a) Very neat hole at side or end of nut.					■						
(b) Irregular (normally) hole anywhere on surface.			■								
(c) Nut split into two holes.						■					
(d) Nut split and jammed into bark crevices.								■			
ACORNS and NUTS											
(a) Acorns found on tree stump in large numbers and split open.						■					
(b) Number of berries hidden, e.g. hollow trunks.			■								
(c) Berries nibbled on branches.			■	■							
(d) Berries scattered under tree with 'peck' marks.										■	
FOLIAGE											
(a) Sprigs of Oak, Hazel, Sweet Chestnut, Beech, Hornbeam, Scots Pine and Larch, lying under tree stripped.						■					
(b) Honeysuckle stripped of bark and leaves.					■						
(c) Superficial barking over small areas.			■								
(d) Deep barking, from first branches.						■					
(e) Areas of grass cropped around holes on river bank.	■										
(f) Piles of reeds or rushes bitten into small lengths at water edge.	■										
SNAIL SHELLS								□			
(a) Smashed shells near large stone.								■			
(b) Neatly nibbled through spiral.			■								
FUNGI											
(a) Nibbled on cap, teeth marks.			■			■					
(b) Areas eaten, no teeth marks.											■

278

The introduction of new species of mammals to Britain

From time to time species of mammals have been introduced, accidentally or deliberately, into our fauna. Many of these have established themselves as successful wild populations and are now considered as natives. Below is a list of introductions. Some species are now extinct while the Reindeer represents a reintroduction of a once indigenous species.

Scilly Shrew (1925)
American Mink (1950)
Rabbit (12th century)
Brown Rat (1730)
Black Rat (12th century)
House Mouse (Roman)
Yellow-necked Mouse (1894)
Golden Hamster (1960)
Common Vole (1805)
Bennett's Wallaby (1940's)

Grey Squirrel (1890)
Edible Dormouse (1890)
*Musk Rat (1929–37)
Coypu (1940)
Fallow Deer (Roman times)
Sika Deer (1900)
Chinese Water Deer (after 1900)
Reindeer (1952)
Chinese Muntjac (after 1900)
*Hog Deer (1940–50)
*Indian Muntjac (after 1900)
*Axis Deer (1940–50's)
*White-tailed Deer (1940's)

*These species have become extinct either because they could not adapt to environmental conditions, or because of a campaign of extermination.

The Golden Hamster and Bennett's Wallaby are two recent escapes. The Golden Hamster may well become a pest and any discovery of this species should be reported to the authorities. The Wallaby does not seem to be causing any harmful effects.

Introductions have had devastating effects in this and other countries because they often have no natural enemies and multiply to pest proportions. However, many of these species have now been absorbed into our fauna and it is difficult to realise just how many species are, like the British themselves, not truly British.

The most exotic species in the British Fauna is Bennett's Wallaby. This species belongs to the Marsupials which are restricted to Australia and parts of the Americas. The group is characterised by the possession of a pouch in which the young are reared.

A CHECK LIST OF BRITISH MAMMALS

Infraclass: Metatheria
Order Marsupialia (Marsupials)
Macropus rufogriseus (Desmarest, 1817) *Wallaby

Infraclass: Eutheria
Order Insectivora (Insectivores)
Family: ERINACEIDAE
Erinaceus europaeus (Linnaeus, 1758) Hedgehog
Family: TALPIDAE
Talpa europaea (Linnaeus, 1758) Mole

Family: SORICIDAE
Sorex araneus (Linnaeus, 1758)	Common Shrew
Sorex minutus (Linnaeus, 1758)	Pygmy Shrew
Neomys fodiens (Pennant, 1771)	Water Shrew
Crocidura suaveolens (Pallas, 1811)	***Lesser White-toothed Shrew
Crocidura russula (Hermann, 1780)	***Greater White-toothed Shrew

Order Chiroptera (Bats)
Family: RHINOLOPHIDAE
Rhinolophus ferrumequinum (Schreber, 1774)	Greater Horseshoe Bat
Rhinolophus hipposideros (Bechstein, 1800)	Lesser Horseshoe Bat

Family: VESPERTILIONIDAE
Myotis myotis (Borkhausen, 1797)	**Mouse-eared Bat
Myotis mystacinus (Kuhl, 1819)	Whiskered Bat
Myotis nattereri (Kuhl, 1818)	Natterer's Bat
Myotis bechsteini (Kuhl, 1818)	Bechstein's Bat
Myotis daubentoni (Kuhl, 1819)	Daubenton's Bat
Vespertilio murinus (Linnaeus, 1758)	Part-coloured Bat
Eptesicus serotinus (Schreber, 1774)	Serotine Bat
Nyctalus noctula (Schreber, 1774)	Noctule Bat
Nyctalus leisleri (Kuhl, 1818)	Leisler's Bat
Pipistrellus pipistrellus (Schreber, 1774)	Common Pipistrelle
Pipistrellus nathusii (Kayserling and Blasius 1839)	Nathusis Pipistrelle
Barbastella barbastellus (Schreber, 1774)	Barbastelle
Plecotus auritus (Linnaeus, 1758)	Common Long-eared Bat
Plecotus austriacus (Fischer, 1829)	***Grey Long-eared Bat

Order Carnivora (Carnivores)
Family: CANIDAE
Vulpes vulpes (Linnaeus, 1758)	Fox

Family: MUSTELIDAE
Martes martes (Linnaeus, 1758)	Pine Marten
Mustela erminea (Linnaeus, 1758)	Stoat
Mustela nivalis (Linnaeus, 1766)	Weasel
Mustela putorius (Linnaeus, 1758)	Polecat Domestic var. Ferret
Mustela vison (Schreber, 1758)	*American Mink
Meles meles (Linnaeus, 1758)	Badger
Lutra lutra (Linnaeus, 1758)	Otter

Family: FELIDAE
Felis sylvestris (Schreber, 1777)	Scottish Wild Cat

Order Pinnipedia (Seals)
Family: PHOCIDAE
Halichoerus grypus (Fabricius, 1791)	Grey Seal
Phoca vitulina (Linnaeus, 1758)	Common Seal
Phoca hispida (Schreber, 1775)	**Ringed Seal

Pagophilus groenlandica (Erxleben 1777)	**Harp Seal
Erignathus barbatus (Erxleben, 1777)	**Bearded Seal
Cystophora cristata (Erxleben, 1777)	**Hooded Seal
Family: ODOBENIDAE	
Odobenus rosmarus (Linnaeus, 1758)	**Walrus

Order Lagomorpha (Rabbits and Hares)
Family: LEPORIDAE

Lepus capensis (Linnaeus, 1758)	Brown Hare
Lepus timidus (Linnaeus, 1758)	Mountain or Blue Hare
Oryctolagus cuniculus (Linnaeus, 1758)	*Rabbit

Order Rodentia (Rodents)
Family: SCIURIDAE

Sciurus vulgaris (Linnaeus, 1758)	Red Squirrel
Sciurus carolinensis (Gmelin, 1788)	*Grey Squirrel
Family: GLIRIDAE (= MUSCARDINIDAE)	
Muscardinus avellanarius (Linnaeus, 1758)	Common Dormouse
Glis glis (Linnaeus, 1766)	*Edible Dormouse
Family: MURIDAE	
Micromys minutus (Pallas, 1771)	Harvest Mouse
Apodemus sylvaticus (Linnaeus, 1758)	Wood Mouse
Apodemus flavicollis (Melchoir, 1834)	***Yellow-necked Field Mouse
Mus musculus (Linnaeus, 1758)	*House Mouse
Rattus rattus (Linnaeus, 1758)	*Black Rat
Rattus norvegicus (Berkenhout, 1769)	*Brown Rat
Family: CRICETIDAE (= MURIDAE)	
Clethrionomys glareolus (Schreber, 1780)	Bank Vole
Arvicola terrestris (Linnaeus, 1758)	Water Vole
Microtus agrestis (Linnaeus, 1761)	Field Vole
Microtus arvalus (Pallas, 1779)	***Common Vole
Mesocricetus auratus (Waterhouse, 1840)	*Golden Hamster
Family: CAPROMYIDAE	
Myocastor coypus (Molina, 1782)	*Coypu

Order Artiodactyla (Deer, sheep, goats, cattle and pigs)
Family: SUIDAE

Sus scrofa (Linnaeus, 1758)	Domestic Pig

Family: CERVIDAE

Cervus elephus (Linnaeus, 1758)	Red Deer
Cervus nippon (Temminck, 1838)	*Sika Deer
Dama dama (Linnaeus, 1758)	***Fallow Deer
Capreolus capreolus (Linnaeus, 1758)	Roe Deer
Muntiacus muntjak (Zimmermann, 1780)	*Indian Muntjac (probably extinct)
Muntiacus reevsi (Ogilby, 1839)	*Chinese Muntjac
Hydropotes inermis (Swinhoe, 1870)	*Chinese Water Deer
Rangifer tarandus (Linnaeus, 1758)	***Reindeer

Family: BOVIDAE
Capra hircus (domestic)   Goat
Ovis aries (domestic)   Sheep
Bos taurus (domestic)   Cattle

Order Cetacea (Whales)
Family: BALAENIDAE
Balaena glacialis (Borowski, 1781)   **Right Whale
Family: BALAENOPTERIDAE
Megaptera novaeangliae (Borowski, 1781)   **Humpback Whale
Balaenoptera physalus (Linnaeus, 1758)   **Common Rorqual
Balaenoptera musculus (Linnaeus, 1758)   **Blue Whale
Balaenoptera acutorostrata (Lacapede, 1804)   **Lesser Rorqual
Balaenoptera borealis (Lesson, 1828)   **Sei Whale
Family: PHYSETERIDAE
Physeter catodon (Linnaeus, 1758)   **Sperm Whale
Family: ZIPHIIDAE
Hyperoodon ampullatus (Forster, 1770)   **Bottle-nosed Whale
Ziphius cavirostris (Cuvier, 1823)   **Cuvier's beaked Whale
Mesoplodon bidens (Sowerby, 1804)   **Sowerby's Whale
Mesoplodon mivus (True, 1913)   **True's beaked Whale
Family: MONODONTIDAE
Monodon monoceros (Linnaeus, 1757)   **Narwhale
Delphinapterus leucus (Pallas, 1776)   **White Whale
Family: PHOCAENIDAE
Phocaena phocoena (Linnaeus, 1758)   *Common Porpoise
Family: DELPHINIDAE
Delphinus delphis (Linnaeus, 1758)   *Common Dolphin
Stenella styx (Gray, 1846)   Euphrosyne Dolphin
Tursiops truncatus (Montagu, 1821)   *Bottle-nosed Dolphin
Lagenorhynchus acutus (Gray, 1828)   *White-sided Dolphin
Lagenorhynchus albirostris (Gray, 1846)   *White-beaked Dolphin
Pseuodcra crassidens (Owen, 1846)   **False killer
Orcinus orcra (Linnaeus, 1758)   *Killer Whale
Globicephala melaena (Traill, 1809)   *Pilot Whale
Grampus griseus (Curvier, 1812)   *Risso's Dolphin

*Introduced. **Vagrant. *** Became extinct, but now reintroduced. ***Probably introduced. *Regular visitor (whales). **Vagrant visitor (whales).

All extinct forms and subspecies have been omitted.
N.B. The American Hoary Bat, *Lasurius cinereus*, was recorded in Orkney in 1847, but it was either blown over in a storm or transported in a ship.

Glossary

Acetabulum: Bowl-shaped depression on each side of the pelvic girdle into which the head of the thigh bone (femur) fits.

Acromion process: The dorsal projection on one side of the bifurcated spine of the scapula.

Alveoli: The holes filled by the roots of the teeth.

Aquatic: Living entirely in water. *See* semi-aquatic.

Arboreal: Term given to an animal that spends most of its time in and around trees, e.g. squirrel.

Auditory bullae (Auditory capsule): Part of the skull in vertebrates covering the inner ear.

Basi-occipital: ⎱ Two bones lying close together on ventral surface.
Basisphenoid: ⎰ Of skull in the mid-line of and anterior to the auditory bullae.

Bicuspid: Tooth having two cusps.

Browse: Eating of leaves, as in some herbivores.

Calcanium: The bone at the base of the foot (as in man) forming the heel.

Carnivore: 1. a member of the order Carnivora.
    ,,   2. A flesh eater.

Cast: Term given to any impression taken from an original source.

Casting: 1. Term given to the annual removal of antlers, as in deer.
    ,,   2. Fox droppings.

Cleaves: Principal toes of deer's foot.

Condyle: A knob of bone which fits into a corresponding socket of bone, forming a joint, e.g. lower jaw into skull.

Coracoid spur: Spur of bone overhanging the glenoid fossa (glenoid cavity) on the scapula.

Couch: 1. Lying-up place of an otter – made of reeds and often in a willow.
    ,,   2. Lying-up place of a deer.

Cranium: Part of skull which encloses brain (brain-case).

Crepuscular: Active at dusk and dawn.

Crotties: Deer droppings.

Currants: Hare droppings.

Den: Stoat or marten home.

Dentary: Term given to the lower jaw.

Dew claws: Those digits on the feet of artiodactyls which generally never reach the ground.

Diastema: Gap (in herbivores) between the incisors or canines and premolars or molars.

Digitigrade: Walking on tips of toes (e.g. cat, fox).

Diurnal: Active by day only.

Drey: Squirrel's nest.

Elytra: Wing cases of beetles; often found in droppings and owl pellets.

Environment: Those conditions in which an animal lives.

Feral: Term given to those animals which have escaped captivity and are able to live 'wild', e.g. Coypu (escaped from fur farms).

Fewmets: Individual deer droppings.

Foliage: Collective name given to green leaves of trees, flowers and ferns.

Fraying: Removal of **ve**lvet from antlers; and also bark from trees.

Gait: Type of locomotion in quadruped animals.

Gallop: Fastest gait.

Grazing: Eating of grass, as in some herbivores, e.g. cattle.

Gregarious: Living in groups or families.

Herbivore: An animal which eats plants.

Hibernation: Winter season during which some mammals become dormant, results in low body temperature, and is preceded by gluttonous feeding to store body fat, e.g. dormouse.

Holt: Otter's breeding den.

Hop: A gaity typical of many small mammals; enables them to push the body off the ground, from a standstill position using the hind feet.

Ilium: Dorsal part of hip-girdle; joined, sometimes fused to the sacral vertebrae (see Fig. 5:2).

Incisor: Most anterior-placed tooth in mouth of mammals. Chisel-shaped, and lies on the premaxilla of each jaw, used for seizing food.

Insectivore: 1. A member of the order Insectivora.

,,   2. An insect eater.

Interparietal: The most posteriorly placed bone on the dorsal surface of the skull; forming, especially in the carnivores, the major part of the sagittal crest.

Ischium: Ventral part of hip-girdle, projecting backwards.

Jugal: Anterior bone forming part of zygomatic arch (cheek-bone).

Kennel: The lying-up place of a fox above ground.

Lair: Deer's resting-place.

Latrine: The place, often a mound or pit, used for regular placing of droppings.

Maxilla: 1. Large bone of the upper jaw of mammals, which carries all the upper teeth, except the incisors.

,,   2. Sometimes used for the whole of the upper jaw.

Metacromion process: The ventral projection of the bifurcated spine of the scapula; not present in all mammals.

Migrate: To move from one place to another, normally at the change of seasons, to gain some advantage of food or weather.

Moult: Normal seasonal loss of hair, giving rise to colour change, e.g. stoat.

Musk: Scent which is very prominent in the mustelids, which is emitted from two glands at the base of the tail.

Myxomatosis: A disease of the rabbit.

Nasals: Bones protecting the nasal passages.

Nocturnal: Active at night only.

Obturator foramina: The gap between the pubis and ischium in the hip-girdle.

Omnivore: Animal eating both plant and animal food.

Os innominatum: (means the nameless bone) all the bones forming the pelvic girdle.

Orbit: Cavity in the skull holding the eye.

Palatine: Bone forming the posterior part of the hard palate, the anterior part being formed by the maxilla and premaxilla.

Plantigrade: Walking on the soles of the feet.

Posterior nares: Hindmost part of the nasal region.

Predator: Animal preying on others.

Prehensile: Having a tail which can effectively be used as a fifth limb, e.g. Harvest mouse.

Premaxilla: Bone of the upper jaw and carrying the incisors.

Prey: Animals killed by others for food.

Prickings: The tracks of a hare.

Pubic symphysis: The point at which the two halves of the pelvis join, ventrally.

Pubis: Ventral part of hip-girdle, projecting forward.

Register: Where two tracks completely or almost overlap, i.e. hind feet placed in or almost in same position as fore.

Ring: Circular patch worn by the Roe buck when courting doe.

Runs: Regular pathways used by many small mammals, especially rodents, e.g. voles.

Rut: Time of courtship and mating.

Sacrum: Group of sacral vertebrae fused together, and united to, or fused with the pelvis.

Sagittal crest: Ridge on top of the cranium dividing it into two halves, well developed in the carnivores.

Semi-aquatic: Species living a part of its life in water.

Slot: Term for a deer's track.

Smears: Marks made by the fur of small mammals, and especially rats. Often seen under beams in barns and warehouses.

Splay: Term used to describe the spread seen in tracks.

Spraints: Otter droppings.

Squamosal: Posterior bone forming part of the zygomatic arch.

Stop: The breeding burrow of a rabbit.

Stride: The distance between two consecutive placings of a given limb, i.e. the distance between the track of one limb, and the following track of that limb.

Subterranean: Underground.

Sutures: Fixed joints between two bones, e.g. Maxilla and Premaxilla.

Taciturn: Silent.

Terrain: Nature of the land surface.

Terrestrial: Living on land.

Territory: That area that an animal defends from others of the same species, to ensure adequate food, etc.

Thicket: A tangle of shrubs or trees.

Tine: One of the prongs of a deer's antler.

Track: A single footprint in the ground.

Trail: The pattern of tracks left by a moving animal. According to the relationship between the various tracks it is possible to determine the pace at which the animal is moving.

Tricuspid: Tooth having three cusps.

Trot: The diagonally opposite feet moving together in a swing-over manner alternately. A medium pace.

Tympanic bullae: See *Auditory bullae.*

Unguligrade: Walking on tip of horny hoofs, e.g. deer, pigs.

Unicuspia: Tooth having only one cusp.

Velvet: The soft skin which covers a deer's growing antlers.

Vestigial: An organ whose size, structure and function has diminished.

Vibrissae: (Whiskers). Stiff hairs projecting from the face (and sometimes – limbs), of most mammals; they act as touch receptors.

Walk: The animal's body never leaves the ground, there always being one or two feet on the ground. This is one of the slowest paces.

Wallow: The place where a deer rolls.

Warren: Term given to a rabbit's dwelling place.

Zygomatic arch: (*Cheek-bones*) Made of two bones, the jugal and squamosal.

Bibliography

Adams, L. E. (1903). A contribution to our knowledge of the mole (*Talpa europaea*). *Mem. Manchr. Lit. Phil. Soc.* **47**, no. 4.

Adams, L. E. (1913). The Harvest Mouse. *Wildlife* **2**, 7–18.

Anon. (1963). *The Coypu Advisory leaflet*, No. 479. Min. Agric. Fish & Food. H.M.S.O.

Anon. (1965). Foxes' insect diet. *New Scientist.* **25**, 616.

Barret-Hamilton, G. E. H., and Hinton, M. A. C. (1910–21). *A history of British mammals*. London, Gurney and Jackson (3 volumes).

Beirne, B. P. (1947). The History of the British Land Mammals. *Ann. Mag. Nat. Hist.* ser. 11, **14**, 501–14.

Bell, T. (1837). *A history of British quadrupeds*. London, Van Voorst.

Bentley, E. W. (1959). The distribution and status of *Rattus rattus* L. in the United Kingdom in 1951 and 1956. *J. Anim. Ecol.* **28**, 299–308.

Berwin 'What do foxes eat'. *Gamekeeper.* **205**, 923–4.

Blackmore, M. (1948). *Mammals in Britain*. Collins.

Booth, Y. Spencer (1956). Shrews (*Crocidura cassireridum*) on the Scilly Isles. *Proc. Zool. Soc. Lond.* **126**, 167–70.

Brown, J. C., and Twigg, G. I. (1965). Some observations of Grey Squirrel dreys in an area of mixed woodland in Surrey. *Proc. Zool. Soc. Lond.* **144**. 131–4

—(1969). Studies on the pelvis in British Muridae and Cricetidae (Rodentia). *J. Zool. Lond.* (1969), **158**, 81–132.

Brown, L. E. (1966). Home range and movement of small mammals. *Symp. Zool. Soc. Lond.* No. **18**, 111–42.

Brown, R. W. Rates of Soil formation on Man-Made surfaces. Ph.D. Thesis. *Univ. of London.*

Buckhurst, E. A. The status of the Sika deer (*Cervus nippon* (Temmink)) in the Poole basin. *Proc. Dorset Nat. Hist. Arch. Soc.* **86**, 96–101, 2 figs.

Burton, M. (1968). *Animals of the British Isles*. Warne & Co.

Buxton, A. (1948). Roe deer and their fairy rings. *Country Life.* Lond. **104**, 1, 266–7.

—(1949). Roe deer and their fairy rings: a sequel. *Country Life.* Lond. **106**, 1, 367–8.

Carne, P. H. (1958). Wild deer in Southern England. *The Field.* **211**, 695–6.

—(1959). Japanese deer in Britain. *The Field.* **213**, 185.

—(1960). Fallow deer. *Countryman.* **5**, 311–14.

Chard, J. S. R. (1936). *British Animal Tracks*. London, C. Arthur Pearson.

—(1964). *The Roe Deer*, Forestry Commission leaflet **45**, H.M.S.O. 1964.

Church, H. F. (1957). The Times of Emergence of the Pipistrelle. *Proc. Zool. Soc. Lond.* **128**, 600–2.

Clark, S. P. (1970). Field experience of Feral Mink in Yorkshire and Lancashire. *Mammal Review.* Vol. **12**, 41–7.

Classens, A. J. M., and O'Gorman, F. (1965). The Bank vole (*Clethrionomys glareolus*, Schreber), a mammal new to Ireland. *Nature*, Lond. **205**, 923–4.

Condry, W. (1954). The Polecat in Wales. *Oryx.* **2**, 238–40.

Cook, D. (1963–4). Notes on Essex mammals, 1963–64. *Essex Nat.* **31**, 273–7.

Corbet, G. B. (1960). Wood mice at high altitude in Scotland. *Proc. Zool. Soc. Lond.* **133**, 486–7.

Corbet, G. B. (1964). *The identification of British Mammals*. Brit. Mus. (Nat. Hist.)
—(1966). *The Terrestrial Mammals of W. Europe*. Foulis.
Cotton, K. E. (1963). The Coypu. *River Bds. Ass. Yb.* 1963, 31.
Cranbrook, Earl of. Notes of foraging groups of Serotine bats. (*Eptisicus serotinus*, Schreber). *Trans. Suffolk Nat. Soc.* **13**, 15–19.
Cranbrook, Earl of, and Crowcroft, P. (1958). The white toothed shrews of the Channel Islands. *Ann. Mag. Nat. Hist.* ser. 13, 1, 359–64.
Crowcroft, P. (1957). *The Life of the Shrew*. London, Reinhardt.

Darling, F. F. (1947). *Natural History in the Highlands and Islands*. London, Collins.
Davis, R. A. (1960). A note on the distribution of Coypu (*Myocastor coypus*) in Great Britain. *J. Anim. Ecol.* **29**, 397.
—(1961). A simple live-trap for small mammals. *Proc. Zool. Soc. Lond.* **137**, 631–3.
—(1963). Feral coypus in Britain. *Ann. appl. Bio.* **51**, 345–8.
Day, M. G. (1968). Food habits of British Stoats (*Mustela erminea*) and Weasels (*Mustela nivalis*), *J. Zool. Lond.* (1968), **155**, 485–97.
Dean, C. D., and O'Gorman, F. (1969). The spread of Feral Mink in Ireland. *Irish Nat. J.* **16**, (7), 198–202.
Delany, M. J. (1961). The ecological distribution of small mammals in north-western Scotland. *Proc. Zool. Soc. Lond.* **137**, 107–26.

East, K. (1965). Notes on the opening of Hazel nuts (*Corylus avellana*) by mice and voles. *J. Zool.* **147**, 223–4.
Ellison, N. F. The Coypu in the Lake District. *Fld. Nat. N.S.* **10**, 41–3.
Elmhirst, N. F. (1938). Food of the Otter in the marine littoral zone. *Scot. Nat.* **1938**, 99–102.
Emlen, J. T. (1957). Dropping boards for population studies of small mammals. *J. Wildlife manag.* **21**, 300–14.
Erlinge, S. (1967). Home range of the otter (*Lutra lutra* L.) in Southern Sweden. *Oikos.* **18**, 186–209. Copenhagen, 1967.

Fairley, J. S., and O'Donnel, T. (1970). Notes from the Mammal Society. The distribution of the Bank vole (*Clethrionomys glareolus*) in south-west Ireland. *J. Zool. Lond.* **161**, 273–6.
Fooks, H. A. (1958). The Roe deer. London. *Forest. Comm. Tech. notes.* No. **6**.

Garnis, H. (1967). *The Natural History of Europe*. Ed. Joyce Pope and A. Meldnis. Paul Hamlyn.
Gerell, R. (1967). Food selection in relation to habitat in Mink (*Mustela vison*, Schreber) in Sweden, *Oikos.* **18**, 233–43. Copenhagen, 1967.
Glue, D. J. (1967). Prey taken by the Barn owl in England and Wales. *Bird study.* **14**, 169–83.
Godfrey, G. K. (1962). *Moles*. Sunday Times Publications Ltd.
Godfrey, G. K., and Crowcroft, P. (1960). *The Life of the Mole*. London, Museum Press.
Grubb, P., and Jewell, P. A. Social grouping and home range in Feral Soay Sheep.
Guldsbury, P. A. (ed.). *Predatory Mammals in Britain* (Council for Nature, 1967).

Harrison, J. L. (1960). A simple live-trap for squirrels. *J. Mammal.* **41**, 142–3.

Harting, J. E. (1880). *British animals extinct within historic times.* London, Trubner.

—(1895). The Harvest mouse. *Zoologist.* ser. 3, 418–25.

Haydn, J., and Kirby, P. (1954). Bats in the Bishop's Stortford area. *Oryx.* **2**, 325.

Hewer, H. R., and Neal, E. G. (1954). Filming Badgers at Night. *Discovery.* **15**, 121–4.

Hewson, R. (1948). Some observations on the Orkney vole, *Microtus o. orcadensis* (Millais). *Northway. Nat.* **23**, 7–10.

—(1969). Couch building by the Otter (*Lutra lutra* L.). *J. Zool.* vol. 159 (*Notes from the Mammal Society* 1969).

Hooper, J. (1962). *The Bats.* Sunday Times Publications Ltd.

—(1962). *Horseshoe Bats.* Sunday Times Publications Ltd.

Hooper, J. H., and Hooper, W. M. (1956). Habits and movements of cave-dwelling bats in Devonshire. *Proc. Zool. Soc. Lond.* **127**, 1–26.

Howard, W. E. (1957). Amount of food eaten by small carnivores. *J. Mammal.* **38**, 516–17.

Hurrel, Elaine (1962). *Dormice.* Sunday Times Publications Ltd.

Hurrel, H. G. (1962). *The Fox.* Sunday Times Publications Ltd.

—(1962). *The Pine Marten.* Sunday Times Publications Ltd.

Illingworth, F. (1949). 'Reindeer for Scotland'. *The Field*, 2nd April. Vol. **193**, no. 5021, pp. 377–8.

Jenkins, D. (1962). The present status of the wild cat (*Felis silvestris*) in Scotland. *Scot. Nat.* **70**, 126–38.

Johnston, H. H. (1903). *British Mammals.* London, Hutchinson.

Kelway, P. (1944). *The Otter Book.* London, Collins.

Kirk, J. C., and Wagstaffe, R. (1943). A contribution to the study of the Scottish Wild cat (*Felis silvestris grampia Miller*). Part I. Size and weight. *Northw. Nat.* **18**, 271–5.

Knight, M. (1962). *Hedgehog.* Sunday Times Publications Ltd.

Larina, N. I. (1958). (On the diagnostic problem of closely related species *Apodemus sylvaticus* Linnaeus and *A. turiais* Pallas.). *L. Zool. Th.* **37**, 1719–32.

Laurie, E. M. O. (1946). The Coypu (*Myocastor coypus*) in Great Britain. *J. Anim. Ecol.* **15**, 22–34.

Lawrence, M. J. (1969). Some observations on non-volant locomotion in Vespertilionid bats. *J. Zool. Lond.* **156**, pp. 309–17.

Lawrence, M. J., and Brown, R. W. (1967). A brief consideration of the identification of European Mammals from their tracks, trails and signs. *Acta. Zool. et Path.* **43/1967**, pp. 3–43.

Leffrich, A. W. The national badger survey. J. Northampt. *Nat. Hist. Soc.* **35**, pp. 365–9.

Leutscher, A. (1960). *Tracks and signs of British Wild Animals.* Cleaver Hume Press.

Linn, I. (1962). *Weasels.* Sunday Times Publications Ltd.

Lindgren, E. J. (1966). *The herd of Reindeer in the Glenmore, Cairngorm Forest Park.* H.M.S.O. Edinburgh.

Lloyd, H. G. (1959). The distribution of squirrels in England and Wales. *J. Anim. Ecol.* **31**, 157–65.

Lloyd, J. Ivester (1953). Otters – Their slides. *The Field*, **201**, 23.

Lockie, J. D. (1961). The food of the Pine Marten, *Martes martes*, in West Ross-shire, Scotland. *Proc. Zool. Soc. Lond.* **136**, 187–95.

Lowe, V. P. W. (1961). A discussion on the history, present status and future conservation of Red deer (*Cervus elaphus*) in Scotland. *Terre et la Vie.* **108**, 9–40.

Matheson, C. (1962). *Brown Rat.* Sunday Times Publications Ltd.

—(1963). The distribution of Red Polecat in Wales. *Proc. Zool. Soc. Lond.* **140**, 115–20.

Matthews, L. H. (1952). *British Mammals.* London, Collins.

McMillan, N. F. (1965). The water shrew in Orkney. *Proc. Zool. Soc. Lond.* **145**, 147–8.

Millais, J. G. (1904–6). *Mammals of Great Britain and Ireland.* London, Longmans Green. 3 vols.

Miller, G. S. (1912). *Catalogue of the mammals of Western Europe.* London, B.M. (Natural History).

Miller, R. S. (1954). Food habits of the Wood mouse, *Apodemus sylvaticus* (Linne, 1758), and the Bank vole, *Clethrionomys glareolus* (Schreber, 1780), in Wytham Woods, Berkshire. *Saugetiek Mitt.* **2**, 104–14.

Moffat, C. B. (1938). The mammals of Ireland. *Proc. Roy. Irish Acad.* **44B**, 61–128.

Morris, P. A., and Harper, J. F. (1965). The occurrence of small mammals in discarded bottles. *Proc. Zool. Soc. Lond.* **145**, 148–53.

Morrison-Scott, T. C. S. (1939). A key to the British bats. *Naturalist, Lond.* 33–6.

Murie, O. J. (1954). *A Field Guide to Animal Tracks.* Boston, Houghton Mifflin. Co.

Neal, E. G. (1949). *The Badger.* London, Collins. New Naturalist Series.

—(1955). *Badgers in Woodland.* Forestry Commission leaflet No. **34**. H.M.S.O.

—(1962). *Otters.* Sunday Times Publications Ltd.

—(1962). *Badgers.* Sunday Times Publications Ltd.

Perry, R. (1953). *The Watcher and the Red Deer.* London, Hodge & Co.

—(1962). Reindeer in the Cairngorms. *The Shooting Times and Country Magazine*, Nov. p. 1392.

Phillips, G. C., and East, K. (1961). The relative efficiency of small mammal traps. *Proc. Zool. Soc. Lond.* **137**, 637–40.

Phillips, W. A. A., and Blackmore, M. (1969). Mouse-eared bats *Myotis myotis* in Sussex. *Notes from the Mammal Society No. 21. J. Zool.* Vol. 162, p. 4.

Pickvance, T. J., and Chard, J. S. R. (1960). Feral muntjac in the West Midlands. *Proc. B'gham. Nat. Hist. Soc.* **19**, 1–8.

Prior, R. (1968). *The Roe Deer of Cranbourne Chase* (an ecological survey). Oxford University Press.

Rowe, F. P. (1960). Golden Hamsters (*Mesocricetus auratus* Waterhouse) living free in an urban habitat. *Proc. Zool. Soc. Lond.* **134**, 499–503.

—(1968). Further records of free living Golden Hamsters (*Mesocricetus auratus*). *J. Zool.*, Vol. 165, Part **4**, 529–30.

Ryder, S. R. (1962). *Water Voles.* Sunday Times Publications Ltd.

Sergeant, D. E. (1951). The status of the Common Seal (*Phoca vitulina*) on the East Anglian coast. *J. Mar. biol. Ass. U.K.* **29**, 707–17.

Shorten, M. (1946). A survey of the distribution of the American grey squirrel (*Sciurus carolinensis*) and the British red squirrel (*Sciurus vulgaris leucourus*) in England and Wales in 1944–5. *J. Anim. Ecol.* **15**, 82–92.

—(1954). *Squirrels.* Collins, London.

Siivonen, L. *Pohylum Nisakkaat.* (Mammals of Northern Europe.) Otava. Helsinki.

Simpson, G. G. (1945). The principles of classification and a classification of mammals. *Bull. Amer. Mus. Nat. Hist.* **85**, 1–114.

Snaffle (1904). *The Roe Deer*, London, E. M. Harwar.

Southern, H. N., and Crowcroft, W. P. (1956). Terrestrial habits of the Water vole (*Arvicola amphibius*). *Proc. Zool. Soc. Lond.* **126**, 166–7.

Southern, H. N. (1964). *The Handbook of British Mammals.* Blackwell Scientific Publication.

Speakman, F. J. (1954). *Tracks, trails and signs.* G. Bell & Sons Ltd.

Stebbings, R. E. (1970). A bat new to Britain (*Pipistrellus nathusii*) with notes on its identification and distribution in Europe. *J. Zool. Lond.* **161**, pp. 282–6.

—(1967). Identification of bats of the genus *Plecotus* in England. *J. Zool. Lond.*, **153**.

—(1968). Bechsteins bat (*Myotis bechsteini*) in Dorset. (1966–7). *J. Zool.*, Vol. **155**, pp. 228–31.

—(1965). *Plecotus austriacus* in Dorset. *Nature, Lond.* **206**, 314–15.

Stephens, M. (1957). *The Otter Report.* London, Univ. Fed. Anim. Welfare.

Stephens, M. N. (1957). *The natural history of the otter.* 88 pp. Tunbridge Wells, Kent.

Stevenson, J. H. F. (1959). *Mink in Britain.* 3rd ed. Exeter, Pitts.

Taylor, J. C. (1968). The use of marking points by Grey Squirrel. *J. Zool. Lond.* **155**, pp. 246–7.

Taylor, W. L. (1946). The wild cat (*Felis silvestris*) in Great Britain. *J. Anim. Ecol.* **15**, 130–3.

—(1939). The distribution of wild deer in England and Wales. *J. Anim. Ecol.* **8**, 6–9.

—(1948). The distribution of wild deer in England and Wales. *J. Anim. Ecol.* **17**, 151–7.

—(1952). The Polecat (*Mustela putorus*) in Wales. *J. Anim. Ecol.* **21**, 272–4.

—(1956). Pine Martens in Britain. *Countryman.* Idbury. **53**, 277–81.

Taylor Page, F. J. (1972). Field Guide to British Deer. *Mamm. Soc. Brit. Isles.*

—(1962). *Red Deer.* Sunday Times Publications Ltd.

—(1962). *Roe Deer.* Sunday Times Publications Ltd.

—(1962). *Fallow Deer.* Sunday Times Publications Ltd.

Tegner, H. S. (1951). *The Roe Deer*. London, Batchworth.

Tetley, H. (1945). Notes on British Polecats and Ferrets. *Proc. Zool. Soc. Lond.* **115**, 212–17.

Thomas, D. H. (1939). *Tracks in the Snow*. London, Hodder and Stoughton.

Thompson, H. V. (1953). The Edible Dormouse (*Glis glis*, L.) in England 1902–1931. *Proc. Zool. Soc. Lond.* **133**, 490–4.

—(1953). The Edible Dormouse (*Glis glis*, L.) in England, 1902–1951. *Proc. Zool. Soc. Lond.* **122**, 1017–24.

—(1958). *British Wild Mink. Ann.*

Thompson, H. V., and Worden, A. N. (1956). *The Rabbit*. London, Collins.

Tinbergen, Von N. (1965). Von den Vorratskammeran des Rotfuches. Sonderdruck aus Zeitschrift fur tierpsychologie. *Band 22, Heft 2* (**1965**), S. 119–49 (English Surnames).

Tittenson, A. M. (1969). Red squirrel dreys. *J. Zool. Soc.* Vol. **162**, p. 4.

Topsell, E. (1607). *The historie of the foure-footed beastes*. London, Jaggard.

Utsi, M. N. P. (1957). The future of reindeer in Scotland. *Oryx*, pp. 40–2.

Van den Drink, F. H. (1967). *A Field Guide to the Mammals of Britain and Europe*. Collins, London.

Venables, U. M. (1943). Observations at a Pipistrelle bat roost. *J. Anim. Ecol.* **12**, 19–26.

—and Venables, L. S. V. (1960). A Seal survey of Northern Ireland 1956–7. *Proc. Zool. Soc. Lond.* **133**, 490–4.

Vesey-Fitzgerald, B. (1949). *British Bats*. London.

Walton, K. C. (1964). The distribution of the Polecat (*Putorius putorius*) in England, Wales and Scotland. 1959–1962. *Proc. Zool. Soc. Lond.* **143**, 333–6.

—(1968). The distribution of the Polecat (*Putorius putorius*) in Great Britain 1963–1967. *J. Zool. Lond.* **55**, 237–40.

Warwick, T. (1934). The distribution of the musk rat (*Fiber zibethicus*) in the British Isles. *J. Anim. Ecol.* **3**, 250–67.

Watson, A. (1955). The winter food of six Highland Foxes. *Scot. Nat.* **67**, 123–4.

—and Hewson, R. (1962). *Mountain Hares*. Sunday Times Publications Ltd.

Watts, C. H. S. (1968). The food eaten by Woodmice (*Apodemus sylvaticus*) and Bank Voles (*Clethrionomys glareolus*) in Wytham Woods, Berkshire. *J. Anim. Ecol.* **37**, 25–41.

Whitehead, G. K. (1949). Chinese Water Deer. *The Field*. **193**, 301.

—(1954). Deer from Asia at home in England. *The Field*. **203**, 663.

—(1954). Epping Forest and its Deer. *Country Life*. **116**, 810–11.

—(1962). Muntjac deer in England. *The Gamekeeper and Countryside*. Oct., No. **781**, pp. 12–13.

Yalden, D. W. (1965). Running in the Mole, *Talpa europaea*. *Proc. Zool. Soc. Lond.* **144**, Part 1, 131–52.

Index

295

297